Contributions to the Doctrine of Signs

RESEARCH CENTER FOR LANGUAGE AND SEMIOTIC STUDIES

INDIANA UNIVERSITY

Thomas A. Sebeok, *Chairman,*
 and Acting Director of Publications

Contributions
to the
Doctrine of Signs

Thomas A. Sebeok

Published by
INDIANA UNIVERSITY, BLOOMINGTON
and
THE PETER DE RIDDER PRESS, LISSE

INDIANA UNIVERSITY PUBLICATIONS

STUDIES IN SEMIOTICS

Thomas A. Sebeok, *Editor*

Yin May Lee, *Assistant to the Editor*

Volume 5

Copyright © 1976 by Indiana University
All rights reserved

ISBN 87750-194-7

Library of Congress Catalog Card Number 75-39428

Research Center for Language and Semiotic Studies, P. O. Box 1214, Indiana
University, Bloomington, Indiana 47401 U.S.A.
The Peter de Ridder Press, P.O. Box 168, Lisse, The Netherlands

Printed in the United States of America

For Charles Morris

Table of Contents

vii

Foreword

The expression *doctrine of signs*, for the title of this collection, was selected with deliberation to emblematically align the arguments embodied in these eleven essays with the semiotic tradition of Locke and Peirce rather more closely than with others that prefer to dignify the field – often with premature strategic intent – as a 'theory' or even a 'science'. For Locke, a doctrine was hardly more than a body or system of principles or tenets loosely constituting a department of knowledge. Things, Actions, and Signs were for him "the three great Provinces of the intellectual World, wholly separate and distinct one from another". The mind makes use of signs both in the contemplation of things and in actions for the attainment of its ends; moreover, it does so for "the right ordering of [the one and the other] for its clearer Information". The business of the doctrine of signs, or semiotics, he asserted at the very end of his "celebrated *Essay*", was to consider matters such as these.

Peirce, as is well known, redefined Locke's term as "the doctrine of signs", but with an immediate and most important qualification, describing it as "quasi-necessary, or formal", meaning by this "that we observe the characters of such signs as we know, and, from such an observation, by a process which I will not object to naming Abstraction, we are led to statements, eminently fallible, and therefore in one sense by no means necessary, as to what *must be* the characters of all signs used by a 'scientific' intelligence, that is to say, by an intelligence capable of learning by experience". Thus semiotics was launched as an observational science, with a double aim: its tasks to find out not merely what *is* in the actual world, but also what *must be*.

Progress in this direction has been very slow, not the least because of the strange fate of Peirce and of the rich harvest of his solitary reflections, a combination of historical circumstances that Nagel aptly described as "a misfortune for [Peirce] himself as well as for the subsequent history of philosophy".

In the hundred years or so that have passed since 1867 — when Peirce's "On a New List of Categories" was first published, including his delineation of "a trivium of conceivable sciences", that is, of speculative grammar, critical logic, and speculative rhetoric, and his attendant seminal division of representations into icons, indices, and symbols — some of the most interesting developments in semiotics have centered upon a problem seriously taken up by Morris, paramount contributor of the mid-century: "how to distinguish animal sign-behavior from that of man". Characteristically, Morris recommended our going beyond the existing literature, for the knowledge to be gained "must be the product of specially designed experimentation", which, furthermore, as it is obtained, will greatly and significantly enrich the account of biological evolution.

Some of those who have thus striven to elucidate crucial processes at the interface of nature and culture were unaware that they belonged to a wider community of scholars who shared their most cherished goals. Jakob von Uexküll was one of the greatest cryptosemioticians of this period: a superb biologist, he was a teacher of Konrad Lorenz and thus came to be enshrined a prime ancestral figure of ethology (a label that stands for little else than diachronic semiotics with preponderantly phylogenetic concerns). What busy inquirers into verbal semantics — linguists, logicians — have probed and profited from Uexküll's masterful *Bedeutungslehre*? What student of sign operations in man has bothered to inquire into the phenomenological basis of Uexküll's 'subjective environmentology', and has grasped its implication for the doctrine in general or its particular kinship to, say, Husserl's "Zur Logik der Zeichen (Semiotik)"? Apart from the cursory attention Stepanov paid to him in the strict context of biosemiotics — a subject which, by the way, Eco quite erroneously consigns to "the lower limit of semiotics because it concerns itself with the communicative behavior of non-human (and therefore non-cultural) communities", whereas, in fact, biological foundations lie at the very epicenter of the study of both communication and signification in the human animal — Uexküll, so far, figures only in the historiography of the life sciences, but not yet in that of our "science qui étudie la vie des signes au sein de la vie sociale", Saussure's parochial utopia, where Uexküll's achievements manifestly also belong. In a special study, already in preparation, I intend to spell out my reasons for this claim, and to similarly assess the contributions of a host of 'neglected' giants (another such was Galen) who, in my view, helped contour the doctrine of signs, each from his own coign of vantage.

Why has the progress of the doctrine of signs toward the status of a genuine theory, in the proper sense of that much abused word (especially in linguistic writings of the 1960s), been so thwartingly laborious? Why has the essential identity of ethology and diachronic semiotics not been explicitly recognized decades ago? Why is the inherently and obviously semiotic nature of the genetic code, as well as of what the late Tomkins called 'the metabolic code', still a matter of idle controversy? The answer to these questions is that precisely one century and a decade has intervened to separate the earliest semiotic efforts of Peirce – who, on December 28, 1908, confided to Lady Welby that he had himself "been entirely absorbed in the very same subject since 1863" – from the publication date of the single most important paper in semiotics of our times, Thom's 1973 sketch of the theory of symbolism. In this epochal, if excessively laconic, essay, the author decisively demonstrates that man's allegedly unique *facultas signatrix* is in fact compounded of features among which "on n'en trouve aucun qui ne figure soit dans la matière inanimée, soit dans les formes les plus humbles de la vie". While, as the writings assembled in this book, and in a previous selection of mine, *Perspectives in Zoosemiotics* (1972), plainly and amply bear out, I reached this same conclusion long ago, my views represent nothing more than distilled opinion, whereas the distinguished topologist's arguments are a solidly based side-product of a mathematical theorem of great sophistication, with special relevance to both biology and semiotics. Morphogenetic processes can now be modeled mathematically in their qualitative aspect, and to develop the general properties which such models *must have*; thus it becomes feasible for the first time, in a technical way, to satisfy, with minimal fallibility, Peirce's criteria alluded to above. The breadth of application of Thom's ideas – called catastrophe theory – is of enormous range, and encompasses soft sciences such as those concerned with the generation of signs, inclusive of verbal signs. Although the models are still crude as measured against the very complex states of affairs they are intended to represent, I believe they point in the unique direction which all branches of semiotics are bound to traverse, and the route – in Kuhn's sense – to 'normal science' in the decades ahead. If this is so, my book is to be read as mopping-up work, which, however, as Kuhn rightly insisted, can, in itself, prove quite fascinating in the execution, as indeed it has to me.

*   *   *

All of the papers in this third of my collections published over the last four years were written from a more or less strictly circumscribed semiotic perspective; they were designed as preliminary fragments to be reworked and rounded out in coherent fashion within the frame of a book on the subject as a whole I have in preparation for Penguin. The same holds for the contents of two previous collections: the first, on animal communication (1972), already mentioned; and the second on verbal art, which appeared under the title *Structure and Texture* (1974). (A fourth book, being readied for press, will gather up writings on miscellaneous anthropological topics, notably religion.)

In the Foreword to the 1972 volume I remarked: "As I reread these pieces, I can see that I have often repeated myself. The idea I wanted to express and to convey is set forth in somewhat different guises, with other examples, and with varying shades of emphasis, but the core remains the same. Redundancy is in the nature of any autodidactic exercise" – and, I am now tempted to add, is mostly in the eye (or ideology) of the beholder. This holds true, in a measure, for some of the articles reprinted here as well, but I do not think that is necessarily a bad thing: any reader who cares to follow me can see for himself how the conceptions I hold as central are revised with variations that mark their ripening, while those I regard as peripheral tend to fall by the wayside – this is notably so in my analysis of sign tokens and types. The demonstration of their ubiquity is what matters in the end.

In the "Web", I have already recorded my indebtedness to my two teachers in semiotics, Charles Morris and Roman Jakobson. I know of no one else, living or dead, who has enjoyed a comparable opportunity of sharing my, it appears, singular lot of having studied with both of these men who have shaped, each in his own way, the intellectual climate of the world we inhabit – especially the world of signs. I have previously tried to suggest, by appropriate metonymies, what I owe to Jakobson – by having dedicated to him my 1974 book, and, in more detail, in my recent article on "Roman Jakobson's Teaching in America".

I wish now to dedicate this book to Charles Morris, with affectionate admiration. He, more than anyone else I know, meets my standard of the good and the true. As the author of the *Nicomachean Ethics* put it, speaking of virtue as a means to an end, namely happiness: "Human good is activity of soul in accordance with virtue in a complete life." Aristotle's maxim could hardly have found a more perfect embodiment!

Salzburg, May 13, 1976

1

Semiotics: A Survey of the State of the Art*

1. THE SCOPE OF SEMIOTICS

The subject matter of semiotics[1] – ultimately a mode of extending our perception of the world – is the exchange of any messages whatever and of the systems of signs which underlie them; hence, alongside such fields as social anthropology (which deals with the exchange of mates), and economics (which deals with the exchange of utilities, viz., goods and services), semiotics is most commonly regarded as a branch of the communication disciplines.[2] Some investigators prefer to emphasize the study of the systematic – rather than the transactional – aspects of the repertory of signs (noumena vs. phenomena).[3] Whichever approach one may favor, however, the key concept of semiotics remains always the 'sign'.

*   This article is reprinted, with minor alterations, from *Current Trends in Linguistics*, Vol. 12, *Linguistics and Adjacent Arts and Sciences*, ed. by Thomas A. Sebeok (The Hague: Mouton, 1974), Tome 1, pp. 211-64. The article was begun in 1969 and essentially completed in 1971.
[1]   For a discussion of this term and its congeners, see the next Chapter.
[2]   Cf. Lévi-Strauss (1958: 326): "Dans toute société, la communication s'opère au moins à trois niveaux: communication des femmes; communications des biens et des services; communication des messages. Par conséquent, l'étude du système de parenté, celle du système économique et celle du système linguistique offrent certaines analogies. Toutes trois relèvent de la même méthode; elles diffèrent seulement par le niveau stratégique où chacune choisit de se situer au sein d'un univers commun."
[3]   This differential emphasis between empirical and analytic approaches is discussed by Valesio (1969). Prieto also notes that there are two tendencies in contemporary semiotic researches: one emphasizing communication, the other signification (his own work following the former); see his 1968 article, and his

Messages may be emitted and/or received either by inorganic objects, such as machines,[4] or by organic substances, for instance, animals, including man, or by some of their component parts (e.g., ribonucleic acid, mRNA, that serves as an information-bearing tape 'read' by particles, called ribosomes, that travel along it, carrying amino acid sequence information [Ičas, 1969: 8]); one may also speak of information, for instance, in cardiovascular functioning, where messages are conveyed from peripheral vessels to the brain, relayed thence to the heart and back to the brain (Adey, 1967: 21). The interaction of organic beings with inorganic things (such as communication between a man and a computer) can also be treated as a semiotic problem. However, this survey will, in the main, be restricted to the semiotic manifestations of whole living systems.

A further distinction could provisionally be drawn between terrestrial and extraterrestrial communication. Exploration of the latter is shared by fields such as mathematics, exobiology, and radioastronomy with science fiction.[5] Since, at present, the study of cosmic message exchanges remains a discipline without a subject matter, this survey must be further confined to semiotic behavior on earth.

Message interchanges are most conveniently – if anthropocentrically – treated in two vast domains: in man and in other living systems; (also, of course, in their interactions, for instance, as regards semiotic processes that enter into the training, taming, and domestication of animals[6]). By 'other living systems', usually are meant animals other than man, but plants and fungi can also be said to be the sources

four contributions cited *ibid.*, p. 144. Marxist philosophers naturally stress the communication process as the starting point in the analysis of the sign; cf. i.a., Schaff, 1962: 155-211; and Resnikow, 1968: 38.

[4] Cf. Wiener, 1950: 85-88: "... it is quite possible for a person to talk to a machine, a machine to a person, and a machine to a machine ... the new machines will not stop working merely because we have discontinued to give them human support". For technical details, see, e.g., Gorn, 1968.

[5] On extraterrestrial semiotic processes as a scientific problem, see the summary of the literature in David Kahn, 1967, Ch. 26 and p. 1130. On semiotic processes in science fiction in general, see Krueger, 1968; a particular example, by a well-known linguist (whom Krueger failed to mention), is Hockett's "How to Learn Martian" (1955). An Institute for Extraterrestrial Linguistics exists, since 1969, in Heidelberg, as reported in *Linguistische Berichte*, No. 4, p. 88 (1969).

[6] Cf., e.g., Hediger, 1968, esp. Chs. 8 and 9; and Zeuner, 1963. Hediger, p. 120, for example, writes: "Training a circus animal means teaching it, by specialized handling and continuous use of effective cues, until it performs certain actions at a special personal signal. These actions, in their elements, are well known to the animal, but in freedom they would never be caused by the same stimuli, and never

and/or destinations of messages, notably in their interrelations with certain animals;[7] further, the biological status of such eminently communicative Protozoa as cellular slime molds (Acrasiales) is still in doubt (Bonner, 1963; see also Bleibtreu, 1968: Ch. 7).

Anthroposemiotics, that is, the totality of man's species-specific signaling systems, was the first domain concretely envisaged and delineated, under the designation *semiotic*. For most investigators, from 1960 to this day, both notions still remain synonymous. The second domain, *zoosemiotics*, which encompasses the study of animal communication in the broadest sense, was named and comprehensively outlined only in 1963. It would now seem more accurate to consider anthroposemiotics and zoosemiotics, separately and conjointly, as two principal divisions of semiotics, having in common certain essential features but differing especially as to the fundamental and pervasive role that language plays in the former in contradistinction to the latter. A third domain, *endosemiotics* – which studies cybernetic systems within the body – will not be examined in detail on this occasion; it is enough to say now that, in this field, the genetic code plays a role comparable to that of the verbal code in anthroposemiotic affairs (for reasons specified in Masters, 1970), and that it is still broadly true that the coding and transmission of information of differences outside the body is very different from the coding and transmission inside (Bateson, 1970); the field of transducer physiology, which studies the conversion of outside signals to their initial output inside, is, as yet, a totally undeveloped science (but see now the pioneering article of Tomkins, 1975).

2. HISTORICAL OUTLINE OF THE FIELD[8]

The discipline of *semiotics* – referring in earliest usage to medical concerns with the sensible indications of changes in the condition of

---

performed under the same conditions." Again, p. 128, he writes: "During the course of training the animal learns a lot of human signals and expressions and, conversely, the trainer develops an understanding of the animal's expression and signals." In semiotic terms, then, to tame and train an animal is to come to share, at least in part, its repertory of signs, and vice versa; in domestication, the diachronic dimension is superimposed.

[7] One particularly interesting community of interacting plants and animals involves milkweeds belonging to the family of Asclepiadaceae, a group of insects, the Danaidae, and blue jays, in a complex and subtle semiotic ecosystem; cf. Brower, Brower, and Corvino, 1967.

[8] For a partial sketch of the history of semiotics, cf. the Appendix (pp. 285-310)

the human body – constituted one of the three branches of Greek medicine. For the Stoics, the term acquired a broader meaning as a basic division of philosophy, including logic and the theory of knowledge. Hellenistic philosophy – not only among the Stoics, but also in its Epicurean and the Skeptic varieties – centered around a theory of signs, and was anticipated by Aristotle, who, in turn, was influenced by Plato, the Sophists, and several Greek physicians (such as Asclepiades, Erasistratus, Herophilus, all mentioned by Sextus[9]). In the Middle Ages,[10] a comprehensive and very keen theory of signs (known as *scientia sermocinalis*), embracing grammar, logic, and rhetoric, was elaborated by a number of scholars. "Within this development two streams can be distinguished: the dominant tendency was to interpret sign-processes within the framework of the Platonic and Aristotelian metaphysics; this was countered by a progressively growing attempt to assimilate semiotic to empirical science and philosophy. The first direction was carried on by Leibniz, the second by the British empiricists" (Morris, 1946: 286).

Leibniz gave his main attention in semiotics to the syntactical study of sign-structures. He regarded even the calculus as part of an all-embracing theory of signs and as an illustration of the fruitfulness of semiotic. His ideas of a universal system of signs (the *characteristica universalis*) have been variously carried forward by symbolic logicians and others such as Boole, Carnap, Frege, Gomperz, Husserl, Lambert, Peano, Russell, Tarski, Whitehead, and notably Peirce.[11]

The British empiricists (Francis Bacon, Bentham, Berkeley, Hobbes, Hume, and notably Locke), on the other hand, were variously concerned with the semantic dimension primarily. The Stoic term *semiotic* was reintroduced, in 1690, into English philosophical discourse by John Locke, in his *Essay Concerning Humane Understanding*.

---

to Morris, 1946. A full history of this field is yet to be written, but cf. now Jakobson, 1975.

[9] Cf. the account, summarized after Sextus Empiricus, of "Aenesidemus' Theory of Signs", constituting Appendix C (pp. 266-68) of Ogden and Richards, 1938. On sign theories of the Stoics and Epicureans, see Stough, 1969: 102-04, 125-28.

[10] On medieval linguistic study, see Bursill-Hall, 1971.

[11] On Peirce: see below; on Husserl: see Ogden and Richards, 1938: 269-72, and Schaff, 1962: 162-73; on Russell: Schaff, 1962: 273; on Frege: Schaff, 1962: 273-74; on Gomperz: Schaff, 1962: 274-77. Karl Söder's 1964 dissertation, "Beiträge J. H. Lamberts zur formalen Logik und Semiotik", is known to me only through Albrecht, 1967: 68-69, 253.

Locke declared the "doctrine of signs" as that branch of his tripartite division of all sciences "the business whereof is to consider the nature of signs, the mind makes use of for the understanding of things, or conveying its knowledge to others". For communication and for recording of our thoughts, "signs of our ideas are . . . necessary: those which men have found most convenient, and therefore generally make use of, are *articulate sounds*. The consideration, then, of *ideas* and *words* as the great instruments of knowledge, makes no despicable part of their contemplation who would take a view of human knowledge in the whole extent of it. And perhaps if they were distinctly weighed, and duly considered, they would afford us another sort of logic and critic, than we have been hitherto acquainted with" (Locke, 1690: Bk. IV, Ch. XXI, §4).

The preceding passage contains lingering echoes of the introductory paragraphs of Antoine Arnauld and Claude Lancelot's *Grammaire générale et raisonnée*, first published in 1660. In a third, revised edition, that appeared in 1676, the Port-Royal grammarians had written: "Parler, est expliquer ses pensées par des signes, que les hommes ont inventez à ce dessein. On a trouvé que les plus commodes des ces signes, estoient les sons et les voix . . . on a inventé d'autres signes pour les rendre durables et visibles, qui sont les caracteres de l'ecriture. . . . Ainsi l'on peut considerer deux choses dans ces signes: La premiere; ce qu'ils sont par leur nature, c'est à dire, en tant que sons et caracteres. La seconde, leur signification: c'est à dire, la maniere dons les hommes s'en servent pour signifier leurs pensées" (Brekle, 1966: 5). The pertinence and import of this capital workshop for the history of semiotics – not only of the Port-Royal *Grammar*, but also and especially of Arnauld and Pierre Nicole's *Logic* (1662) – are only now coming to be appreciated (cf. Brekle, 1964; and see fn. 88, below).

The real founder and first systematic investigator of modern semiotic, however, was the subtle American philosopher, Charles Sanders Peirce (1839-1914).[12] Convinced that many passages of Locke's *Essay* "make the first steps in profound analyses which are not further developed" (2.649), Peirce took over from him the term *semiotic* with its definition as the 'doctrine of signs', and devoted a

---

[12] On Peirce's semiotics in historical perspective, see also Morris, 1946: 287-91; and Ogden and Richards, 1938: 279-90, where pertinent extracts from his correspondence with Lady Welby are also included. On the latter, see also Lieb, 1953. For Peirce's review of Lady Welby's *What Is Meaning?* (1903), see Peirce, 8.171-175.

"lifelong study" to the nature of signs, that is, "the doctrine of the essential nature and fundamental varieties of possible semiosis". He viewed himself as "a pioneer, or rather a backwoodsman, in the work of clearing and opening up . . . *semiotic*", and added: "I find the field too vast, the labour too great, for a first-comer. I am, accordingly, obliged to confine myself to the most important questions" (5.488).

Peirce explicitly connected sign-processes with processes involving mediation or 'thirdness', as in the following passage: "It is important to understand what I mean by *semiosis*. All dynamical action, or action of brute force, physical or psychical, either takes place between two subjects . . . or at any rate is a resultant of such actions between pairs. But by 'semiosis' I mean, on the contrary, an action, or influence, which is, or involves, a cooperation of *three* subjects, such as a sign, its object, and its interpretant, this tri-relative influence not being in any way resolvable into actions between pairs . . . . my definition confers on anything that so acts the title of a 'sign' " (Peirce, 5.484).

Because of his idealism, the complexities of his argument, and especially the fact that his terminology is not constant — "raising doubts as to whether or not he has changed his thesis with his terms" (Weiss and Burks, 1945) — Peirce's writings are somewhat hard to understand. This difficulty has given impetus to an ever-growing secondary exegetical literature.[13]

In the semiotic domain, it was basically his contention that "the entire universe . . . is perfused with signs, if it is not composed exclusively of signs" (Peirce, 5.448n), and that every "thought . . . is in itself essentially of the nature of a sign" (5.594) or, at least, that thinking never occurs without the presence of some feeling, image, conception, or other representation which serves as a sign.[14] In his view, furthermore, "a law is in itself nothing but a general formula or symbol" (5.107), and man himself "is the thought", or, in other words, a human being "is a sign himself" (5.314; 6.344). A sign is to be understood only "in terms of some other more comprehensive and rational sign which welded the totality of things and beliefs together into a fixed and perfect whole" (Weiss, 1940), and, "Finally, as what anything really is, is what it may finally come to be known to be in the ideal state of complete information, so that reality depends on the

[13] Cf., i.a., Fitzgerald's selected bibliography in his 1966 book.
[14] Peirce, 5.283: "When we think . . . we ourselves, as we are at that moment, appear as a sign."

ultimate decision of the community; so thought is what it is, only by virtue of its addressing a future thought which is in its value as thought identical with it, though more developed" (5.316).

Peirce's ultimate classification (c. 1906) of signs into sixty-six different kinds developed slowly but persistently over some forty years. It was in 1867, in his paper "On a New List of Categories", that he first stated his now famous fundamental triad that — with intermediate and hybrid forms determined subsequently (cf. Wells, 1967, esp. #2a) — has proved to be of such high utility in several recent studies of both human and animal communication (for anthroposemiotic applications, see Jakobson, 1964, 1965, 1967; for zoosemiotic applications, Sebeok, 1967d). Peirce initially asserted that there were three kinds of signs (or, as he then called them, 'representations'): (1) *likenesses* (a term soon abandoned in favor of *icons*), or "those whose relation to their objects is a mere community in some quality", the Platonic notion that the signifier 'imitates' the signified; (2) *indices*, or "those whose relation to their objects consists in a correspondence in fact", that is, pointing, ostension, or deixis as a mode of signification, as the footprint that Crusoe found in the sand "was an Index to him of some creature"; and (3) *symbols* (which are the same as *general signs*), or "those the ground of whose relation to their objects is an imputed character", which he later called 'laws', meaning conventions, habits, or natural dispositions of its interpretant or of the field of its interpretant.[15]

Some three and a half decades afterwards, he incorporated this trichotomy (B) into a broader scheme,[16] yielding the following sets of sign relations displayed in Table 1, on p. 8.

It is fair to remark that the more Peirce elaborated and refined his scheme,[17] the more it became a challenge to his successors to devise

---

[15] By 'interpretant' Peirce appeared to mean the interpreter's reaction to the sign, that is, the sign's transmutation into an inferred neural code. On information processing in the nervous system in general, see the *Proceedings of the International Union of Physiological Sciences*, Vol. 3 (see Bibliography). More particularly in regard to the mechanisms of speech, see Brain, 1961; Luria, 1967, 1974.

[16] On the three trichotomies yielding ten classes of signs, plus what Peirce called 'degenerate' signs, see Peirce, 2.233-273. This is also discussed by Bense, 1965, and further elaborated in his 1967 book.

[17] Where *Rheme* is defined as "a Sign which, for its Interpretant, is a Sign of qualitative Possibility, that is, is understood as representing such and such a kind of possible Object", that is, roughly, a *term* or propositional function; a *Dicent* is "a Sign, which, for its Interpretant, is a Sign of actual existence", or roughly a

applications to particular semiotic systems, most of all to the pattern of language. One notably useful distinction in his scheme, however, was that the very same word could stand for different varieties of (*A*) signs in themselves:

As it is in itself, a sign is either of the nature of an appearance, when I call it a *qualisign*; or secondly, it is an individual object or event, when I call it a *sinsign* . . . ; or thirdly, it is of the nature of a general type, when I call it a *legisign*. As we use the term 'word' in most cases, saying that 'the' is one 'word' and 'an' is a second 'word', a 'word' is a legisign. But when we say of a page in a book, that it has 250 'words' upon it, of which twenty are 'the's, the 'word' is a sinsign. A sinsign so embodying a legisign, I term a 'replica' of the legisign. The difference between a legisign and a qualisign, neither of which is an individual thing, is that a legisign has a definite identity, though usually admitting a great variety of appearances. Thus, &, *and*, and the sound are all one word. The qualisign, on the other hand, has no identity. It is the mere quality of an appearance, and is not exactly the same throughout a second. Instead of identity it has *great similarity*, and cannot differ much without being called quite a different qualisign.[18]

TABLE 1

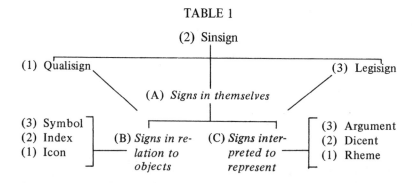

(2) Sinsign

(1) Qualisign   (3) Legisign

(A) *Signs in themselves*

(3) Symbol	(B) *Signs in re-*	(C) *Signs inter-*	(3) Argument
(2) Index	*lation to*	*preted to*	(2) Dicent
(1) Icon	*objects*	*represent*	(1) Rheme

---

proposition; and an *Argument* "is a Sign which, for its Interpretant, is a Sign of law". See Peirce, 2.250-252. The English philologist J. P. Postgate, in his Inaugural Address on "The Science of Meaning", unsuccessfully attempted to introduce *rheme* as a technical term in semantics, which he then proposed to relabel *Rhematology*; see Bréal (1900: 329).

[18] Peirce, in a 1904 letter to Lady Welby, cited in Ogden and Richards, 1938: 282; also Peirce, 8.334. Some of the distinctions made there were then developed in a 1906 article under the title, "Prolegomena to an Apology for Pragmaticism" (= Peirce, 4.530-572). A 'sinsign' (2.245) is perhaps better known

The above triple trichotomies yield ten classes of signs, labelled and illustrated by Peirce (Table 2):

TABLE 2

A-B-C	Name of Sign	Example
1-1-1	Qualisign	A feeling of 'red'
2-1-1	Iconic Sinsign	An individual diagram
2-2-1	Rhematic Indexical Sinsign	A spontaneous cry
2-2-2	Dicent Sinsign	A weathercock
3-1-1	Iconic Legisign	A diagram, apart from its factual individuality
3-2-1	Rhematic Indexical Legisign	A demonstrative pronoun
3-2-2	Dicent Indexical Legisign	A street cry
3-3-1	Rhematic Symbol (or Symbolic Rheme)	A common noun
3-3-2	Dicent Symbol	Proposition
3-3-3	Argument	Syllogism

Ten classes of signs, summarized in tabular form by Weiss and Burks, 1945, after Peirce, 2. 254-263.

It is indeed difficult to appreciate the utility of assigning a demonstrative pronoun in any natural language, for instance, to the category of a Rhematic Indexical Legisign, which "is any general type or law, however established, which requires each instance of it to be really affected by its Object in such a manner as merely to draw attention to that Object". This formulation ignores the evident fact that every demonstrative pronoun constitutes a different nodal point in a special network of verbal signs (Benveniste, 1969). Wells thinks, moreover, that Peirce's notion of symbol, though original, is fruitless, because of the way in which he generalizes his concept of the mind, which "permeates and infects what he says of the symbol". It is only his notion of index that Wells (1967: # 2b) deems both novel and fruitful.[19]

---

as a *token* (4.537) (which Peirce sometimes called an Actisign), in contrast to *type*, or 'legisign' (earlier Famisign; cf. 8.363) (see further Section 3, below). In 1906, Peirce (4.537) also named a legisign he called *tone*, which he defined as "an indefinite significant character such as a tone of voice", and which he regarded as neither a token nor a type; this may constitute the earliest explicit recognition of paraphonetic features as a part of semiotics.

[19] The notion of the icon is related to the Platonic process of *mimesis*, which

On the other hand, such passing strictures are not to be mistaken for an adequate critique of Peirce's work in semiotic. As another important contributor to semiotic remarked later, Peirce's "classification of signs, his refusal to separate completely animal and human sign-processes, his often penetrating remarks on linguistic categories, his application of semiotic to the problems of logic and philosophy, and the general acumen of his observations and distinctions, make his work in semiotic a source of stimulation that has few equals in the history of this field" (Morris, 1946: 290).

Since the bulk of Peirce's pertinent work, completed soon after the turn of the century, was published posthumously, it could hardly have come to the attention of his contemporary, Ferdinand de Saussure (1857-1913), the Swiss linguist who, at about the same time, conceived the need for a general science of signs which he tentatively designated *sémiologie*.[20] This he thought indispensable for the interpretation of language, as well as of all other systems of signs in their interrelation with language: "Puisqu'elle n'existe pas encore, on ne peut dire ce qu'elle sera; mais elle a droit à l'existence, sa place est déterminée d'avance. . . . Par là, non seulement on éclairera le problème linguistique, mais nous pensons qu'en considérant les rites, les coutumes, etc., comme des signes ces faits apparaîtront sous un autre jour, et on sentira le besoin de les grouper dans la sémiologie et de les expliquer par les lois de cette science" (Saussure, 1960: 33, 35).

Saussure's originality consisted of the recognition of the vital importance for linguistics of a comparative analysis and classification of the different sign systems, since such a confrontation is alone capable of revealing "what properties are shared by verbal signs with some or all other semiotic systems and what the specific features of language are" − in brief, that which can alone enable us to discriminate what is necessary from what is contingent in various systems of communication,

---

Aristotle broadened (in the *Poetics*, IV) from a chiefly visual representation to embrace all of cognitive and epistemological experience. For semiotic implications of this axiological category, cf. Morawski, 1970.

[20] The notion of semiotics, and its designation as *la sémiologie*, were first recorded in a note of Saussure's dated November, 1894; (cf. Godel, 1957: 275). Prieto's remark that Saussure seemed "Le premier à concevoir cette science" (1968: 93), is, of course, absurdly inaccurate. Saussure was even anticipated, in spirit if not in terminology, by Rudolf Kleinpaul, who published a well-reasoned and abundantly illustrated 456-page work on nonverbal communication a few years earlier (1888).

notably in language (Jakobson, 1969: 78; cf. pp. 68, below). The task
Saussure set for himself was not to decide whether linguistics was
more closely allied to psychology or to sociology, or even to find its
place among existing disciplines, but to raise the issue to an entirely
new level and to pose the problem in fresh terms, as shown in the
following key citation:

La langue est un système de signes exprimant des idées et par là,
comparable à l'écriture, à l'alphabet des sourds-muets, aux rites
symboliques, aux formes de politesse, aux signaux militaires, etc., etc.
Elle est seulement le plus important de ces systèmes.
   On peut donc concevoir *une science qui étudie la vie des signes au*
sein de la vie sociale; elle formerait une partie de la psychologie sociale,
et par conséquent de la psychologie générale; nous la nommerons
sémiologie (du grec *sēmeîon* 'signe'). Elle nous apprendrait en quoi
consistent les signes, quelles lois les régissent. . . . La linguistique n'est
qu'une partie de cette science générale, les lois que découvrira la
sémiologie seront applicables á la linguistique, et celle-ci se trouvera
ainsi rattachée à un domaine bien défini dans l'ensemble des faits
humains.
   C'est au psychologue à déterminer la place exact de la sémiologie;[21]
la tâche du linguiste est de définir ce qui fait de la langue un système
spécial dans l'ensemble des faits sémiologiques . . . si pour la première
fois nous avons pu assigner à la linguistique une place parmi les sciences,
c'est parce que nous l'avons rattachée à la sémiologie (Saussure,
1960: 33-34).

In contrast to Peirce — who was heir to the entire tradition of
philosophical analysis of signs — Saussure's point of departure and
constant center of attention was language; for him, the notion of the
sign was primarily a linguistic fact, that somehow expanded to
encompass the other processes of human, in particular social, signaling
behavior. As for Locke before him, and for many other scholars after
him — for instance, Bloomfield, who asserted that "Linguistics is the

[21] Here Saussure refers to Adrien Naville, *Nouvelle classification des sciences*
(1901: 104), who recorded this early version of his Geneva colleague's views on
the subject: Saussure insists on the importance "d'une science très générale, qu'il
appelle *sémiologie*, et dont l'objet serait les lois de la création et de la
transformation des signes et de leur sens. La sémiologie est une partie essentielle
de la sociologie. Comme le plus important des systèmes de signes c'est le langage
conventionnel des hommes, la science sémiologique la plus avancée c'est la
linguistique ou science des lois de la vie du langage." Cf. Godel, 1957: 181.

chief contributor to semiotic" (1939: 55), or Weinreich, who called natural human language "the semiotic phenomenon par excellence" (1968: 164) – for Saussure language occupied pride of place among all semiotic systems. A contemporary critic, Roland Barthes, going a step further, deems it necessary to "face the possibility of inverting Saussure's declaration: linguistics is not a part of the general science of signs, even a privileged part, it is semiology which is a part of linguistics: to be precise, it is that part covering the *great signifying unities* of discourse. By this inversion", adds Barthes (1968: 11), "we may expect to bring to light the unity of the research being done in anthropology, sociology, psycho-analysis and stylistics round the concept of signification." [22] The validity of this enthusiastic reversal of the semiotic hierarchies can be contemplated, if at all, only if zoosemiotics – the signaling behavior of all the speechless creatures – is left out of account; we shall, therefore, reject it without further discussion, as not fitting to the scope of this article.

What is the precise nature of the relationship of language to the other human semiotic systems? It appears that, for Saussure, the answer to this question lay in his well-known conception of the 'arbitrary' character of the linguistic sign. In general, he asserts that the prime target of semiotics will be "l'ensemble des systèmes fondés sur l'arbitraire du signe", and it is just in consequence of this that language acquires its position of preeminence: "on peut . . . dire que les signes entièrement arbitraires réalisent mieux que les autres l'idéal du procédé sémiologique; c'est pourquoi la langue, le plus complexe et le plus répandu des systèmes d'expression, est aussi la plus caractéristique de tous; en ce sens la linguistique peut devenir le patron général de toute sémiologie, bien que la langue ne soit qu'un système particulier" (Saussure, 1960: 110). Thus, while Saussure clearly insisted on the notion that linguistics had a necessary relationship with semiotics – a relationship, moreover, in which semiotics was superordinate – he failed to define its exact character beyond asserting the principle of the

[22] Genette explicates this reversal of Saussure's formula in his 1969 article. On semiotics as unification of science, see further Morris, 1946: 223-27, where this idea appears in two senses: semiotics is said to provide a comprehensive language for talking about sign phenomena, instead of looking at them piecemeal, and to provide an instrument for analysis of the relations between all special scientific languages; cf. also Hjelmslev, 1953. On the Unity of Science movement, the associated *International Encyclopedia* and Institute, see Feigl, 1969; for glimpses of the role of Morris, cf. Feigl, 1969: 647-48, 656-57, 659-60.

"arbitrariness of signs", which he regarded as a pervasive feature of all systems of expression, especially of language. In sum, for Saussure, semiotics remained a programmatic science, and its salient traits were those that he identified with his linguistic model (*le patron général*).

For several decades after the epoch of Peirce and Saussure, the further development of the science of signs was stimulated by the joint and separate work of C.K. Ogden and I.A. Richards, who were under the direct influence of Jeremy Bentham. Their volume, *The Meaning of Meaning* (1938),[23] proposed to distinguish the signification of signs represented in scientific discourse (referential or 'symbolic' terms) from those characteristic of non-scientific discourse (emotive or expressive terms), an emphasis which has proved fruitful in the consideration of semiotic issues in connection with aesthetics in general and literary and other art theory in particular. They also introduced the so-called context theory of meaning (for a critical review see Hotopf, 1965: 253-64), which brought mental process into the definition of the sign. This was done as follows (according to a later formulation by Richards): "A sign . . . works by being a member of certain kind of interpretative context in the mind — let us write it *abcq*. When *abc* . . . recurs without *q* — such is the fortune and overwhelming important characteristic of these interpretative contexts — the effect is in certain respects as though *q* also had recurred. And *q*, then, is what *a* (the sign) is of, what it signifies, or represents" (Richards, 1933); in other words, whenever an object experienced together with another causes us to think of that other, then it acts as a sign of the other, and these objects are said then to form a context. Richards' still later statement, that "meaning is *delegated efficacy*" (1936: 32), moves more in a behavioristic direction, but a detailed account of how the sign exercises this delegated efficacy was left for the next major contributor to semiotics, Charles Morris, to supply. Richards himself concluded, in 1936 (p. 34), that "no one knows" how signs work. In passing, it should also be pointed out that the collaborative work of Ogden and

---

[23] This book — the substance of which first appeared in periodical form during 1920-22 — passed through numerous editions (1923[1], 1938[5]), with constant revisions; references are made, throughout, to the 1938[5] edition. Supplements included Malinowski's influential piece on "The Problem of Meaning in Primitive Languages" (1923), and the interesting but hitherto neglected essay by Crookshank, on "The Importance of a Theory of Signs and a Critique of Language in the Study of Medicine" (1923). There is a brief account of Ogden and Richards' views on the modes of signifying in Morris, 1946: 69-72.

Richards, and, after the death (in 1957) of his senior partner, the later work of Richards especially, fell "mainly in the sphere of the educator's interest in semiotic" (Morris, 1964: 296).

Morris, in a succession of articles and books, has consistently aimed to lay the foundation for a comprehensive and fruitful science of signs.[24] Most concise and lucid in form, his exposition of 1938, *Foundations of the Theory of Signs*, remains one of the classics of the field. In this monograph, he introduced his "very useable and useful trichotomy", which "has a Peircean basis" (Wells, 1967: #3), namely, the division of semiotics into syntactics, semantics, and pragmatics.[25] When there is signification, there is (a) a sign, which has (b) a meaning or an object, and which has (c) this meaning or this object for an interpreter of the sign. Accordingly, he defines syntactics as "that branch of semiotic that studies the way in which signs of various classes are combined to form compound signs", that is, syntax treats signs in abstraction from their objects and their users. He next defines semantics as "that branch of semiotic which studies the signification of signs", that is, semantics takes signs and objects into account, but not interpreters. At last, he defines pragmatics as "that branch of semiotic which studies the origin, the uses, and the effects of signs", that is, pragmatics takes all three factors into account.[26] Logicians usually claim that the pragmatic relationship presupposes the semantic and the syntactic, and that the semantic presupposes the syntactic, but that, on the other hand, "the syntactic relationship does not presuppose the semantic and the pragmatic", and that "the semantic relationship may be studied without reference to the pragmatic" (e.g., Bocheński, 1968: 33). In the language development of the child, for example, the semantic aspect always implies the syntactic, but this hierarchy seems to be just the opposite in the case of Washoe, the young female chimpanzee that has been taught to communicate by gestures based on the standard American Sign Language of the deaf (Gardner and

[24] For a complete listing of Morris' relevant publications, see Morris, 1964: 92-93. On Morris and his works, see Rossi-Landi, 1953, 1974. (Morris' writings on the general theory of signs appeared in 1971, as *Approaches to Semiotics* 16 [The Hague: Mouton].)
[25] This aspect of semiotics was illuminatingly applied by Greenberg (1964) to the many-faceted relations between ethnology and linguistics. Weinreich (1968: 169), on the other hand, thought that this tripartition "turned out to be of little use in connection with natural sign phenomena".
[26] For definitions of these other terms employed by Morris, see the Glossary (pp. 345-56) appended to his *Signs, Language and Behavior* (1946).

Gardner, 1969). In other words, the eidetic meaning of a sign invariably implies an operational meaning along with it for the human, but not necessarily so for the animal; David McNeil has summarized the situation aptly: "A child will retain grammar even when speaking utter nonsense, whereas a chimpanzee apparently will exclude grammar even when conveying perfect meaning" (in Pfeiffer, 1969: 399; cf. Bronowski and Bellugi, 1970; and Brown, 1970).

Another trichotomy introduced by Morris, cross-cutting the former (cf. Sellars, 1950) distinguishes pure, descriptive, and applied semiotics. Pure semiotics is said to elaborate "a language to talk about signs", and Morris' own books may be regarded as outstanding exemplars of this genre. Descriptive semiotics studies actual signs; almost all zoosemiotics is descriptive in this sense. Applied semiotics "utilizes knowledge about signs for the accomplishment of various purposes".

These distinctions were found to be eminently applicable not only to sign-processes at the level of human behavior, but also to those that occur in the speechless animals. The possibility of such an extension of semiotics was explicitly envisaged, but not elaborated, by Morris himself (1946: 52-55, V). This was tried much later by the zoologists Peter Marler (1961) and W. John Smith (1968) (also anticipated by Yerkes and Nissen, 1939), and was also attempted, in a substantially wider framework in a series of papers, by myself (e.g., Sebeok, 1972). Marler held that the application of syntactics to animal communication is particularly clear, that semantics is of doubtful value in this sphere; but he was most interested in animal pragmatics, which he helped develop (although he was anticipated in this effort, in some ways, by J. B. S. Haldane) with the aid of still another set of distinctions drawn by Morris, namely, that among identifiors (that signify a location in space or time), designators (that signify characteristics or stimulus-properties of stimulus-objects), appraisors (that signify something as having a preferential status for behavior), and prescriptors (that signify the requiredness of certain response-sequences). These (non-exhaustive) categories of signs, that influence the behavior of their interpreters in different ways, were then applied by Marler (1956) in an analysis of vocal communication in the chaffinch: "in essence, given a knowledge of the response of other animals to the signal, and of the other circumstances in which that same response is given", Marler could "infer the nature of the 'message' transmitted by the signal".

Morris was close to two of his linguist colleagues at the University of Chicago: Manuel J. Andrade and Leonard Bloomfield. His basic view of the relation between semiotics and linguistics was that the former provides the metalanguage for the latter, "and that the terminology of linguistics is to be defined by linguists on the basis of the terms of semiotic" (Morris, 1946: 221). In 1946, he also introduced the very general notion of a *lansign-system* (*ibid.*, 35ff). roughly equivalent to language, but applicable as well to such speech surrogates as script, more or less formalized transforms such as symbolic logic and mathematics, and "perhaps to the arts" (1964: 60). In 1964, he observed that while recent work in linguistics had been in the syntactical study of certain lansign-systems (viz., the natural languages), he now sensed — correctly, as it turned out — a growing movement to extend the study of language to take into account its semantic and pragmatic aspects as well; in this, he saw a clear parallel in the development of logic in this century. He also reemphasized that linguistics is a part of semiotics, citing in support of this hierarchy, besides Bloomfield's, the authority of Saussure, Hjelmslev, and Greenberg.

In addition to his monograph cited above, Morris carried forward Peirce's dictum that, to determine the meaning of any sign, "we have . . . simply to determine what habits it produces". Accordingly, his book, *Signs, Language and Behavior*, was produced in the attempt to describe and differentiate signs in terms of the dispositions to behavior which they cause in their interpreters. In other words, semiotics is here tied to a particular theory of behavior — although it also draws upon the results of the insights of logicians, especially of Rudolf Carnap — which stresses the response to the stimulus, while the stimulus situation is disregarded: Morris' starting point here seems to have been "an analysis of indexical signs, as opposed to conventional symbols. The modification consists in this that a definite response to an utterance ceases to be considered the meaning of that utterance; it is replaced in that role by the type of response, i.e., a regular and potential response. The theory is, as it were, a behaviorist, external aspect of associationism: the association of thoughts and/or ideas is replaced by a relationship between acts or types of behaviour" (Pelc, 1969).

Morris' latest statement, *Signification and Significance*, while retaining his commitment to a variety of behavioristic psychology, aims at a synthesis of semiotics and axiology, the theory of value. It explores the relation of signs and values, and assesses their place in human action.

At this point, I must record my over-all agreement with the late

Uriel Weinreich's assessment (1968: 166) that "the reduction of sign phenomena to some more general kind of behavioral phenomenon have produced no marked success in either theory or research practice. A sign type is not always — perhaps only rarely — correlated with a class of specific stimuli or of overt responses". If this has a certain application to Morris' efforts to couple semiotics to behaviorism, the criticism holds *a fortiori* regarding the attempts of experimental psychologists to specify the meaning of individual signs in terms of attitudes taken towards them, emotions induced by them, productive of subjective connotations of strength or weakness, warmth or coldness, friendliness or unfriendliness, or further signs automatically evoked by them — by such techniques as a semantic differential or a free-association test, the former reviewed at length by Weinreich.[27]

In the decades that followed the publication of Saussure's *Cours*, linguists were too busy with problems internal to their discipline — particularly those attendant on the development of structuralism — to pay more than perfunctory attention to semiotics, although some linguistically oriented scholars, working in adjacent disciplines and concerned with questions of foundations, made fertile exploratory contributions to sign systems other than languages (e.g., a system of garments, certain of the verbal arts, etc.; I shall return to some of these in Section 3), more or less inspired by general principles of semiotic analysis.

One of the rare exceptions was the Belgian linguist Eric Buyssens, who undertook a serious, original, and reasonably comprehensive essay (1943) to realize "le voeu de Saussure", to confront languages with other (human) sign systems.[28] Buyssens introduces the term *seme*, defining this as "tout procédé idéal dont la réalisation concrète permet la communication", the adjective *semic*, and the phrase *semic act*, meaning the concrete embodiment of a seme. Semes — not signs,[29]

---

[27] See Osgood, Suci, and Tannenbaum, 1957; and Weinreich's review article, 1958; also Snider and Osgood, 1969. On behaviorism and semiotics in general, see also Wells, 1967, esp. II.

[28] Whether he was successful was challenged by representatives of the Geneva school, e.g., Frei, 1963. See also Buyssens, 1967, the first part of which constitutes a somewhat modified and augmented edition of Buyssens, 1943; and, in the same tradition, Pohl, 1968, especially the first volume, *Le symbole, clef d'humain*.

[29] But cf. Prieto 1968: 125: "le terme 'signe' . . . est sans doute synonyme de 'sème' ". Nevertheless, he finds 'sign' an ambiguous notion and advocates, with Buyssens, the adoption of 'seme' instead. On Saussure's conception of *sème*, see Engler, 1968: 44.

which, according to Buyssens, cannot be isolated, and can be defined solely as semic function – are then classified by a double criterion: according to the sensory modality involved, such as auditory, visual, and the like, or modalities (since semes like etiquette may combine words, gestures, perfumes, décors); and according to their etiology, which depends on the kind of relation between the form and the meaning of a given seme. This can be *intrinsic*, "existant antérieurement entre deux faits", which I take to be iconic and/or indexic; or *extrinsic*, where the relation exists "uniquement en vue de la communication", or is 'arbitrary', in Saussure's sense. Some semes may have a mixed character.

Among intrinsic semes, Buyssens cites the following:

l'art, la publicité imagée, certains symboles, certains gestes, les histoires sans paroles, les dessins qui à l'envers de certains postes récepteurs de radio indiquent l'endroit où il faut relier l'antenne, la prise en terre, le pick-up ou le réseau; les dessins qui, sur les machines-outils destinées à l'exportation, indiquent la fonction des manettes, pédales, leviers, boutons, interrupteurs; les enseignes parlantes; les dessins qui, par exemple, sur le ferry-boat *Londres-Istamboul*, indiquent à l'entrée de chaque salle sa destination: un serveur pour le restaurant, une dame sur un tabouret pour le bar, etc.

Among extrinsic semes, he cites:

le discours et ses transcriptions . . . ; les signalisation routière, ferro-viaire et maritime; les sonneries de clairon, de trompette ou de cor; les batteries de tambour; les signaux auditifs par sifflet, sirène, cloche, gong, canon; les signaux optiques par fusées, lampes, phares, bouées, fumées; les symboles des mathématiciens, physiciens, chimistes, logi-ciens; les notations commerciale, musicale et prosodique; les modèles de quantité de documents officiels (billets de banque, pièces d'identité, affiches, etc.); les taches de couleurs par les quelles on marque dans les campagnes les itinéraires touristique; la croix rouge sur fond blanc des services sanitaires; le coup de sonnette du visiteur; la sonnerie de téléphone et son signal 'occupé', etc., etc. (Buyssens, 1943: 46).

A mixture of intrinsic and extrinsic semes is found, among other structures, in etiquette, and in maps, blueprints, and the like.

In concluding, Buyssens claims to have demonstrated that there is no difference at all, in principle (*de nature*), between (natural) languages and other *sémies*, that is, sets of semes opposed to each other by normal and significant differences; the superiority of speech is, for him, merely a quantitative matter.

The well-argued, adequately illustrated, if somewhat quaint booklet of Buyssens has been virtually ignored by other linguists, possibly because of its appearance during World War II; nevertheless, it still repays careful reading. Curiously enough, however, when, some thirteen years later, Buyssens himself described (1956) the system of 460 gestures used by members of a Cistercian religious order, he abandoned all of his theoretical apparatus and treated it conventionally as a system of signs.[30]

To date, the most explicit and formalized exposition of the Saussurean heritage, however, is the theory of Glossematics, as embodied in the writings of two Danish linguists, Louis Hjelmslev (1953) and H. J. Uldall (1957), in which semiotic notions played a leading role, and with all sorts of ramifications (which will not be discussed here). Glossematic theory is based on the over-all assumption that the properties of all semiotic systems – accounted for in terms of a moderately complex algebraic apparatus – are based on a small set of primes, such as class and component, function, necessary and not necessary functive, both/and and either/or functions, and the empirical assumption of two non-conforming planes – content and expression – that consist, each, of two nonconforming hierarchies, form and substance. (See further, Mulder and Hervey, 1972, and Parkinson, 1975.)

In its final stages, the algebra of functions proposed by both Hjelmslev and Uldall was conceived as a highly general and uniform framework for the description of human behavior. In her Introduction to the second edition of Uldall's 1957 work, Eli Fischer-Jørgensen (1967) emphasized the differences between Hjelmslev's and Uldall's conception of the scope of glossematics. She points out that for Uldall glossematics was "a formal theory, which is not defined by any specific material, but designed explicitly to be used for all human activity", whereas for Hjelmslev glossematics was a linguistic theory, "which, implicitly, may serve also as a model for other humanistic disciplines" (1967: x-xi). At first blush, all this brings to mind Noam Chomsky's skepticism toward such universality; how worthwhile is it to rise to a level of abstraction where there are "plenty of other things incorporated

---

[30] Cf. Clelia Hutt's recent study on the Trappists (1968). Partly in the tradition of Buyssens, to whom he owes the observation "qu'il existe des procédés de signalisation a-systématiques", are several articles by Mounin; see, e.g., 1959.

under the same generalizations which no one would have regarded as being continuous with language or particularly relevant to the mechanisms of language?" (Chomsky, 1967: 73.) It is, indeed, one of the crucial questions of semiotics whether such generalizations, represented by the glossematicians (and again in such works as Barthes', e.g., 1968), merely express a methodological attitude, at best providing a uniform frame of reference for some or all of the behavioral sciences, or incorporate genuine empirical insights. The glossematicians would presumably argue that a systematic confrontation of language with other – both less and more complex – semiotic systems would reveal peculiarities of linguistic structure, that a study of this kind presupposes a uniform frame of reference, and that the issue boils down to the care one exercises in the selection of a common point of view so that "these sciences are concentrated around a linguistically defined setting of problems" (Hjelmslev, 1953: 69).

In the glossematic conception, natural languages are distinguishable and distinguished from non-language by specific properties, as follows: they belong to the class of semiotic systems exhibiting two planes with a diverging form; further, the content of languages can be manifested by all possible content substances, or, in other words, a language is that semiotic system which is able to express everything that can be expressed at all. Accordingly, says Hjelmslev:

In practice, a language is a semiotic into which all other semiotics may be translated – both all other languages, and all other conceivable semiotic structures. This translatability rests on the fact that languages, and they alone, are in a position to form any purport whatsoever; in a language, and only in a language, we can "work over the inexpressible until it is expressed" (Kierkegaard). It is this quality that makes a language usable as a language, capable of giving satisfaction in any situation . . . . There is no doubt that it rests on a structural peculiarity, on which we might be able to cast better light if we knew more about the specific structure of non-linguistic semiotics. It is an all but obvious conclusion that the basis lies in the unlimited possibility of forming signs and the very free rules for forming units of great extension (sentences and the like) which are true of any language . . . in general, a language is independent of any specific purpose (Hjelmslev, 1953: 69).

As Manfred Bierwisch (1972) has rightly pointed out, it is at this juncture that Hjelmslev and Chomsky converge in the tradition of Cartesian linguistics, and come to grips with what the latter has sometimes called the "creative aspect of language use", which is thus claimed to be the specific property that distinguishes language from all other semiotic systems; ('creativity', in Chomsky's sense, seems to refer to the appropriateness of language to any new situation).

Hjelmslev, in his concluding statement, makes the claim that "semiotic structure is revealed as a stand from which all scientific objects may be viewed" (1953: 81), and indeed, by the middle of the past decade, we witnessed, as Jakobson has recently observed, "a spontaneous and rapid international development of the new discipline which encompasses a general theory of signs, a description of the different sign systems, their comparative analysis and classification" (1969: 78). Scientific workshops in several countries[31] – particularly in France, Italy, Poland, the U.S.A., and the U.S.S.R. – are now conducting researches in a wide variety of semiotic problems, involving multifarious academic disciplines. (It must be admitted, however, that certain of these – somewhat in the manner of Monsieur Jourdain – have pursued semiotic goals, "il y a plus de quarante ans", without knowing it!)

In the United States, the first conference on semiotics[32] was held on May 17-19, 1962 (Sebeok, Hayes, and Bateson, 1964). Initially convened to discuss merely the twin topics of paralinguistics and kinesics, the inquiry and debate were soon widened to take in other areas of nonverbal communication, although there was throughout a centripetal tendency to view problems with constant reference to language. It was only in the final discussion session of this three-day meeting – in the last minutes of the conference, in fact – that Margaret Mead, in her usual incisive fashion, succeeded in crystallizing the thoughts of the some sixty scholars, of most diverse backgrounds, around the 'semiotics'[33] label. "It would be very nice", she said,

---

[31] Hjelmslev's line of thinking about semiotic and allied notions is currently carried forward, in Europe, by Greimas (and his students, especially in France and in Italy) – see fifteen of his collected essays (1970), six of which have also appeared in Italian as *Modelli semiologici* (1968); and, in the U.S., by Lamb and his students – see, e.g., his *Outline of Stratificational Grammar* (1966) – and by Chafe, who reviewed (1968) Lamb's *Outline*, and who gives further references (p. 603) to Lamb's works and his own; see also Fleming, "Stratificational Theory: An Annotated Bibliography" (1969).

[32] The conference, sponsored by the U.S. Office of Education, was held on the Bloomington campus of Indiana University.

[33] Editorial comment on the word 'semiotics' appears in my Preface to Sebeok, Hayes, and Bateson, 1964.

if we could go away from here with at least a preliminary agreement on the use of some phrase that we could apply to this whole field. Kinesics and paralinguistics, after all, are two. . . . We are, I think, conceivably working in a field which in time will include the study of all patterned communication in all modalities, of which linguistics is the most technically advanced. If we had a word for patterned communications in all modalities, it would be useful . . . many people here, who have looked as if they were on opposite sides on the fence, have used the word 'semiotics'. It seems to me the one word, in some form or other, that has been used by people who are arguing from quite different positions. . . . A lot of people are not going to spend their time on this field unless it is set up for exploration at all levels and in all modalities, but with a great deal of help from linguists (Mead, 1964: 275).

This pioneer interdisciplinary conference was deliberately organized as a pentad. Its five foci were: medicine, that is, communication without words between patient and doctor (Ostwald, 1964[34]); psychology, in particular, research on extralinguistic phenomena (Mahl and Schulze, 1964); pedagogical perspectives in paralinguistics and kinesics (Hayes, 1964); cross-cultural perspectives (La Barre, 1964); and emotive language (Stankiewicz, 1964[35]). The published transactions also included a general statement by Miss Mead, summarizing the highlights of the symposium and pointing the way for "continuing work on the multi-modal analysis of communication". She affirmed that, "in inaugurating the new science" of semiotics, we must act on behalf of man, by which she meant to disavow any manipulative applications (Mead, 1964; see also Mead, 1969 for a later version of her views on semiotics).

In the very year when this initial systematic American effort appeared in book form, Soviet scholars were holding the first of a continuing series of colloquia on semiotics in Kääriku (near Tartu, in Estonia), under the leadership of Juri M. Lotman.[36] While detailed

[34] A revised version of this paper has appeared (1968).

[35] Stankiewicz is currently expanding this paper into a monograph, to appear in the *Studies in Semiotics* series.

[36] The principal writings of Soviet semioticians centered around Lotman (who is Chairman of the Russian Literature Department at the State University of Tartu) have hitherto appeared under his editorship in *Trudy po znakovym systemam*, Vols. 2, 3 (cf. also Venclova, 1967), 4, and 5. See also Julia Kristeva's 1967 (reprinted 1969b, with 10 other essays) essay, which takes the writings of the Soviet semioticians as her point of departure. For a panoramic view of semiotics in the U.S.S.R., see Faccani and Eco, 1969; Papp, 1969; and especially the survey

information about this meeting is lacking,[37] a report of the next one, which was held on August 16-26, 1966 (and attended also by two U.S. participants), has been published (Venclova, 1967). According to this account, the meeting was devoted, in the main, to the area of semiotics that has been called in French 'systèmes secondaires modelants', that are (in the narrow sense) complex macrostructures composed of a natural language as their infrastructure and having at least a text coded with prefabricated units and constructions as their secondary super-structure.[38] The products of verbal art evidently belong here and elevate the study of the poetic function of language to the status of semiotic inquiry; likewise, the semiotic interpretation of myths and other kinds of oral tradition falls within this sphere. The approximately thirty communications presented tended to divide into eight groups: typology of texts; semiotics of folklore; poetics; typology of cultures; problems of mythology; semiotics of space and time in modeling systems; artistic models in a communicative frame; and general problems of semiotics.

---

by Segal, in Jurij M. Lotman and Boris A. Uspenskij (eds.), 1973, pp. 452-70.

[37] Three of the papers presented at the Tartu colloquium of May 10-20, 1968 have appeared in *Semiotica*, Vol. 1: Ivanov, 1969; Kristeva, 1969a, and Lotman and Pjatigorskij, 1969.

[38] 'Systèmes secondaires modelants' is a translation from the Russian of an expression proposed by A. A. Zaliznjak, V. V. Ivanov, and V. N. Toporov, in reference to the framework used in their collaborative work on Belorussian myths and rites, *Slavjanskie jazykovyie modelurujuščie semiotičeskie sistemy* (1965: 6-8). The notion of a secondary modeling system, in the broad sense, refers to an ideological model of the world where the environment stands in reciprocal relationship with some other system, such as an individual organism, a collectivity, a computer, or the like, and where its reflection functions as a control of this system's total mode of communication. A model of the world thus constitutes a program for the behavior of the individual, the collectivity, the machine, etc., since it defines its choice of operations, as well as the rules and motivations underlying them. A model of the world can be actualized in the various forms of human behavior and in its products, including linguistic texts – hence the emphasis on the verbal arts – social institutions, movements of civilization, and so forth. If I understand the notion fully, it is akin to the thematic principle that some American and other anthropologists have – with more artistic insight than scientific rigor – referred to as *ethos*, the integrating or summative pattern of a culture; cf. Kroeber and Kluckhohn, 1952, esp. pp. 165-71. For broad applications, especially in the sociology of literature, see further Żołkiewski, 1969. The relevant literature is reviewed, with particular reference to folklore, in Voigt, 1969b. For the relation to linguistics, see Pawlowski, 1974.

In 1965, a gathering was convened in Warsaw, but the first full-scale international conference on semiotics — with representatives from Czechoslovakia, Denmark, France, the German Democratic Republic, Italy, Poland, the U.S.A., and the U.S.S.R. in attendance — took place on September 12-18, 1966, at Kazimierz nad Wisła (in Poland). By that time, the Collège de France's Laboratoire d'Anthropologie Sociale had established its Section de Sémio-linguistique, led by A. J. Greimas, with the blessing and collaboration of Lévi-Strauss, Benveniste, and Barthes. Polish leadership was provided by Stefan Żółkiewski and his associates, especially Maria Renata Mayenowa.[39]

A remark of Mayenowa's reflected the mood of this conference; she later wrote:

it is only recently that semiotics has begun to constitute itself as an autonomous field of research superimposed on the several disciplines dealing with specific sign systems. However, since these disciplines, with the sole exception of linguistics, are themselves of recent origin, more or less contemporary with semiotics, we cannot as yet be said to have developed adequate and universally accepted theories for sign systems, other than those developed in linguistics for the natural languages (1967: 59-64; cf. Sebeok, 1967b).

Nevertheless, the conferees were confident that the time had come to advance semiotics by two practical and interrelated actions: the creation of an International Association for Semiotics; and provision for a periodical publication. It was decided to hold a new meeting in Warsaw in 1967, to finalize arrangements for the proposed organization, and to immediately authorize the setting up of a suitable publication outlet. Unfortunately, the 1967 meeting had to be postponed to 1968, at which time an international political crisis prevented the holding of more than a rump session in Warsaw. Eventually, however, an organizational meeting was called in Paris, on January 21, 1969, and there the Association Internationale de Sémiotique (International Association for Semiotic Studies) was born.[40]

[39] U.S. participants were: Henry Hiż, Roman Jakobson, Krystyna Pomorska, Meyer Schapiro, and myself; Noam Chomsky submitted a written communication. The proceedings of the conference, including the full texts of the papers delivered or sent, have appeared, in 1970, as Vol. 1 in the Series Maior of *Janua Linguarum* (The Hague: Mouton).
[40] The address is: 23 via Melzi d'Eril, Milano, Italy. In 1975, the officers were as

The Association has announced three aims: to promote semiotic researches in a scientific spirit; to advance international cooperation in this field; and to collaborate with local associations (which had already been formed in France, Italy, Poland, and the U.S.S.R.). It proposes to achieve these goals by organizing national and international meetings, and through its sponsorship of an international quarterly, *Semiotica*.

Semiotica – which is doubly co-sponsored by UNESCO'S Conseil International des Sciences Sociales and its Conseil International de Philosophie et des Sciences Humaines – represents a direct outgrowth of *Studies in Semiotics – Recherches Sémiotiques*, authorized by the Kazimierz assembly and constituting a regular section throughout eleven issues (Vol. 6, Nos. 2-6, 1967; Vol. 7, Nos. 1-6, 1968) of the bilingual periodical, *Social Science Information – Information sur les Sciences Sociales*. It was produced under the joint auspices of a Standing Committee on Publications, established at Kazimierz, entrusted to the editorial care of A. J. Greimas (Editor-in-Chief, 1967), Juri M. Lotman, Thomas A. Sebeok (Editor-in-Chief, 1968), and M. W. Skalmowski (1967; replaced by Jerzy Pelc in 1968). Effective 1969, this relatively modest initial effort has been transformed into a full-scale independent monthly, renamed *Semiotica*, edited by Thomas A. Sebeok.[41]

Furthermore, the journal is being supplemented by *Approaches to Semiotics*, *Advances in Semiotics*, and *Studies in Semiotics*, to accommodate book-length contributions, such as original monographs, collections, relevant conference proceedings, important reprintings and

follows: President: Cesare Segre (Italy); Honorary President, Emile Benveniste (France); Vice-Presidents: Roman Jakobson (U.S.A.), Jurij M. Lotman (U.S.S.R.), and A. Ludskanov (Bulgaria); Secretary General: Umberto Eco (Italy); Executive Secretary: Julia Kristeva (France); Treasurer: Jacques Geninasca (Switzerland); and *ex officio*: Thomas A. Sebeok (U.S.A.). Its directors include: Eliseo Verón (Argentina); Nicolas Ruwet (Belgium); Decio Pignatari (Brazil); A. Ludskanov and M. Yanakiev (Bulgaria); Paul Bouissac and René Lindekens (Canada); F. Miko and Ivo Osolsobě (Czechoslovakia); Holger S. Sørensen (Denmark); Emile Benveniste and Julia Kristeva (France); Erhard Albrecht and Manfred Bierwisch (German Democratic Republic); Hans-Heinrich Lieb and Hansjakob Seiler (German Federal Republic); J. Cohen and D. MacKay (Great Britain); Iván Fónagy and György Szépe (Hungary); Benjamin Hrushovski (Israel); Umberto Eco and A. Rossi (Italy); Shigeo Kawamoto (Japan); Teun A. van Dijk (The Netherlands); Jerzy Pelc and S. Żółkiewski (Poland); Mihai Pop (Romania); Bertil Malmberg (Sweden); Jacques Geninasca (Switzerland); S. Bayrav (Turkey); Henry Hiż and Roman Jakobson (U.S.A.); and Jurij M. Lotman (U.S.S.R.).
[41]   For current members of the Editorial Committee, see Ch. 10, fn. 3, on p. 185.

translations. The fourth volume in the first-mentioned series is a republication of the most consequential contents of the eleven issues of *Studies in Semiotics — Recherches Sémiotiques*, published in order to make them conveniently available under a single cover.[42]

The founding of the Association, with the concurrent establishment of multiple publication outlets, will undoubtedly serve as a rallying point and perhaps as a catalyst for all interested individuals and groups who have a serious concern for the notion of the sign; the year 1969 may thus well turn out to have been a milestone in the history of semiotics.

3. TOWARDS A CLASSIFICATION OF SIGNS AND SIGN SYSTEMS

It must have become apparent from the foregoing that while numerous attempts were made by philosophers and philosophically inclined linguists, throughout the history of semiotics, to classify signs or systems of signs,[43] none of them has as yet enjoyed universal and permanent acceptance. What follows is a non-exhaustive survey of what seem to me important criteria that must be taken into account in working toward a reasonably holistic categorization — surely a task to be completed in the distant future. The interrelationships among the classes that are suggested here are clearly of the kind that are convertible into Euler-Venn diagrams: that is, they overlap; this approach to classification seems to me unavoidable at this stage in the development of semiotics (cf. Lenneberg, 1969). The ensuing attempt differs from previous ones chiefly insofar as it lays heavy emphasis on semiotically relevant data from current ethological literature (Sebeok, 1972).

In biology, as Ralph Gerard has suggested, it is useful to conceive of a material system — an org — in one of three ways: its 'being', or

---

[42] *Essays in Semiotics/Essais de sémiotique*, ed. by Julia Kristeva, Josette Rey-Debove, and Donna Jean Umiker (The Hague: Mouton, 1971).

[43] One of the more thoughtful attempts was Bally's "Qu'est-ce qu'un signe?" (1939). Spang-Hanssen's "Recent Theories on the Nature of the Language Sign" (1954; but completed in 1948), is the most comprehensive survey of 'recent' psychological sign theories (Ogden and Richards, Karl Britton, Bertrand Russell, Charles W. Morris), as well as of 'recent' linguistic theories (Ferdinand de Saussure, Leo Weisgerber, Alan H. Gardiner, Karl Bühler, Eric Buyssens, Leonard Bloomfield, Louis Hjelmslev). See also Mahmoudian's entry on "Signe" in Martinet's *La linguistique: Guide alphabétique* (1969). Jakobson has recently devoted a special study to the classification of sign systems (1970) — as announced in Jakobson, 1969: 80, fn.

structure, that is, its enduring status in a synchronic sense; its 'behaving', or *function*, 'a repetitive perturbation' along a secular trend; and its 'becoming' or *history*, representing cumulative changes in the longitudinal time section (Gerard, 1957; 1960). A semiotic system – a sign – can likewise be fruitfully examined from each of these three points of view: we can ask, what is a sign, how does the environment and its turbulences impinge upon it, and how did it come about? Functional classifications of the sign are empirical, extrinsic; they are based upon variations at different nodal points in an expanded communication model. A structural identification of the sign is analytic, intrinsic; it utilizes types of associations potentially inherent in the architecture of the sign itself. The problem of becoming introduces diachronic considerations of two sorts: we can focus on the evolution of sign systems in phylogeny, or consider their development in ontogeny. What follows is organized according to this scheme, but diachronic considerations are omitted from this article.

Function

In delineating the scope of the field at the outset, there was an underlying pragmatic implication: when proposing to restrict the discussion to "the semiotic manifestations of whole living systems" (p. 2, above), attention was deliberately focused upon the origin and/or effects of signs or, more generally, the sorts of relationships that can prevail between the source of a message and its destination. The first basic classificatory criterion can, therefore, be constructed in terms of the nature of all possible sources of signs, for it is reasonable to begin to classify where the coding itself begins – at the input end. According to the distinctions introduced in Section 1, these could be provisionally diagrammed as in Table 3:

TABLE 3

SOURCES OF SIGNS

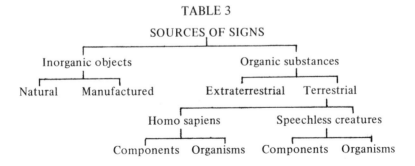

This excessively simplistic scheme becomes at once more complicated as the nature of the sign-receivers — the other end of the feedback loop in the transactional chain — is taken into additional consideration. Man's conspecific messages can, for example, be differentiated as intrapersonal, requiring only one participant engaged with a prospective or imaginary interlocutor (cf. the phenomenon of 'inner speech',[44] or 'internal dialogue'[45]); interpersonal (dialogue, requiring an *alter* besides the *ego*),[46] or pluripersonal[47] — in Eskimo oral tradition, for example, "the myth-teller speaks as many-to-many, not as person-to-person" (Carpenter, 1960). A human message may be directed at a machine,[48] or at a personified supernatural, as in an incantation or a prayer addressed to a deity (Sebeok, 1962b); communication with ancestral spirits is prevalent and commonplace in many cultures, for example, in New Guinea (Eilers, 1967: 34-36). Vice versa, animates may receive signs from the environment — cf. the phenomenon of echolocation (Griffin, 1968) — or fancy receiving them, "as in some of the epigrams of Callimachus and of his imitators, the stone is thought of as carrying on a brief dialogue with the passerby" (Hadas, 1954: 50-51), or again from the location of stars and planets, the length and intersection of lines in the hand, the entrails of sheep, the position of dregs in a teacup — in brief, by those pseudo-semiotic divinatory techniques that are known variously as augury, astrology, palmistry, haruspication, and the like (Kleinpaul, 1888: Ch. III; Kahn, 1967: 92). Animal senders and receivers of signs are either conspecifics, or they belong to two or more different species, one of which may be man (cf. Hediger, 1965, 1967). Accordingly, zoologists tend to classify sign systems first of all into intraspecific vs. interspecific varieties;[49] an animal can direct its

[44] On the genesis and function of inner speech, cf. Egger, 1904, and especially Vygotsky, 1962.
[45] Cf. Peirce, 4.6: "... thinking always proceeds in the form of a dialogue — a dialogue between different phases of the *ego* — so that, being dialogical, it is essentially composed of signs ..." Also, *id.*, 6.338: "All thinking is dialogic in form."
[46] Matson and Montagu, 1967, contains some useful, if recherché, selections viewing human communication as a dialogue.
[47] A pluripersonal group may be centrifugal (one-to-many) or centripetal (many-to-one); see Table D, on p. 277, in Ruesch and Bateson, 1951, and Ch. 11 generally, for a review of different types of coexistent networks of communication. For a discussion of 'pluripersonal' communication in allo-primates, see Altmann, 1967.
[48] Cf. p. 2, fn. 4; and Dewan, 1969, cited on p. 74, below. For a characteristically pessimistic view of "The Future of Man-machine Languages", see Bar-Hillel, 1968.
[49] Thus Wynne-Edwards (1962: 24) writes: "... the primary subdivision in the

messages, moreover, at a *particular* member of its own species, or at an *individual* of another species.[50]

Contact among emitters and receivers is established and maintained by miscellaneous flow-processes that link them across space and time, and our classification of sign systems becomes still further refined as this operationally crucial third factor — the medium of trans- mission — is taken into account. In principle, any form of energy propagation or transfer of matter can serve as a sign carrier, depending on an animal's total perceptual equipment. Sign systems are thus also distinguishable in terms of the channel or channels connecting the input side with the output side. If an animal's sensory capacity allows for the parallel processing of information through multiple input channels, calculable redundancies will be found to prevail (an effect sometimes referred to as 'the law of heterogeneous summation') (Sebeok, 1968: 36), and the application of the rules for switching from one subassembly to another, under particular circumstances, will yield different hierarchical arrangements that render the classification even subtler in consequence of contextual effects.

From the semiotic point of view — to say nothing of an evolutionary standpoint — it is very important to appreciate fully both the advan- tages and the disadvantages of every channel (Table 4) utilized for successful communication in and across all species.

Yet the foundations for a comparative analysis of this kind have barely begun to be laid.[51] For every semiotic system, it would be useful indeed to have a lucid and concise account, comparable with the following characterization of speech: "Speech is produced with the human body alone, without any tool; it is independent from light and can be used day and night; it fills the entire space around the source and does not

---

functions of communication should clearly fall between signals directed at other members of the same species and those . . . directed at other kinds of animals; these divisions are respectively intra- and inter-specific". See further the tabular outline of animal behavior, based on the origin and destination of signals, in Wenner, 1969.

[50] For a remarkable example of the former, cf. the mutual auditory display of shrikes of the genus *Laniarius*: each pair of the species *aethiopicus* "tends to develop a particular repertoire of duet patterns by which they can be distinguished from other pairs in the neighbourhood", as shown in Thorpe, 1963; more generally, see Thorpe, 1968. The extremely complex relation between picarian birds and their mammalian symbionts (ratels, baboons, or humans) furnishes an even more striking illustration of the latter; see Friedmann, 1955.

[51] A typology is adumbrated, in summary fashion, in Sebeok, 1967c. See further Geldard, 1960, as well as Jakobson, 1964, 1967; Sebeok, 1967d.

TABLE 4

CHANNELS

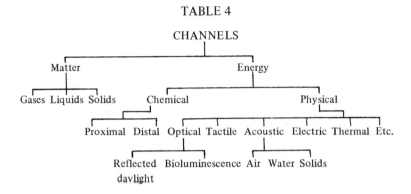

necessitate a straight line of connection with the receiver; it can also be greatly varied from intimate whisper to long distance shouting; and it involves a very small amount of energy" (Lotz, 1950: 712).

Among the criterial design features of speech just cited, Lotz singled out for first mention that signs encoded in this mode can be produced by the human body alone, without recourse to any tools. The use of both ready-made objects and shaped artifacts as tools is known to occur variously throughout the animal world, ranging from moths and spiders through birds, otters, and primates.[52] Chimpanzees of the Gombe Stream Reserve, for instance, build nests, fold selected leaves to facilitate drinking or to wipe their body, use sticks, twigs, and grasses to get termites, ants, or honey, and use them, as well, as olfactory probes; they also use stones to break nuts, and employ both sticks and stones in agonistic displays (van Lawick-Goodall, 1968). The instrumental behavior of these chimpanzees exemplifies a twofold function of tool using in animals and man: a (presumably) primary amplifying function, and a (presumably) secondary semiotic function. When the chimpanzee uses a stone to break nuts, it draws material supplies from its environment to adaptively extend and improve, with relatively moderate expenditure of energy, the manipulatory systems necessary for its existence in its living space. When, on the other hand, it uses a stone in

---

[52] On the use of tools by animals in general, see Hall, 1963 and the comments that followed, in *Current Anthropology* 7: 215-16 (1966); in moths and spiders, Wickler, 1968: 58, 131-32; in birds (viz., Egyptian vulture, *Neophon peromopterus*) reported in *Time*, January 6, 1967, under the heading, "Birds That Throw Stones"; in the California sea otter, *Enhydra lutris*, Hall and Schaller, 1964; in primates, Hall, 1963, and Kortland and Kooij, 1963.

agonistic displays, the primary amplifying function is endowed with a secondary sign function – the behavior has, in the parlance of the ethologists, become ritualized. The instrumental – as opposed to the merely somatic – production of animal signs sometimes takes exceedingly bizarre forms, as in those "wonderful arena birds called bower birds, with their houses and ornamented gardens and their courtship displays that replace plumage with glittering natural jewelry" (Gilliard, 1963).[53]

Both human and animal sign systems can thus be classified into organismal, according to whether they are produced by the body alone, or artifactual, produced by the body amplified. Diverse surrogates for spoken languages (cf. Stern, 1957) can be contrasted in this way (among others, of course): for example, the transposition of speech into whistles is organismal, into drumbeats artifactual, although all these are manifested in the same acoustic substance; or into relatively autonomous graphic systems, or Braille (all in different substances, viz., for the addressee,[54] auditory, visual, tactile).[55] A transitional grouping of implements is constituted by detachable parts of an animal's body itself; thus a particle of dung, or the trace of secretion on the territorial marking place, can function as a sort of synecdoche, with the animal's separated *pars* – that can continue to be efficacious even after the temporary departure or permanent extinction of the source – standing *pro toto*.[56] The identical semiotic process is the basis for contagious – in contrast to homeopathic – magic, where the intended

[53] These birds and their display have evolved, along quite different lines, essentially into builders of avenue-type bowers, and builders of maypole-type bowers, but both types "use display-objects of various circumscribed colours which are collected with great discrimination . . .", according to Marshall, 1954: 170.

[54] For the addresser, of course, the situation may be quite different: a written sign may be encoded chemically (e.g., in ink), but will be decoded visually; cf. Sebeok, 1967d: 1778. Signs encoded visually may be decoded by the blind through the skin of the back; cf. Bach-Y-Rita, *et al.*, 1969.

[55] On speech surrogates in general, see Umiker, 1974 and Sebeok and Umiker-Sebeok, 1976.

[56] Bilz, 1940: 195 develops the *pars pro toto* principle in a double sense: "einmal als Möglichkeit sprachlicher Mitteilungen, indem der Erzähler eine der Teilfunktionen herausgreift und für das *Ganze* setzt, d. h. mit der Komponente das volle Funktionsbild meint oder das ganze Objekt bezeichnet, zum anderen aber verfährt auch *die Natur* in der gleichen Weise, indem sie das ganze Funktionsbild tatsächlich in seine Teilfunktionen aufsplittern kann und nur die eine oder die andere Komponente statt des Ganzen mobilisiert".

victim's nail parings, or the like, act as the indexic signs.[57] Objects used for semiotic display can, moreover, be distinguished further according to whether they are 'Found Objects', like a plucked flower, or matter, as precious metal, wrought into floral shape, to be worn as a brooch; prehistoric artists are said to have discovered, by a semiotic technique that is sometimes called 'épouser les contours' (Giedion, 1960), in natural rock formations the images of the animals they sought.[58]

Another important distinction, also highly relevant to the problem of classification, results from contrasting 'pure' with other sorts of semiotics. Let us recall that Morris specified the task of pure semiotics to be the elaboration of "a language to talk about signs" (cf. p. 15, above). Since it is obviously necessary to use signs for referring to signs in discourse about signs, and since, for this purpose, a signifier (or *signans*, or sign vehicle; see below) is commonly employed as an index of its own sign, such "a language to talk about signs", or a semiotic system specialized for communicating about another semiotic system, can be said to constitute a *metasemiotic* (by analogy with 'meta-language'). The *object semiotic* (by analogy with 'object language') then becomes any 'other' semiotic system communicated about in the metasemiotic.[59] Morris assigned the study of such actual sign systems to descriptive semiotics. Confusingly, however, other scholars refer to the study of phenomena which arise when signs are actually used in the process of communication as applied semiotics (one might call this 'performance'), as against pure semiotics, which then becomes the study of the underlying rules which regulate the objective structure of signs ('competence'). Again, according to a distinction introduced by Jakobson, the object of pure semiotics is the linguistic sign, whereas

[57] Frazer, *The Golden Bough* (1951: 43): "The most familiar example of Contagious Magic is the magical sympathy which is supposed to exist between a man and any severed portion of his person, as his hair or nails . . ."

[58] On semiotic organization by chance, see further O'Brien, 1969. Communication by ready-made objects as signs "where as the vehicle of information serves the presented reality itself", has been called *ostension* by Osolsobě (1967: 101), who explored the significance of "showing things and persons actually existing and present in time and space . . . limited to what is at our disposal at the time of communication just now and just there" in the arts, particularly in the context of the theater.

[59] Variants of this pair of terms were operationally used by Hjelmslev; cf. 1943, Def. 102: metasemiotic, "a scientific semiotic one or more (two) of whose planes is (are) (a) semiotic(s)", and Def. 103: object semiotic, "semiotic that enters as a plane into a semiotic".

applied semiotics deals with such systems of signs as may be embodied, for instance, in cuisine, garments, the products of gardening, or architectural constructs; (as he remarked, "we don't inhabit signs").[60] However, still others prefer to confine the latter expression to merely pedagogical applications. Morris himself intended by applied semiotics to circumscribe the field that utilizes "knowledge about signs for the accomplishment of various purposes", a definition which I then extended to applied zoosemiotics. Since I have found Morris' trichotomy useful, especially in heuristic comparisons of human with animal communication, I prefer it to a bifurcated model and will, at least provisionally, continue to use all three terms – pure, descriptive, and applied – much in the way he has defined them for semiotics and, by implication, *mutatis mutandis*, for zoosemiotics.

Higher organisms are so constructed, both centrally and peripherally, that they are able to – although they need not – draw simultaneously upon two or more repertoires of sign systems. This capability, notably characteristic of man, allows for a high number and many kinds of admixtures of expressions. It also provides another criterion for classifying sign systems, as ranging from 'simple', homogeneous structures to syncretic formations of varying degrees of complexity, the components of which, furthermore, may or may not be patterned symmetrically. This last point can be illustrated as follows: if I assert 'yes', and, at the same time, nod my head affirmatively, my verbal sign is symmetrical – as well as mutually redundant – with my kinesic sign. In a Franz Lehar operetta, a Chinese mandarin sings an aria vigorously disclaiming his alleged susceptibility to bribery, while, simultaneously, he keeps thrusting his palm out behind his back: the audience is given to clearly understand that, of the two asymmetrical, in fact, wholly contradictory message components, the kinesic one is to be interpreted as true and the acoustic one as false.[61]

What Lotz (1950: 717) has called a 'ribbon concept' of communica-

[60] Lecture on "Language in Relation to Other Communication Systems" delivered on October 14, 1968, reported in de Mauro and Grassi, 1969, and witnessed by the author.
[61] A striking illustration of asymmetry between an acoustic and a visual message component was cited by Sebeok in 1962a: fn. 8: "A patient was told under hypnosis she must raise her right index finger to indicate an affirmative answer, left for negative. Brought out of trance, she was questioned by her doctor. Unable to face her emotional problem, she shook her head vigorously in manifest negation, but her right finger shot up, showing that the correct answer was 'yes' ". The problem area has been reviewed and discussed in Ekman and Friesen, 1969a,

tion — a notion which, of course, overlaps, yet is not identical, with what Birdwhistell (e.g., 1968b) and others have called 'multi-modal' communication[62] — seems to characterize most of normal human signaling behavior. Were this imaginary ribbon to be sectioned at any point in time, it would, much more often than not, reveal verbal, paraphonetic, kinesic, proxemic, olfactory, and perhaps other strands of signs mixed together but stacked in a hierarchy suited to the requirements of the global message involved. Signs are combined in appropriate — linguists would say 'grammatical' — ways to yield a compound designatum (or *signatum*, that is, content that is signified; see below). The emotional attitude of a speaker towards his verbal message can be conveyed either by features — emotive, expressive — coded by the language itself (Stankiewicz, 1964), or by accompanying nonverbal features — paraphonetic, kinesic, etc. — that serve to support or belie it (contributing to effects like irony or sarcasm). The revealing character of the nonverbal features when the verbal performance is latent was underscored by Freud (1959: 94) in an often-cited remark: "He that has eyes to see and ears to hear may convince himself that no mortal can keep a secret. If his lips are silent, he chatters with his finger-tips; betrayal oozes out of him at every pore."

The semiotic systems called 'secondaires modelants', or macro-systems — that is, those that imply, by definition, a natural linguistic infrastructure (as discussed in fn. 38) — all constitute elevated cases of syncretism, including those with a predominantly folkloristic and artistic function. Here belong all genres of discourse composed of prefabricated texts, such as myths and the other products of oral tradition; the verbal arts in general and poetry in particular; such hybrid formations — labeled with transitional awareness — as vocal music, circus acts, dramatic performances, sound film; and blended structures of the highest intricacy, as opera. To illustrate: a sound film can partake of four sign systems, one visual and three auditory — language,

---

but the classic treatise on the subject remains Quintilian's *Institutes of Oratory* (see esp. Book XI, Ch. III), from the first century A.D.

[62] Mary Catherine Bateson writes (1968: 10-11) that "we must assume that coded linguistic communication is concurrent with little known types of communication in other modalities, and that the overall system includes rules about the way in which the codes interact and what kinds of code switching are possible". See also the remarks by several participants in the discussions and Bar-Hillel (1970), cited on p. 78, below.

music, and other sound-effects (*'bruit'*);[63] an acrobatic act partakes of at least five, namely, the performer's dynamic behavior, his social behavior, his costume and other accessories, the linguistic accompaniment, and the musical accompaniment (Bouissac, 1968, 1969, 1971). As to the art of the opera,[64] which, in Stender-Petersen's (1949) formulation, irreversibly presupposes the literary, the musical, and the scenic arts, it is a semiotic product that can, indeed, achieve "un degré très élevé d'indépendance raffinée".

Structure

Rulon Wells (1967) tells us that "Semiotic has two groups of affinities. It is connected, on the one hand, with communication, and, on the other, with meaning." If, in this article, I have so far focused on phenomena of usage, particularly those that pertain to miscellaneous transactional relationships, this was not for lack of interest in such facts as intention;[65] therapeutic explorations of man's *paysage intérieur* by

---

[63] Cf. various essays by Metz, in particular 1968b: 113-14. On the semiotic of film, see, i.a., the following works: Metz, 1968a and b; Bettetini, 1968; Garroni, 1968; Wollen, 1969 (esp. Ch. 3, on "The Semiology of the Cinema"); and Worth, 1969; and the special issue of *Sprache im Technischen Zeitalter*, No. 27 (1968), entirely devoted to "Zeichensystem Film – Versuche zu einer Semiotik".

[64] Cf. p. 79, below.

[65] The place of 'intention' – or, more broadly, goal-orientation – in a communication model constitutes an entangled and controversial problem. In the sense of self-awareness – so-called 'subjective teleology' – the notion may be criterial in the definition of all anthroposemiotic systems, and notably characterizes language (as D. M. MacKay is wont to insist, e.g., in his 1961 article, where he points out that semantic questions can find their natural place in information theory if and only if language is pictured in the shape of a *'goal-directed self-adaptive'* diagram). Jakobson (1970: 10), for example, speaks of symptoms as "mere unintended indexes as a subspecies of a vaster semiotic class", and of 'unwitting indexes' as a variety of signs. But this would hardly be pertinent to zoosemiotic systems, as implied in Verplanck, 1962. Evans and Bastian, 1969 convincingly argue against the 'stultifying effects' of the groundless conception of intentionality in the social behavior of the bottle-nosed dolphin and other marine mammals. On the other hand, in the sense of implying explanations – so-called 'objective teleology' – to account for directively organized structures, mechanisms, and patterns of behavior, the concept may not only be appropriate but is perhaps indispensable for the study of communication in all organisms; cf. Ayala, 1968; for the use of teleological conceptions in the analysis and description of behavior generally, see also Miller, Pribram, and Galanter, 1960. On the two kinds of teleology, see the twin articles by Hofstadter, 1941-42 and 1942. Lange-Seidl's arguments (1975: 260f.) have, I think, an *ad hoc* character, and cannot be maintained.

Freud and by Jung (Jung, *et al.*, 1968), Lacan (1966, 1968; Bär, 1971), or Shands (1970a-b, 1971), and other psychiatrists; in those symbolic forms in the dimensions of our *milieu extérieur* studied, among many others, by Ernst Cassirer (1923, 1924, 1929, 1944) and his epigones (e.g., Langer, 1948), or the dialectic 'dramatism' of Kenneth Burke (1966; reviewed by Hymes, 1968b) and those who would apply his model of symbolic action in the various social sciences;[66] or in the fascinating problems of *Weltanschauung*,[67] as advanced by Wilhelm von Humboldt (cf. Miller, 1968: Ch. 2, the influence of Humboldt on Cassirer), reexamined by Edward Sapir (1929) and popularized by Benjamin Lee Whorf (Carroll, 1956), resisted by Max Black (1968: 71-75), and inverted by Adam Schaff, with the assertion that "Reality shapes language..." (1962: 349). It was, rather, because I share Weinreich's judgment that semantic analysis quickly embroils all venturers "in some of the more inconclusive epistemological controversies of social science" (Weinreich, 1968: 165[68]), and because the theories of both reference and meaning remain as opaque and intractable as ever.[69] And if semantic theory is incoherent, hardly reliable when applied to natural languages — save, to a limited extent, in the domain of highly systematic grammatical elements, less so for the more loosely structured vocabulary, but

---

[66] Sociological reflexes are exemplified by Duncan, 1968, reviewed by Hymes, 1969; for anthropological reflexes, see, e.g., the Cornell University Press series on *Symbol, Myth, and Ritual*, ed. by Victor W. Turner, and Peacock, 1968, with a foreword by Hymes, setting it firmly in the Burke tradition. For a more recent survey, see Turner, 1975.

[67] For a review of the *Weltanschauung* problem as a whole, see Rossi-Landi, 1968.

[68] Would that Sørensen's (1967) remark were true in a serious sense: "Since the notion of meaning is a basic notion, one would think that everyone must know the meaning of 'meaning'. This, in point of fact, is what everyone does."

[69] In spite — or just because — of this, I have spared no editorial efforts to obtain adequate coverage of these topics, wherever pertinent, in the *Current Trends in Linguistics* series; the following major chapters have appeared: in Vol. 1, *Soviet and East European Linguistics*, Weinreich, on Soviet "Lexicology" (1963); in Vol. 3, *Theoretical Foundations*, Weinreich, "Explorations in Semantic Theory" (1966); in Vol. 9, *Linguistics in Western Europe*, Ullmann, "Semantics" (1972); in Vol. 12, *Linguistics and Adjacent Arts and Sciences*, three separate chapters, to wit, by Coseriu and Geckeler, "Linguistics and Semantics" (1974); by Clark, "Semantics and Comprehension" (1974); and by Werner, *et al.*, "Some New Developments in Ethnosemantics and the Theory and Practice of Lexical/Semantic Fields" (1974).

practically not at all for compound signs (idioms, sentences in general) — zoosemantic theory, properly speaking, cannot even be asserted to exist.[70] Nevertheless, the nature of the coupling between the moieties that are traditionally and universally recognized as the minimal components of any sign has perennially been a crucial issue for anyone seriously interested in semiotics, and therefore at least a rudimentary acquaintance with the composition of signs is a prerequisite for even their mere classification.

A sign, then, by all accounts — from Stoic philosophy to contemporary thinking — is conceived of as constituted of two indispensable halves, one sensible, the other intelligible: the *signifier*, a perceptible impact on at least one of the sense organs of the interpreter; and the content *signified*. Dante incisively formulated this, in 1305, in his unfinished *Dē vulgarī eloquentiā* (I-3), as follows: "hoc equidem signum sensuale quid est, in quantum sonus est; rationale vero, in quantum aliquid significare videtur ad placitum" ("this sign ... being, as to sound, *sensible* by nature, but *rational* [i.e., intelligible] in so far as it carries some meaning by convention [i.e., arbitrarily]") (1957: 18; 1890: 6). (In medieval Latin, the corresponding pair of terms for signifier and signified was *signans* and *signatum*, rendered by Saussure as *signifiant* and *signifié*, by Morris as *sign vehicle* and *designatum*, etc.). The distinction between the two can be crudely illustrated by the following anecdote: a Danish photographer's apprentice is sent to America to learn to improve his technique in portraiture; there he is told to always have his subjects say *cheese*; upon his return to Denmark, he instructs them to say *ost* — the joke turns on his confusion of the bilingual signifiers with the common (i.e., translatable) signified.

In various systems of signs; notably in language, a sign vehicle can sometimes — when the contextual conditions are appropriate — signify by its very absence, occur, that is, in *zero* form.[71]

A particular occurrence of a sign — what Peirce labelled a 'sinsign' — is now more commonly called a *token*, whereas the class of all occurrences of the sign — Peirce's 'legisign' — is called a *type*. Let us reapply his own illustration: if a page in a book has 250 words upon it,

---

[70] Two papers by W. John Smith (1969a and b) are especially important for emergent zoosemantic theory. Jakob von Uexküll's 1940 *Bedeutungslehre* (1970) is the classic treatise on zoosemantics.
[71] See further p. 118, below.

this is the number of word tokens, whereas the number of different words on the page is the number of word types.[72]

Now the two principal sets of questions that have preoccupied most students of the sign are these: (1) how do particular sign *tokens refer*, how do sign *types* have the constant capacity to *mean*; and (2) what, precisely, is the distinction between the relation of reference, or *denotation*, and the relation of meaning, or *designation*?[73] The theory of verbal reference and the theory of verbal meaning are usually treated together under *semantics*;[74] the word *zoosemantics* was recently coined to accommodate presumably corresponding processes among animals' (Sebeok, 1965). Although an understanding of denotata and designata, and of the differences between reference and meaning, are absolutely essential to explain a vast number of facts of semantics and zoosemantics, there is no consensus among philosophers on any theory according to which the data accumulated by linguists, over many centuries, from the languages of the world, and ethograms, gathered by ethologists, over several decades, in a growing number of species,[75] can be coherently analyzed, ordered, compared, and generally comprehended. A few of the many linguistic, ethnolinguistic, and psycholinguistic attacks on the problems of reference and/or meaning — which could, of course, also be supplemented by the works of countless philosophers and logicians[76] — fall into the following (partially overlapping) groups:

[72] Cf. fn. 18. For a recent exploration of this distinction, see Richards, 1969.

[73] Although most theorists have distinguished the capacity of signs to refer from their actual referring, this particular distinction between *Sinn* and *Bedeutung* derives from Gottlob Frege; see his 1892 article; cf. Husserl's *Bedeutung* vs. *Bezeichnung*, Mill's *connotation* vs. *denotation*, Paul's *Bedenkung* vs. *Benutzung*, Saussure's *valeur* vs. *substance*, etc., etc. For a critical discussion of Frege's sense-reference distinction, see Ch. III in Grossman, 1969. (Another important question, not considered below, is indicated by Rulon Wells in the title of his article exploring the subject, "Meaning and Use" [1954].)

[74] But see the strictures of Quine, 1963: 130: "When the cleavage between meaning and reference is properly heeded, the problems of what is loosely called semantics become separated into two provinces so fundamentally distinct as not to deserve a joint appellation at all."

[75] Niko Tinbergen fixed the 'ethogram' as the starting point of ethological investigation when he proclaimed that "special emphasis should be placed on the importance of a complete inventory of the behavioral patterns of a species" (1951: 78).

[76] Analytic philosophers typically assign the theory of truth and the theory of logical deduction to semantics, on the ground that truth and logical consequence are concepts based on the relation of designation and hence semantic concepts

A) a whole spectrum of 'traditional' approaches, as practiced mainly in Continental Europe and Great Britain, comprehensively reported in several works of Stephen Ullmann;[77]

B) the so-called 'structural' semantics of discourse, as exemplified by the recent book of the semiotician A.J. Greimas[78] (1966; reviewed by Ullmann, 1967; Baumann, 1969);

(Carnap, 1942: 10); this view is developed, for instance, in a series of papers by Donald Davidson (most recently, 1970). According to Ryle (1957), "Answers to this highly abstract question, What are meanings? have, in recent decades, bulked large in philosophical and logical discussions. Preoccupation with the theory of meaning could be described as the occupational disease of twentieth-century Anglo-Saxon and Austrian philosophy." S. J. Schmidt, 1969 is a recent survey of philosophical trends, aware, however, of linguistic contributions as well.

[77] Most recently, in Ullmann, 1972; *q.v.* for references to his other, book-length treatments, including especially his *Semantics: An Introduction to the Science of Meaning* (1962). See also Todorov, 1966; Alain Rey, 1969 (with additional bibliographical indications on pp. 124ff.), and Coseriu and Geckeler, 1974.

[78] The word 'structural', used by Greimas in his title, has only approximate kinship with the same word as used by John Lyons in the title of his book, *Structural Semantics: An Analysis of Part of the Vocabulary of Plato* (1963). Lyons' 'structural' semantics is an attempt to update the concept of *Wortfelder*, or lexical subsystems, developed by J. Trier (cf. Trier, 1931) and others, and is loosely coupled to Chomsky's transformational model (see also Lyons, 1968, esp. Chs. 9 and 10.) The relationship of Weisgerber to structuralism is reviewed in Schaeder, 1969. On the other hand, as already suggested in fn. 31, Greimas appears to have been principally influenced by Hjelmslev, particularly perhaps by the latter's "Pour une sémantique structurale", written in 1957 and published in 1959. Cf. also the Plenary Session, devoted to the question "To What Extent Can Meaning Be Said to Be Structured?", at the Eighth International Congress of Linguists, with important contributions by Hjelmslev and by Wells, followed by an interesting discussion, as published in the *Proceedings*, pp. 636-704 (1958). A second important source of Greimas' semantics was the first English edition of Propp's *Morfologija skazki* (*Morphology of the fairytale*) (1958, 1968²; Russian originals, 1928¹, 1969²), as pointed out by Eleazar M. Meletinskij, in his afterword to the second Russian edition (Moscow: Nauka), and again in his 1969(b) article.

The word *structure*, and its derivatives, *structural, structuralism*, are a-mong the most overburdened clichés of contemporary social thought (es-pecially of France). A few among the seemingly endless references – selected here because of their partial pertinence in the context of semiotic studies – are: Bastide, 1962; Viet, 1965; Ehrmann, 1966; Bierwisch, 1966; Piaget,1968; Ducrot, Todorov, Sperber, Safouan, and Wahl, 1968; Macksey and Donato, 1970. Three elementary introductions may also be consulted: Auzias, 1967; Fages,1968; and Lane, 1970. In all this welter of publications on 'structuralism', and despite the fact that 'structuralism' is intimately linked with modern semiotics, no exhaustive

C) the semantic differential (developed by C. E. Osgood), allied free-association techniques, and psycholinguistic analyses more generally;[79]

D) the method of 'back translation', and related techniques derived from anthropological fieldwork;[80]

E) methods of cognitive anthropology;[81]

F) methods aiming at compatibility with generative-transformational approaches to grammar, particularly to syntax.[82]

A noticeable discrepancy between what a sign type designates and the denotatum of one of its tokens may be responsible, on various levels, for the linguistic processes known as 'figures of speech' (e.g., metaphor), as well as perhaps kindred phenomena found in animals.[83] This is also the mechanism involved in lying, which — certain opinions

---

treatment exploring the interrelationship of the two exists; see, however, the essay by Segre, 1969.

[79] The principal references to the work of Osgood and his associates were given in fn. 27. In general, see the *Journal of Verbal Learning and Verbal Behavior*, Vols. 1 (1962) onwards, *passim*; Brown, 1958, especially Ch. 3, on "Reference and Meaning"; Carroll, 1964, section on "Meaning as a Problem for Psychology", pp. 33-42; and Clark, 1972.

[80] Phillips, 1959-60; Nida, 1964; Chs. 3-5; Nida and Taber (1969); and Nida's article on the "Science of Translation" (1969), with further references given in his fn. 4. [Nida's *Componential Analysis of Meaning* was published, in 1975, in the *Approaches to Semiotics* series.] Some of the problems involved in this approach were anticipated by Susan M. Ervin, in 1965 [1954].

[81] This expression covers roughly the same area in anthropology as 'formal analysis', 'componential analysis', 'folk taxonomy', 'ethnoscience', and 'ethnosemantics'. For the latest collection of readings, containing several of the classic contributions to this approach to semantic analysis, see Tyler, 1969; also, Bendix, 1966; and Werner, *et al.*, 1974.

[82] Examples of various approaches to the semantic interpretation of syntactic structures are: Katz, 1966, 1967; Weinreich, 1966; Bierwisch, 1969. McCawley, 1968, represents a position intermediate between Weinreich's and Katz's, roughly, that deep grammatical structure is the same thing as semantic structure and that, therefore, a separate semantic component of the type envisaged by Katz (and some of his collaborators) is superfluous. Chomsky's "Deep Structure, Surface Structure, and Semantic Interpretation" (1971) convincingly reemphasizes that properties of surface structure do play a role in determining semantic interpretation. Further references will be found in Katz's bibliography and several of the aforementioned papers. Krenn and Müller (1970) assemble a bibliography of 146 items of 'generative' semantics to accompany their note on the subject.

[83] The problem was posed in Bronowski, 1967, thus: "Does any animal language have figures of speech?" and he observes that "This is an interesting question because the answer is not straightforward, and throws light on how we ourselves

notwithstanding – corresponds to various forms of deception found throughout the animal kingdom.[84]

Recognition of the manifold possible relations between signifier and signified has led to corresponding classifications of signs, among which Peirce's maximal scheme, with sixty-six varieties (Weiss and Burks, 1945), was surely the most exuberant. Today, only some half a dozen types of signs are regularly identified and commonly employed (with but roughly comparable definitions). It should be clearly understood, furthermore, that it is not signs that are being classified here at all, but rather aspects of signs. In other words, a sign may exhibit more than one aspect, so that we may recognize differences in gradation. For instance, a symbol, such as an imperative, may also be endowed with signal value; an emblem, such as the U.S. flag, is also partially iconic; or a primarily indexic sign, as a directional arrow, may possess a discernible symbolic component in addition.[85] Aspects co-occur in a definite hierarchy; thus the sign is legitimately, if loosely, labeled after the aspect that ranks predominant.

The following terms seem to occur most frequently in contemporary semiotics (see further Ch. 8, below):

---

couple the ambivalent meanings in human language". If this question means, rephrased in more formal terms, "whether an animal ever uses the same gesture in two different meanings", I am convinced that the answer is yes, and commonly so, for the reasons suggested by Smith, namely, that, although the number of displays in any species of birds and mammals is highly restricted (from about 15 to 45 per species), contextual information "greatly extends the set of events concerning which there can be communication by means of displays" (Smith, 1969b: 149).

[84] Cf. Caws, 1969: "truth ... is a comparative latecomer on the linguistic scene, and it is certainly a mistake to suppose that language was invented for the purpose of telling it." Sturtevant (1947: 48) speculated that "language must have been invented for the purpose of lying"; Hockett asserted that "Lying seems extremely rare among animals", in connection with his design feature # 14, as enumerated in (1966); there is abundant evidence to the contrary (Altmann, 1967: 353-55, under "Prevarication"). On lying as a linguistic problem, see Weinrich, 1966. For the concept of lying in animals in general, see i.a., Ch. 8, on "Lügenerscheinungen im Tierreich", in Kainz, 1961; Hediger, 1968: 150f.; and Lorenz and Leyhausen, 1968: 370 (by Leyhausen). A recent report, furnishing a clear instance of this phenomenon in foxes, will be found in Rüppell, 1969, so that Pfeiffer's claim (1969: 265), that pretense or deceit "is peculiarly primate behavior; it is seen in no other species", is certainly wrong. See further Ch. 9, below.

[85] Cf. Count (1969: 102): "Symbolization ... is supposable as a matter of a continuous (qualitative) degree."

(1) SIGNAL. *When a sign token mechanically or conventionally*[86] *triggers some action on the part of the receiver, it is said to function as a signal.* Writing in connection with alloprimates, C. R. Carpenter defines signaling behavior generally, in many qualities, forms, and patterns, as "a condensed stimulus event, a part of a longer whole, which may arouse extended actions. Signaling activity, in its simplest form, is produced by an individual organism; it represents information; it is mediated by a physical carrier, and it is perceived and responded to by one or more individuals. Like the stimulus event, of which signaling behavior is a special case, this kind of behavior RELEASES more energy than is used in signaling" (Carpenter, 1969: 44; see also Resnikow, 1968). Examples: the exclamation, 'Go!' or, alternatively, the discharge of a gun starting a footrace; sonic bursts emitted by an echolocating marine mammal or a bat.[87]

(2) SYMPTOM. *A compulsive, automatic, nonarbitrary sign, such that the signifier is coupled with the signified in the manner of a natural link. A* SYNDROME *is a configuration of symptoms.* (Both terms have strong, but not exclusively, medical connotations.[88]) Examples: fever is a symptom of disease; Hediger (1968: 144-45) remarks of the excrement of giraffes that, "normally, the falling of faeces should give a typical rustling sound [but] if the excrement is voided in shapeless, pattering portions, this is an important guide to the [zoo] keeper" as to the animal's state of health.[89]

---

[86] "Signals may ... be provided by 'nature', but they also be produced artificially", as pointed out by Kecskemeti (1952: 36).

[87] Let us recall here, in passing, that, according to the well-known and widely influential 'organon model' of Karl Bühler (1934: 28 and *passim*), the *signal* appeals to the destination, whose behavior it governs (i.e., it is an elicitor or inhibitor of action); the *symptom* has to do with the source, whose inner behavior it expresses; and the symbol relates to the designation; cf. fn. 1 pp. 122f., below. For further animal examples of a signal, consult, e.g., Burkhardt, *et al.*, 1967; Sebeok, 1968b-c, 1972, and 1977a; also Sebeok and Ramsay, 1969.

[88] Cf. Ostwald, 1964. The denotata of symptoms and syndromes are generally not the same for the addresser (viz., 'the patient') and the addressee (viz., 'the physician'); for some Freudian implications of this observation, cf. Brown, 1958: 313; cf. also Kecskemeti, 1952: 61. Three fundamental books in this classic area of semiotics are Ruesch, 1957, 1961, and 1972. For a discussion of the distinction drawn by the Port-Royal logicians, see Ch. 8, Section 2.4., below. Cf. also fn. 2, on p. 125, below.

[89] Symptomatic displays – sometimes called 'autonomic effects' – were acutely observed and described by Charles Darwin,1872. In a famous passage, pp. 101-02, he remarked "that the erection of the dermal appendages", in a variety of vertebrates, "is a reflex action, independent of the will; and this action must be

(3) ICON. [90] *A sign is said to be iconic when there is a topological similarity between a signifier and its denotata.* Examples: a painting, an algebraic formula; the hind end of an aphid's abdomen, which, to an ant worker, signifies the head of another ant, and the kicking of the aphid's hind leg represents an imitation of the antennal movement of an ant (Kloft, 1959).

(4) INDEX. *A sign is said to be indexic insofar as its signifier is contiguous with its signified, or is a sample of it.* Examples: a clock; the linguistic categories known as 'deictics', notably the 'shifters' (such as the personal pronouns of English);[91] the tail-wagging 'dance' performed by a bee on a horizontal surface.[92]

(5) SYMBOL. The operative words in the foregoing definitions of icon and index were, respectively, 'similarity' and 'contiguity'. A sign without either similarity or contiguity — but only *with a conventional link between its signifier and its denotata, and with an intensional class*[93] *for its designatum is called a symbol.* (Admittedly, this is the

---

looked at, when occurring under the influence of anger or fear, not as a power acquired for the sake of some advantage, but as an incidental result, at least to a large extent, of the sensorium being affected. The result, in as far as it is incidental, may be compared with the profuse sweating from an agony of pain or terror" in man.

[90] On the notion of the icon, cf. pp. 9f., fn. 19, above; on iconic functions in language, cf. Jakobson, 1965, and Valesio, 1969. Peirce (2.277) distinguished three subclasses of icons: images, diagrams, and metaphors. The theory of diagrams loomed large in Peirce's semiotic researches, and became the subject of several recent U.S. dissertations: Don D. Roberts, "The Existential Graphs of Charles S. Peirce" (University of Illinois, 1963), later published with revisions, as Roberts, 1973; and J. Jay Zeman, "The Graphical Logic of C. S. Peirce" (University of Chicago, 1964). "The investigation of diagrams", Jakobson remarks, "has found further development in modern graph theory", the implications of which, for semiotics, although unmistakable, have never been scrutinized; cf., however, the provocative piece by M. Gardner, 1968, with further references suggested on p. 144.

[91] On the notion of *deixis*, which is, of course, the Greek word for 'indicating', see Frei, 1944; and Lyons, 1968: 275-81. On the notion of shifters, see Jespersen, 1964: 123-24; Sturtevant, 1947: 135-36; and Jakobson, 1963: Ch. 9. Cf. also Peirce, 2.289.

[92] See pp. 133f., below.

[93] An intensionally defined class is one defined by the use of a propositional function; the denotata of the designation are defined in terms of properties shared by all, and only by, the members of that class. Cf. Reichenbach, 1948: 193. In the terminology of Lewis, 1946: 39, intension refers to "the conjunction of all terms each of which must be applicable to anything to which the given term would be correctly applicable". For a standard technical account of the method

most abused term in the set. In consequence, it has either tended to be grotesquely over-burdened,[94] or reduced to such general kinds of behavioral phenomena as 'stimulus',[95] or even to nullity.[96] The term EMBLEM is sometimes used as a partial — more restricted — synonym for symbol, usually formalized in the visual modality; thus one might say that the 'Stars and Stripes' is either the symbol or the emblem of America, but one cannot say that H_2O is a '*chemical emblem'.[97] Symbols are often asserted to be the exclusive property of humans, but the ability of living things to form intensional class concepts obtains far down in phylogenesis, and this capacity for organizing universals from particulars has been provided with a mathematical-neurological rationalization nearly a quarter of a century ago (Pitts and McCulloch, 1947; cf. Arbib, 1971). Both according to the above definition of a symbol, and the more common Aristotelian ones resting on the doctrine of arbitrariness, that were promoted in linguistics especially by William Dwight Whitney and, after him, Saussure,[98] animals undoubtedly do have symbols. I have previously cited this example of 'arbitrariness' in animals: tail movements in a dog designate friendship, in a cat hostility, but in a horse they merely denote the presence of flies; many other illustrations could be readily rehearsed.[99]

(6) NAME. *A sign which has an extensional class for its designatum is called a name.*[100] Thus individuals denoted by the proper name

---

of extension and intension, see especially, Carnap, 1956; and cf. Stanosz, 1970. See further fn. 100, below.

[94] Cf., e.g., the Cassirer, Langer, and Burke references in the bibliography and related citations given in fn. 66, above; also White, 1940, and Kahn, 1969, cited on p. 135, below.

[95] Kantor (1936: 63): "... the term symbol is made to do duty for everything the psychologist calls a stimulus."

[96] Cf. also Ch. 8, below, Section 5.3.3.

[97] For a discussion of the emblem, see pp. 136f., below.

[98] Even Leonard Bloomfield, in *Language* (1933: 145), reemphasized that "the connection of linguistic forms with their meanings is wholly arbitrary". For the controversy engendered by Saussure's principle of the arbitrary nature of the sign, see the references in the headnote (p. 191) to Sechehaye, Bally, and Frei, "Pour l'arbitraire du signe", first published in 1940-1941, as reprinted in Godel, 1969. For a recent review of the tenet of arbitrariness in language, see Bolinger, 1968: 14-17, 240-43, who, long before, wrote an article entitled "The Sign Is Not Arbitrary" (1949). For a more complete survey, see Engler, 1962, and especially Coseriu, 1967.

[99] Cf. p. 137f., below.

[100] An extensionally defined class is one defined by listing the names of the members, or by pointing to every member successively, according to Reichenbach, 1948. See also fn. 93, above.

'Veronica' have no common property attributed to them save the fact that they all 'answer' to 'Veronica'.[101] Names appear to belong to that mode of signifying which Morris labelled *identifiors*. He distinguishes three kinds of these, of which *namors* and *indicators* seem pertinent here. Namors are linguistic identifiors, hence they include singular signs, like proper names. Indicators, on the other hand, are non-linguistic signs; such 'names' are universally incorporated – *ex hypothesi* – into the calls of birds and mammals.[102]

In summary, we can say that the following formal attributes are criterial for the aforementioned categories of sign-aspects: the denotation of a SYMPTOM is tantamount to its cause within the emitter, whereas that of a SIGNAL causes an alteration in the behavior of the receiver; an ICON entails similarity between signifier and signified, whereas the components of an INDEX are in a status of contiguity; a SYMBOL requires the concept of an intensional class, whereas a NAME requires that of an extensional class; finally, an EMBLEM is opposed to a symbol as a category marked by the channel in which it is manifested.

---

[101] See Section 6.2, p. 138, below.
[102] On various kinds of identifiors, see Morris, 1946: 76-77. On the universality of the identification message in all vertebrate displays, see Smith, 1969a-b. For signs indicating individual identity, see the references to Thorpe in the bibliography and on p. 139, below; for further particularly good examples in a large variety of birds, see Armstrong, 1963: 9-12; for scattered illustrations in primates, see Marler, 1965, and van Lawick-Goodall, 1968: 270. On the apparent distinctiveness of individual whale click trains ('signature'), see Backus and Schevill, 1966.

2

'Semiotics' and Its Congeners*

> *... a long-standing result of linguistic study, of whatever period or school, is the denial of the existence of perfect synonyms. ... Synonyms are the most probable substitutes, in any given situation – but in one situation only, which is an important limitation* (Hill, 1958: 412).

A theory of signs was variously developed on the part of the Epicureans, and especially the Stoics, as a way of proceeding by inference from what is immediately given to the unperceived, and was thus analogous to a doctrine of evidence, particularly medical. Bodily motions were interpreted as a sign of the soul, blushing as a sign of shame, and fever as a sign, viz., symptom – later considered as an 'unintended index' – of a disease. Since none of the many works of the Stoic logicians and semanticists, those of Chrysippos (c. 280-206 B.C.) included, nor a full account of their Epicurean critics, is extant – their ideas are known to us largely through such surviving sources as Sextus Empiricus and Diogenes Laërtius, that postdate by nearly half a millennium their greatest period of efflorescence – the detailed nature of their philosophy of language remains "the most tantalizing problem in the history of semantics" (Kretzmann, 1967: 363; the fullest relevant exposition is Weltring's 1910 dissertation). In any event, the Greek doctrine of signification, with strong medical overtones (in

* This article is reprinted from the English version, originally drafted in December, 1971, and published in *Linguistic and Literary Studies in Honor of Archibald A. Hill, I: General and Theoretical Linguistics*, ed. by Mohammad Ali Jazayery, Edgar C. Polomé, and Werner Winter (Lisse: The Peter de Ridder Press, 1976), pp. 283-95. Various versions have appeared in other languages, to wit: Hebrew, Italian, Japanese, Polish, Portuguese, Romanian, and Russian.

47

special reference to Galen), acquired the designation *semeiotiké*, from *sēma* 'sign', *sēmeiōtikos* 'observant of signs'.

At the end of the 17th century, the Greek word *semeiotiké* was injected into the mainstream of English philosophical discourse by John Locke (1632-1704). Locke declared the "doctrine of signs" to be that branch of his tripartite division of all sciences – namely, logic, physics, and ethics – "the business whereof is to consider the nature of signs, the mind makes use of for the understanding of things, or conveying its knowledge to others" (1690, Bk. IV, Ch. XXI, §4). Specialists like Aaron (1955: 309) find Locke's use of *semeiotiké* for that part of philosophy which is logic rather perplexing, because the Gassendists seemingly made no use of the term, and because there is no evidence, either, that Locke, who was a physician by profession, came across the word in his medical studies and converted it to his own uses; (he certainly does not explicitly connect it with symptomatology). Russell (1939), however, has convincingly argued that Locke adapted *semeiotiké* from neither logical nor medical writings, but from writings on Greek music. His immediate source was probably John Wallis' 1682 edition of Ptolemy's *Harmonics*; (although Russell does not mention this, the fact that the word does not occur in Locke's first draft of the *Essay*, in 1671, strengthens his argument). Wallis, Locke's friend and former mathematics professor in Oxford, appears, in turn, to attribute the term *semeiotiké*, as the art of musical notation, to Marcus Meibomius, with two references to the latter's *Antiquae musicae auctores septem* (1652).

The English word, and some of its congeners, first appear, nearly two centuries later, in the works of C. S. Peirce (1839-1914), as *semeiotic* (1.444), rarely *semeotic* (8.377), but most commonly as *semiotic* (never, however, as far as I have been able to determine, as *semiotics*). Moreover, he also uses *semeiosy*, "or action of a sign" (5.473), and, of course, *semiosis*, pluralized as *semioses* (5.490); (he claims that its variant, *semeiosis*, "in Greek of the Roman period, as early as Cicero's time, if I remember rightly, meant the action of almost any kind of sign" [5.484]). Peirce undoubtedly took the term "*semiotic* (*semeiotiké*)" over, with its attendant definition as the "quasi-necessary, or formal, doctrine of signs" (2.227), directly from the usage of Locke, of whose work he had written elsewhere: "The celebrated *Essay Concerning Humane Understanding* contains many passages which. . . make the first steps in profound analyses which are not further developed" (2.649). In a famous remark, Peirce viewed himself as "a pioneer, or rather a backwoodsman, in the work of clearing and opening up what I call *semiotic*, that is, the doctrine of the essential nature and fundamental varieties of possible semiosis..." (5.488).

Although Peirce makes repeated references (e.g., in 4.353) to J.H. Lambert (1728-1777), he seems, puzzlingly enough, not to have explicitly mentioned the latter's ten masterful chapters on "Semiotik oder Lehre von der Bezeichnung der Gedanken und Dinge" (Lambert, 1764: 5-214), where the cardinal principles of communication and signification are well grasped and lucidly set forth in a consistently semiotic frame (cf. Söder, 1964), prefiguring his own opus in several important respects, including his very use of the term *semiotic*.[1] In fact, as was pointed out by Resnikow (1968: 189), despite Lambert's interesting contributions, "beeinflussten seine Arbeiten die Entwicklung der logisch-semiotischen Probleme kaum". In common German usage, until lately, *Semiotik* continued to mean symptomatology. To cite only one example, Rudolf Kleinpaul, the author of one of the first and most comprehensive books on nonverbal communication, employed the term with its conventional meaning: "Die Mediziner haben eine Wissenschaft, die sie *Semiotik* nennen, die Lehre von den *Kennzeichen* der Krankheiten oder, wie wir gewöhnlich sagen, der Symptomen..." (Kleinpaul, 1888: 103), although, he quickly added, "Es wäre nun wohl schön, wenn...auch die Gesundheit ihre *Semiotik* hätte" (106). Husserl, on the other hand, equated *Semiotik* with "Logik der Zeichen", as spelled out in his important essay on the subject written in 1890 (Husserl, 1970: 340-73). The usage of Hermes (1938), who meant by *Semiotik* pure general syntax, in contradistinction to descriptive syntax, seems highly idiosyncratic. Nowadays, the impact of American Pragmatism, especially of Peirce, and of quasi-behavioristic social science, namely, semiotic, particularly as represented by Morris, is such in Germany that *Semiotik* has come to be equated overwhelmingly and, it would seem, conclusively, with the "Allgemeine Theorie der Zeichen" (cf., e.g., Bense, 1967).

Meanwhile, back in America, *semiotic* became commonplace in philosophical usage, and beyond, through the incentive and persuasive

---

[1] Peirce (in 5.178, but unindexed) does refer to Lambert's "large book in two volumes" on logic ("and a pretty superficial affair it is"), clearly meaning the *Neues Organon*, in whose second volume the *Semiotik* appeared; Peirce's set is still at The Johns Hopkins, although there are no annotations in it (Max H. Fisch, personal communication).

stimulation provided by Charles Morris in a series of publications dealing with various aspects of the general theory of signs, particularly his now classic 1938 monograph, *Foundations of the Theory of Signs*, and his more elaborate 1946 book, *Signs, Language and Behavior* (both included, among others, in Morris, 1971). According to Read (1948: 85), neither *semiotic* nor *semeiotic* had appeared in print during Peirce's lifetime, but, of course, he did use variants of the term, ca. 1908, in his correspondence with Lady Victoria Welby (a part of which was first published in Ogden and Richards, 1923: 281f.; cf. Peirce, 8.342). Read cites a Polish mathematician, Leon Chwistek, as having actually used *semeiotics*, rendering in English his German *Semantik*, in 1924; but *semiotic* was not truly launched in printed English until its appearance in the work of Morris.

Morris (1971: 106) told his readers that " 'Semantics' is perhaps the most widely accepted name for the discipline which studies signs. 'Semiotic', the term here chosen, was used by the Stoics, John Locke, and Charles Peirce. Linguists and logicians restrict 'semantics' to a part of the whole field, namely the part which deals with the significata of signs. Hence we use 'semiotic' as a general term; 'semantics' will be employed for that part of semiotic which deals with significata". Morris' terminology was immediately and prestigiously propagated by Carnap (1942: 9), who assigned "The whole science of language", consisting of syntax, semantics, and pragmatics, a tripartite distinction previously introduced by Morris, to *semiotic*.

Leaving aside here a detailed treatment of the entangled historical interplay of *sem(e)iotic* with *semantics*, and most of their multifarious rivals — some of the lexicographical aspects are expertly discussed by Read (1948) — it does seem worthwhile to enumerate, in this connection, at least those that can be traced back to Greek *sēmeion*: *sem(e)iology*, the only terms in the set I return to below; Reisig's *Semasiologie* (1839-), in English, *semasiology* (1877-); Benjamin H. Smart's *sematology* (1831-), and the perhaps independent coinage of Bühler, *Sematologie* (1934: 34f.), which, employed by the latter with a meaning very close to that of *semiotic*, have both more or less disappeared now; and Noreen's *semology*, (cf. Lotz, 1966: 58, 61f.), currently popular in certain American linguistic circles (e.g., Joos, 1958 or Lamb, 1966: 31f.). One should also mention, in passing, Lady Welby's *sensifics* (1896), and her much better known *significs*, that, in 1917, became the rallying cry of a group of Dutch scientists calling themselves the *significi* (Mannoury, 1969).

Then there is the curious case of *semiotics*, which belongs to the form class of '-*ics* words' that once preoccupied Hill, who demurred that "at least a part of the confusion which learners experience in handling the -*ics* words. . .is caused by the fact that no dictionary makes clear that the final -*s* in these words, no matter what its origin, is not identical with the familiar plural morpheme of nouns which happens to be homonymous with it" (1948: 11). As I have already observed, Peirce never used *semiotics* at all, and neither does Morris, who, in fact, requested the editor of the *Approaches to Semiotics* series, in which his collected writings were recently republished, to add a special "Terminological note" to his book to account for the divergence between his usage and that of the series (Morris, 1971: 9-10). Almost every true *semiotician* – another Morris coinage (1971: 81), to label a practitioner of the art – working in the Peirce tradition, notably, the philosophers clustering around the Charles S. Peirce Society (see the eleven volumes of their *Transactions* 1965-), as well as such prominent linguist partisans and promoters of Peirce as Roman Jakobson (1971d, *passim*), assiduously shun *semiotics*, which they tend to regard as a barbarism. Nevertheless, the term has cropped up in print all along, including in some peculiar ghostly manifestations: thus, in the Index of Subjects to the 5th volume of the Peirce papers (p. 425), there is an entry "Semiotics", but in the paragraph referred to (488) this form does not occur; perhaps the same gremlin is responsible for the identical entry in the Index of Subjects to Bocheński's monograph (1968: 134), but the sole variant that I have been able to locate in his text is *semiotic* (30ff.). Each of the sporadic occurrences of *semiotics*, since the 1940s, must be presumed to have been impelled by an identical mechanism of analogical recreation on the model of what Hill has called the -*ics* words of English, most probably *semantics* (Michel Bréal's late 19th century coinage of which was itself antici- pated, in 17th century English, by *semantick*). Its eventual diffusion and, since the mid-1960s, its increasing acceptance, or as Hermann Paul might have put it, the summation of repetitive shifts in idiolects culminating in a novel Language Custom, must surely be ascribed to the forceful intervention of one individual, Margaret Mead, who, on May 19, 1962, in the final moments of the first American conference ever held on aspects of the emerging field, announced: "It would be very nice if we could go away from here with at least a preliminary agreement on the use of some phrase that we could apply to this whole field. . . .If we had a word for patterned communications in all modalities, it would be useful. I am not enough of a specialist in this field to know what words to use, but many people here, who have looked as if they were on opposite sides of the fence, have used the word 'semiotics'. It seems to me the one word, in some form or other, that has been used by people who are arguing from quite different positions" (Sebeok, Hayes, and Bateson, 1964: 275). I then wrote in the editorial Preface: "Implying the identification of a single body of subject matter, this summative word was incorporated, overburdened as it is, and not without remonstrations from several quarters, into the main title of our work", that is, *Approaches to Semiotics* (Sebeok, Hayes, and Bateson, 1964: 5). This same phrase was later selected to serve as the over-all title of a series designed to accommodate book-length contributions to the theory of signs (Sebeok, 1969a). On the other hand, at the formative meeting, on January 21, 1969, of what was to become the International Association for Semiotic Studies (IASS), the issue what to call the Association's journal was hotly debated, in part because of its intended bilingual character, but in part also because the by then very real rivalry of the synonyms *semiotic/ semiotics* had become acute. The matter was ingeniously resolved by naming our fledgling journal *Semiotica*. My impression of the present state of affairs is that *semiotics* has made irreversible inroads over its competitor, and is likely to entirely replace *semiotic* within a decade or so, in spite of a residue of strong, variously rationalized, scholarly predilections in this regard. Furthermore, a minute holdout dismisses both, in favor of *semeiotics*, on the argument that "The spelling is better etymology than semiotics, and it avoids the ambiguity of semi-. Semi-otics would be nonsense" (Count, 1969: 76n.).

In broad strokes, then, it can be recorded that the family of labels that has become attached to the theory of signs is *sem(e)iotic(s)*. In the Soviet Union, where the discipline flourishes with unmatched concentration and distinction (Meletinsky and Segal, 1971), and where the first colloquium devoted to its foundations was held in 1962 – almost coincidentally with our own initiatory efforts – the favored terms are likewise *semiotic(s)*. It is interesting to note, however, that the famed center of semiotic studies, established about 1964 at the University of Tartu, where lectures and summer courses on the structural study of secondary systems giving rise to models are offered at regular intervals, publishes its Proceedings under the revivalistic banner *Semeiotiké* (subsequently echoed in the title of Kristeva, 1969b), subtitled, in Russian, "Works on Systems of Signs", which is then explicitly rendered, both in English and Estonian, on the verso of the half-title page, as "Works on Semiotics – Tööd semiootika alalt" (Lotman, 1964-). In Poland, a country which has contributed heavily to the advancement of the theory of signs, and where the impetus for the IASS actually germinated, a clear preference is shown for *semiotics*; cf. the name of the International Conference on Semiotics (convened in Poland, in September, 1966), and M. R. Mayenowa's report about "Semiotics Today" (reprinted in Kristeva, *et al.*, 1971: 57-62), or the usage of Polish logicians, as reflected, e.g., in the studies of Pelc (1971, *passim*) and his associates. The situation is much the same throughout the rest of the Slavic world; and the word used in Hungarian is likewise *szemiotika* (cf. Voigt, 1969a: 377f.).

In contrast to what might be called the 'Locke-Peirce-Morris pattern', outlined so far, that prevails generally in America, as it does, too, in both Northern and Eastern Europe, there exists quite another tradition, widespread throughout the Romance areas, but not confined to them, since reflexes of it occur in English, particularly British. This tradition, that I shall refer to as the 'Saussure pattern', actually has two different sources: originally, Greek medicine; then, superimposed much later, the direct heritage of Ferdinand de Saussure (1857-1913). Synchronically, we are dealing here with the simultaneous multilingual interplay of polynymy (involving several similar forms) and polysemy (involving several connected meanings). Let French serve as the Romance prototype (data from Robert, 1967: 1633): there are two forms, a. *sémiologie* and b. *séméiologie*, both with two definitions, 1. "Partie de la médecine qui étudie les signes des maladies", and 2. "Science qui étudie la vie des signes au sein de la vie sociale", or "Science étudiant les systèmes de signes (langues, codes, signalisations, etc.)", in brief, 1., meaning symptomatology, dated 1752 (*Dictionnaire de Trévoux*), and 2., meaning the general theory of signs, illustrated by a quotation from Saussure, dated about 1910. This information can be displayed as a simple matrix:

Forms	a.	b.
Meanings	1.	2.

There are also two additional forms, dated 1555, c. *sémiotique*

(Ambroise Paré, livre XX bis, 23),[2] and d. *sēmeiotique*, both with
essentially the same two definitions, 1. "Sémiologie", and 2. "Théorie
générale des signes", or reconverted into an expanded matrix:

Forms	a.	b.	c.	d.
Meanings	1.		2.	

The situation is, *mutatis mutandis*, the same in the other Romance
languages: in Italian, however, forms c. and d. are polarized in respect
to meanings 1. and 2., that is, *semiotica* has come to refer to the theory
of signs, whereas *semeiotica* continues to be confined to the medical
context; in Romanian, on the other hand, *semiologie* means only
"parte a medicinii care se ocupǎ cu diagnosticarea bolilor dupǎ
simptomele lor", whereas a Romanian form c. is used for a meaning 2.
(e.g., Golopenţia-Eretescu, 1971; on increasing activity in this field in
Romania, cf. also Pop, 1972); in Brazilian Portuguese, the preferred
term is *semiótica*, with an awareness that "Na Europa, a Semiótica é
chamada de Semiologia. . . " (Pignatari, 1971: 27).

Meaning 1. need not detain us (cf. Barthes, 1972); our prime
concern is with *sémiologie* in the secondary sense, which, as every
linguist knows, was launched by Saussure. In one variant, the key
citation read:

La langue est un système de signes exprimant des idées, et par là,
comparable à l'écriture, à l'alphabet des sourds-muets, aux rites
symboliques, aux formes de politesse, aux signaux militaires, etc., etc.
Elle est simplement le plus important de ces systèmes.

On peut donc concevoir *une science qui étudie la vie des signes au
sein de la vie sociale*: elle formerait une partie de la psychologie
générale: nous la nommerons *sémiologie* (du grec *sēmeîon* 'signe'). Elle
nous apprendrait en quoi consistent les signes, quelles lois les régissent.
Puisqu'elle n'existe pas encore, on ne peut dire ce qu'elle sera: mais elle
a droit à l'existence, sa place est déterminée d'avance. La linguistique
n'est qu'une partie de cette science générale, les lois que découvrira la
sémiologie seront applicables à la linguistique, et celle-ci se trouvera

---

[2] Besides its medical use, French *sémiotique* was also used, towards the middle
of the 19th century, in a military context: "Art de faire manoeuvrer les troupes
en leur indiquant les mouvements par signes . . ." (Alain Rey, personal communication), a sense for which sometimes *sémantique* was also used (Rey, 1969: 6).

ainsi rattachée a un domaine bien défini dans l'ensemble des faits humains (Saussure, 1967: 46-49).

After the word *sémiologie*, the *Cours* has a footnote reference to a book by Naville (1901: 104), who recorded this early version of his Geneva colleague's views on the subject: Saussure insists on the importance "d'une science très générale, qu'il appelle *sémiologie*, et dont l'objet serait les lois de la creation et de la transformation des signes et de leur sens. La sémiologie est une partie essentielle de la sociologie. Comme le plus important des systèmes de signes c'est le langage conventionnel des hommes, la science sémiologique la plus avancée c'est la *linguistique* ou science des lois de la vie du langage" (cf. Godel, 1957: 181). The notion, and its designation as *sémiologie*, appear to have been first recorded in a note of Saussure's, dated November, 1894 (Godel, 1957: 275). Beginning 1916, and especially after the monographic treatment of the subject by Buyssens (1943), the word spread throughout French scientific, viz., linguistic discourse, and is now featured in such standard texts as those by Barthes (1964), Mounin (1960), and Guiraud (1971). However, this seemingly straightforward story has recently become considerably muddled by a double crossover: while *sémiologie* has come across the English Channel, in the guise of *semiology*, meaning 'semiotic', *semiotic* has travelled in the opposite direction, returning across the Atlantic, by a zigzag track, to revitalize *sémiotique*, meaning 'sémiologie'. Thus Barthes' influential essay, *Éléments de sémiologie*, was published in England (1967a) (and subsequently distributed in America [1968] as well) under the title, *Elements of Semiology*, and this is the term that, reinforced by the prestige of Parisian intellectual life, now turns up regularly in British newspapers and magazines, such as *The Times Literary Supplement*, and in an outpouring of volumes on the most diverse verbal and nonverbal arts, ranging from architecture ("Semiology of Architecture", Part I of Jencks and Baird, 1969; in a comparable context, see Spanish *semiología*, in Gandelsonas, *et al.*, 1970) to cinematography; a nice illustration of the latter emerges from the contrast of an English chapter, on "The Semiology of the Cinema" (Wollen, 1969: 116-62), with an American essay, published simultaneously, on "The Development of a Semiotic of Film" (Worth, 1969). At the same time, *sémiotique* occurs with such frequency in French (e.g., cf. Kristeva, *et al.*, 1971), that one scholar has even issued a prescriptive caution: for *semiotics*, "La meilleure traduction française reste: sémiologie. Le terme *sémiotique* a pénétré en français . . . pour désigner la sémiologie en général – usage à déconseiller . . . " (Mounin, 1970: 57n.)! Summarizing once more: in British English, the form *semiology* seems to be firmly established, whereas its success in American English, in competition with *semiotic(s)*, appears negligible; in French, *sémiologie* now has a rival in *sémiotique*, with the eventual outcome of the competition still in doubt.

Even in the narrow sense, excluding, that is, their medical uses, *semiotic, semiotics, semiology*, to mention only the three most common English congeners, are by no means wholly interchangeable. While every contributor to *Semiotica* – to stick with a parochial illustration – may indulge his personal taste when attaching a label to the theory of signs, his terminology within the same piece of discourse will not oscillate *ad libitum*, for his initial selection will have signaled to his sophisticated readership whether he has chosen to align himself with the Locke-Peirce-Morris tradition, the Mead variation, or the Saussurean pattern of thought and action. And while these words may – though they need not, of course – all share the same denotatum, the intellectual ambiance evoked by each is so different that Hill's dictum about synonymy, featured in the epigraph to this article, is reconfirmed once again.

A few scholars have deliberately kept the denotatum of *semiotic* distinguished from that of *semiology*. Such was the eventual English practice, notably, of Hjelmslev (1953: 85, 87), who provided these formal definitions: for *semiotic* (Danish *semiotik*) – "hierarchy, any of whose segments admits of a further division into classes defined by mutual relation, so that any of these classes admits of a division into derivatives defined by mutual mutation"; and for *semiology* (Danish *semiologi*) – "metasemiotic whose object semiotic is a non-scientific semiotic". Hjelmslev, moreover, used *semiotics* as well, although casually and informally (1953: 69), and was responsible for the introduction, with formalization, of *metasemiotic* (vs. *object semiotic*) and *metasemiology*. His select followers seek to perpetuate the cleavage: "The independent science that is sought turns out to be rather an immanent semiology – the science that studies semiotics [*sic*] , or sign systems in general" (Francis Whitfield, in Hill, 1969: 258); and, sporadically, others: "It may be useful," a social anthropologist pleads, "to retain *semiology* to describe the study of *semiotics*, used as the plural [!] of *semiotic*. In its turn, a *semiotic* is a sign system" (Ardener, 1971: lxxxvi, n. 16). In French, denotata of *sémiotique* and *sémiologie* are variously distinguished from one another, for instance, by Kristeva (1969b, 1970), and by Mounin, who, as already mentioned, objects to the designation of "la sémiologie en général" by the term *sémiotique*, although he would appear to be content if the employment of it were restricted "pour désigner un système de communication non linguistique particulier: le code de la route est une sémiotique, la peinture en est peut-être une autre, etc." (Mounin, 1970: 57n). In Italian, the meaning of *semiologia* on the one hand is sharply differentiated from that of *semiotiche* on the other, by the author of the most interesting textbook on the subject so far, not at all on the basis of existing usage, but, so to say, *ex cathedra*, in order to establish a convention – how viable this will be remains to be seen – intended to clarify ensuing discussion (Eco, 1968: 384).

In conclusion, I should like to adjoin, very briefly, two sets of observations:

1. In 1963, I set afloat a new compound, *zoosemiotics*. Since its first appearance in *Language*, I tried to keep track of its passage from a linguistic context to all sorts of other scientific texts and, eventually, to fiction and comic strip, as well as of its transmutation from English into other Indo-European and Finno-Ugric languages, and Japanese. My accounts of these events (Sebeok, 1968e, 1970a) can be regarded as companion pieces to this article.

2. A comment on another related term, *asemasia*: Jackson, in his paper on affections of speech, expressed reservations about the term aphasia, on the cogent grounds that "there is, at least in many cases, more than loss of *speech*; pantomime is impaired; there is often a loss of defect in symbolising relations of things in any way", and went on to say that "Dr. Hamilton proposes the term Asemasia, which seems a good one" (Jackson, 1932: 159). His somewhat recondite reference is to Allan McLane Hamilton, a prominent neurologist who practiced in New York City, and who had written a book on nervous diseases, wherein he remarked: "It has occurred to me that the word 'aphasia,' as at present used, has too restricted a meaning to express the various forms of trouble of this nature, which not only consist of speech defects, but loss of gesticulating power, singing, reading, writing, and other functions by which the individual is enabled to put himself in communication with his fellows. I would, therefore, suggest 'asemasia' as a substitute for 'aphasia' " (Hamilton, 1878: 161n.). It is possible, as Jakobson claims (1971d: 289), that Hamilton not only proposed but actually coined this term as a cover for the general deficit of semiotic

activities beyond the merely verbal, but, if so, he was anticipated by Steinthal, who had recognized, at least by 1871, that "die Aphasie. . .erweitert sich. . .zur allgemeinen Mangel an Erkenntniss von Zeichen, Asemie" (Steinthal, 1881: 458).

3

Is a Comparative Semiotics Possible?*

Il y a un double mouvement, une aspiration de la nature vers la culture, c'est-à-dire de l'objet vers le signe et le langage, et un second mouvement qui, par le moyen de cette expression linguistique, permet de découvrir ou d'apercevoir des propriétés normalement dissimulées de l'objet, et qui sont ces propriétés mêmes qui lui sont communes avec la structure et le mode de fonctionnement de l'esprit humain (Lévi-Strauss, to Charbonnier, 1961).

Même les sciences de l'homme ont leurs relations d'incertitude (Lévi-Strauss, 1962b).

Many early anthropologists were certain that there were universal patterns of culture or universal categories which underlay all cultures; thus Adolf Bastian — who was, incidentally, a staunch critic of Darwinism — contended that, by general law, the "psychic unity of mankind" everywhere produced "elementary ideas" (*Elementargedan-*

* The argument developed in this article was first presented in an impromptu talk delivered in January, 1967, in a seminar held at the Collège de France, under the joint auspices of Claude Lévi-Strauss, Roland Barthes, and A.J. Greimas. Dedicated to Claude Lévi-Strauss, the article appeared in *Échanges et communications: Mélanges offerts à Claude Lévi-Strauss à l'occasion de son 60ème anniversaire*, ed. by Jean Pouillon and Pierre Maranda (The Hague: Mouton, 1968), pp. 614-27; see also Sebeok, 1972, pp. 106-21; and a recent Hungarian version in *A Jel Tudománya*, ed. by György Szépe and Özséb Horányi (Budapest: Gondolat, 1975), pp. 417-26. Grateful acknowledgement is hereby made to the National Science Foundation for a Senior Post-doctoral Fellowship with tenure, in 1966-67, at the Center for Advanced Study in the Behavioral Sciences and the University of California (Berkeley), and for a Research Grant (GB-5581) awarded by the NSF Program in Psychobiology.

ken; cf. Hugo Schuchardt's [1912] concept of a linguistic *elementare Verwandtschaft*, derived directly from Bastian) which, responsive to different external stimuli, then gave rise to areal divisions and, at a further stage of evolutionary development, to cultural variation in history proper; compared to the basic laws, however, he considered the latter of subordinate significance (Lowie, 1937).

Contemporary anthropologists have, on occasion, furnished partial lists of items that seem to occur in every human society known to history or ethnography, and have shown that, when some of these – notably language – are analyzed in detail, the resemblances among all cultures are found to be very numerous indeed: "For example, not only does every culture have a language, but all languages are resolvable into identical kinds of components. . . " (Murdock, 1945). On the other hand, while Kluckhohn (1953) has underlined that "linguistics alone of all the branches of anthropology had discovered elemental units . . . which are universal, objective, and theoretically meaningful", he has also questioned whether comparable units are, "in principle, discoverable in sectors of culture less automatic than speech and less closely tied . . . to biological fact". Whatever one may think about the underlying assumptions here about the nature of the relationships between the biological and the social sciences – I join with the view outlined by Tiger and Fox (1966) and endorse the research strategy this implies (cf. Glass, 1967) – an unambiguous resolution of this apparent quandary emerges with the consistent application throughout cultural and social anthropology of the systems concept that is the cornerstone of all modern linguistics. This was pithily reformulated by Lévi-Strauss (1962a) when, with the aim of disposing of such vague notions as 'archetypes' or a 'collective unconscious', he emphasized the validity of latent relational as against patent substantial invariance: "seules les formes peuvent être communes, mais non les contenus". The more general slogan of Gregory Bateson (Sebeok, 1968b: Ch. 22), "The pattern is the thing", once more underlines what all linguists know, that any typology must be constructed by a rigorous elimination of redundancies from the systems assumed to be topologically equivalent. When viewed in this way, any two cultures are seen as superficially different representations of one abstract structure, namely, of human culture; and it is this isomorphism which accounts for the feasibility of communication across cultures. The search for universals thus once again turns out to be a search for the 'psychic unity of mankind', that is, for the fundamental laws which govern human behavior.

In no domain has this search been more diligent – and, after several false starts, more productive – than in linguistics, beginning with Roger Bacon's dictum, "grammatica una et eadem secundum substantiam in omnibus linguis, licet accidentaliter varietur". The early decades of the nineteenth century were suffused by a creative fervor as linguists of that era pursued their single-minded quest to consolidate and order the enormous quantities of concrete language data which had been amassed in the eighteenth century, chiefly under the impetus of Leibniz. Their engrossment with the diversification of language through time and with the concomitant reconstruction of extinct stages of languages by the comparative-historical method temporarily overshadowed, if never quite extinguished, an antecedent tradition of 'philosophical' grammar with which the seventeenth- and eighteenth-century students of language were deeply concerned (cf. Sebeok, 1966). As early as 1808, Friedrich von Schlegel – who was a pupil of Georges Cuviers, the founder of comparative anatomy – proposed a program of investigation animated by a biological metaphor which crudely foreshadowed the key notion of general ethology, that behavior unfolds with morpho-logical growth and differentiation (as a consequence of genetic programming; see, e.g., Lorenz, 1965): "Comparative grammar will give us entirely new information on the genealogy of language, in exactly the same way in which comparative anatomy has thrown light upon natural history" (Pedersen, 1962). The rewarding preoccupation of the past century with problems of linguistic kinship left its scars on the striving for typology in that era, of which perhaps Marr's theory of stadialism – developed through the 1920s, as a misconceived Marxist and equally perverted scientific effort to correlate linguistic (especially morphological) types ordered as pseudoevolutionary stages, with psychological and societal stages arranged in parallel manner – was the last and most thoroughly discredited survival (Thomas, 1957).

An initial impression of rich and seemingly inexhaustible diversity – assigned primacy by empirically inclined anthropological and other descriptive linguists of (roughly) the second quarter of our century – is now again being gradually superseded by the growing conviction of pervasive and significant invariance in the midst of surface variety. The history of linguistic thought has ever oscillated between a predominant preference for data collecting and the view that languages are separate objects to be described, compared, and inter-preted, as against a concentrated search for universals of language and their defining properties. This latter goal – especially in its contempo-rary development – necessarily involves an understanding of the neuro-physiological (Darley, 1967) and the even more broadly biological (Lenneberg, 1967; Sebeok, 1968b: Ch. 21) characteristics of man, his modes of perception, categorization, and transformations, in order to account for the behavior of this unique language-using species and, more immediately, for the processes of linguistic ontogeny. As Zvegintsev (1967) has insisted, the study of language universals becomes meaningful "only when viewing them as interconnected with other sciences, and the results of this study acquire equal importance both for linguistics proper and for other sciences".

The study of language universals – whether substantive, as traditionally pursued (and as exemplified in Greenberg, 1963, and by Greenberg, 1966), or formal, as recently proposed by generative grammarians (Katz and Postal, 1964; Chomsky, 1965) – reveals that all known natural languages are relatively superficial variations on a single underlying theme – what Humboldt, in 1821, explicitly recognized as "an intellectual instinct of the mind" (Cowan, 1963) – a model which is, moreover, both species-specific and species-consistent. The fruitless (but apparently still not altogether resolved) antithesis between 'innate' and 'acquired' categories of behavior (cf. Hinde, 1966) is reconcilable in our domain if we assume that the universal glotto-poetic scheme (deep structure, intended as an approximation to the Humboldtian notion of 'inner form') is hereditary, while the environment contributes the behavioral variability (reflected in surface structures or 'outer forms'). In other words, the development of a normal neonate's faculty of language, which presumably includes a set of the universal primes of the verbal code, is wholly determined by the genetic code, but in such a way that this identical genetic blueprint can then find a variety of expressions in phenogeny through space and time. The feedback from man's environment to his genetic constitution, the interaction between his nature and his culture, yields the thousands of natural languages, but neither parameter can account for more than a portion of the formative rules which led to their creation. The conclusions seem inescapable that the faculty of language – *le langage* – survived only once in the course of evolution, that its basic ground plan has remained both unaltered in and peculiar to our species, and that the multiform languages – *les langues* – concretely realized in human societies became differentiated from each other later on through the miscellaneous, more or less well recognized, processes of historical linguistics.

While language, in its several concrete manifestations, notably speech (but also in its derivatives and transductions, e.g., into script or electrical pulses) is, of course, man's signaling system *par excellence*, indeed, the hallmark of his humanity (or, as Simpson [1966] put it, "the most diagnostic single trait of man"), it is by no means his sole method of communication – only a particular, uniquely adaptive case. The other devices at his disposal, together with those properly linguistic, constitute an important part of semiotics, rapidly burgeoning into an autonomous field of research. The term *semiotic*,[1] confined in earliest usage to medical concerns with the sensible indications of changes in the condition of the human body, that is, symptomatology, later came to be used by the Stoics with a broader meaning and seems to have been introduced into English philosophical discourse by John Locke, in Chapter XXI of his *Essay Concerning Humane Understanding* (1690). Locke considered the doctrine of signs as that branch of his tripartite division of all sciences "the business whereof is to consider the nature of signs, the mind makes use of for the understanding of things, or conveying its knowledge to others". For communication and for recording of our thoughts, "signs of our ideas are . . . necessary: those which men have found most convenient, and therefore generally make use of, are *articulate sounds*. The consideration, then, of *ideas* and *words* as the great instruments of knowledge, makes no despicable part of their contemplation who would take a view of human knowledge in the whole extent of it. And perhaps if they were distinctly weighed, and duly considered, they would afford us another sort of logic and critic, than what we have been hitherto acquainted with."

The real founder and first systematic investigator of semiotic, however, was the subtle and profound American philosopher, Charles Sanders Peirce: "I am, as far as I know", he observed, "a pioneer, or rather a backwoodsman, in the work of clearing and opening up what I call *semiotic*, that is, the doctrine of the essential nature and fundamental varieties of possible semiosis; and I find the field too vast, the labour too great, for a first-comer. I am, accordingly, obliged to confine myself to the most important questions" (Peirce, 1934 [c. 1906]). It is, incidentally, to Peirce that we owe the classification of signs into icons, indexes, and symbols which (with some essential modifications) has proved to be of great utility in several recent studies

---

[1] See the previous Chapter for a more thorough discussion of the term and its congeners.

of both human (Jakobson, 1964, 1965, and 1967) and animal communication (Sebeok, 1967d; see further Ch. 8, below).

The unique place of semiotic among the sciences — not merely one among the others, "but an organon or instrument of all the sciences" — was stressed by Charles Morris, who proposed (1938) to absorb logic, mathematics, as well as linguistics entirely in semiotic. Morris' trichotomy of semiotic into syntactics, semantics, and pragmatics has also proved generally very useful and particularly so in stimulating various approaches to animal communication (cf. Marler, 1961, and Altmann's and Sebeok's chapters in Altmann, 1967). "The whole science of language", Rudolf Carnap then reaffirmed in 1942, "is called semiotic", and, in 1946, Morris introduced further refinements that are valuable for mapping out the field of animal communication (Sebeok, 1967a), such as the distinction among pure semiotic, which elaborates a language to talk about signs, descriptive semiotic, which studies actual signs, and applied semiotic, which utilizes knowledge about signs for the acomplishment of various purposes. The variant form *semiotics* — by analogy with *semantics* and its congeners, rather than with *logic* and its congeners — seems lately to have gained currency on the initiative of Margaret Mead, as a term that might aptly cover "patterned communications in all modalities" (Sebeok, Hayes, and Bateson, 1964).

As a scientific discipline, general semiotics is still in its infancy. When Saussure postulated (in one version of his posthumous book, 1967 [1916]) the existence of a science devoted to "la vie des signes au sein de la vie sociale", he further remarked that, since *sémiologie* (as he called it then; nowadays the French term is being increasingly replaced by *sémiotique*, because the former more commonly means "symptomatology') did not yet exist, no one could foretell what it would be like; one could only be certain that linguistics would be a part of it and that the laws of the former would apply to it as well. Even today, semiotics lacks a comprehensive theoretical foundation but is sustained largely as a consistently shared point of view (Barthes, 1964), having as its subject matter all systems of signs irrespective of their substance and without regard to the species of emitter or receiver involved. As Mayenowa (1967) has correctly observed, since the semiotic disciplines, excepting only linguistics "are themselves of recent origin, more or less contemporary with semiotics, we cannot as yet be said to have developed adequate and universally accepted theories for sign systems, other than those developed in linguistics for the natural languages". It remains to be seen whether a general theory of semiotics can be constructed such that the problems and solutions relating to the natural languages can themselves be reformulated in an interesting way. At present, the trend continues in the opposite direction, that is, the descriptions of other sign systems tend to more or less slavishly imitate – despite occasional warnings, e.g., by Lévi-Strauss (1945) – and more often than not quite erroneously, the narrow internal models successfully employed by linguists. The literature of semiotics is thus replete with mere restatements rather than solutions of problems, and the need for different kinds of theory at different levels of 'coding' appears pressing.

Man's total communicative repertoire consists of two sorts of sign systems: the anthroposemiotic, that is, those that are exclusively human, and the zoosemiotic, that is, those that can be shown to be the end-products of evolutionary series. The two are often confused, but it is important to distinguish the purely anthroposemiotic systems, found solely in man, from his zoosemiotic (Sebeok, 1967e) systems, which man shares with at least some ancestral species.

Anthroposemiotic systems are again of two types: first, language, plus those for which language provides an indispensable integrating base; and second, those for which language is merely – and perhaps mistakenly – thought to provide an infrastructure, or at least an analytical model to be approximately copied. Obvious examples of systems of the first type are furnished by any of the arts qualified, for this very reason, as verbal (Stender-Petersen, 1949), where a particular natural language necessarily intervenes between the source of a message and its destination (cf., several articles in Lotman, 1965 and 1967). Among such complex macrostructures, that may be considered secondary semiotic systems (cf., however, the discussion of Kristeva, 1967), belong also forms, for instance (cf. T. Tsivian, in Lotman, 1965), of normative etiquette behavior, as well as those assemblages of objects that man has elevated to the status of sign systems as he filtered them through his languages. Thus clothing serves at once a protective and a communicative function, and food satisfies both a need for calories and a craving for information: the nomenclature of fashion (Barthes, 1967b) or of cooking (Lévi-Strauss, 1966) is the untranslatable *signans*, to be understood in relation to the use to which the objects are put in this or that society, in brief, to the corresponding transmutable *signatum*. (It is interesting to note in passing that clothing, in its duple function, is not a universal, but bodily adornment, constituting a system of signs with no evident protective function, is.)

To the contrary, such is not the case when addresser and addressee are coupled, e.g., in the acoustic channel by music (Ruwet, 1967), in the visual channel by chalk marks (internationally used by men's tailors), or in the chemical channel by manufactured perfumes (Sebeok, 1967d): semiotic systems of this type, although uniquely human, do not imply any particular linguistic code. Myth and ritual, which function *in situ* as mutually redundant (although not necessarily homologous, cf. Lévi-Strauss, 1956) components of a single culture complex, illustrate, in the sense implied here, typological opposites.

Zoosemiotic systems found in man, *inter alia*, are sometimes classified under such labels as paralinguistics and kinesics (see bibliography of Hayes, in Sebeok, Hayes, and Bateson, 1964), proxemics (Hall, 1968), or simply in terms of the sensory channels used, as gustation for proximal and olfaction for distal chemical signaling (Sebeok, 1967d), or tactile (Frank, 1957), more specifically cutaneous (Moles, 1964), communication. Although there seems to be no compelling reason to assume, and some evidence (supporting intuition) to the contrary, that sign-systems of this sort are language-like in any but trivial ways — chiefly arising from the evident fact that they, like language, are classified as semiotic disciplines — yet they are often prejudicially modelled according to one fashionable theory of language or another. Thus kinesics, to take one glaring example (but others could readily be cited), was deliberately and closely drawn by analogy with a design considered temporarily serviceable by a dominant school of American descriptivists of the late 1940s. This adherence has severely constrained the presentation of a wealth of valuable data on body motion, as well as distorted, in consequence, the proper perspective on kinesics in the hierarchy of semiotic systems in general. The particularism of linguistics of the previous generation, already mentioned, has led even one of the acutest observers of human postures and movements, Birdwhistell (e.g., 1963), to deny altogether the existence of universal gestures, and this in spite of Darwin's (1872) empirical analysis of displays, including a thorough treatment of human expressions, and Birdwhistell's own avowed attitude when he first began to formulate a research strategy without the benefit of linguistics. As a matter of fact, and as one would expect *a priori*, recent pilot studies have confirmed that Darwin was quite correct in asserting that certain human expressions do occur cross-culturally and are probably universal: for instance, film documents of flirting girls from five cultures "show in principle the same type of facial expression and ambivalent behavior" (Eibl-Eibesfeldt and Hass, 1967).

There are, indeed, compelling reasons for sharing Chomsky's skepticism (1967) for studying animal communication systems, human gestures, and language within the same framework, unless one is willing to rise to a level of abstraction where there are "plenty of other things incorporated under the same generalizations which no one would have regarded as being continuous with language or particularly relevant to the mechanisms of language". To establish this level of abstraction is precisely the challenge of semiotics, but diachronic continuities are not material to the theory. Tavolga (Sebeok, 1968b: Ch. 13) is also quite correct when he states that it is "erroneous to use the methods and theory developed for the study of human language in the investigation of a kind of communication found in another species at a different organizational level", and in his insistence that levels of integration in behavior are qualitatively different, requiring, as such, "distinctive instrumentation, experimental operations, and theoretical approaches". Nevertheless, his assertion that "communication does not exist as a single phenomenon" simply does not follow; on the contrary, highly insightful cross-phyletic comparisons have already been made (e.g., by Marler, 1967), and will, we may confidently anticipate, continue to be made, provided that the analytical framework used is that of a well developed theory of signs and not just of linguistic signs.

Parenthetically, it should be pointed out that the claim that a semiotic system, at any given time, functions independently of the processual forces that led to its formation (cf. the linguistic opposition of synchrony to diachrony) is not to say that a holistic analysis of, say, human gestures can afford to ignore their evolutionary antecedents. These can be traced in painstaking detail at least to the zoosemiotic behavior of primitive primates and insectivores, as Andrew (1963) has persuasively shown that many human facial displays have evolved from such mechanisms as responses by which vulnerable areas are protected and those associated with respiration or grooming. On the other hand, there are two schools of thought about the origin of language: "There are those who, like Darwin, believe in a gradual evolution, but there have been others who have believed that speech is specifically a human attribute, a function *de novo*, different in kind from anything of which other animals are capable" (Pumphrey, 1951). At any rate, there can be no facile generalizations overarching both language and the many well identified zoosemiotic systems found in man, such as the territorial, including temporal, spacing mechanisms he shares with the rest of the organic world (Hall, 1968).

The question now arises whether a truly comparative science of signs is possible. We have argued that all natural languages are elaborations from a single template. If this is so, it would appear that the linguists' knowledge of 'deep structure' suffers from the handicap of being restricted to a sample of one. The rules of language can, in some measure, be described; but, being unique, can they be explained, in the sense that these are logically deducible from a higher-level set of semiotic laws? The study and characterization of man's other semiotic systems, and especially of the signaling behavior of the two million or so other extant species, are such immediately appealing tasks because they can perhaps point the way to an escape from the dilemma posed by the necessity for extrapolation from a sample of one and, in this way, enable us to discriminate what is necessary and what is contingent in systems of communication. This hope has fuelled my own researches in these areas and motivated both the assembly of a volume on human communication (Sebeok, Hayes, and Bateson, 1964) and a collection of papers on animal communication that includes exploratory inquiries concerning their implications for anthropology, psychology, linguistics, and the theory of communication (Sebeok, 1968b; see now Sebeok, 1977a for an expanded and updated version of the latter).

Ultimately, however, zoosemiotics as a whole must face the identical problem of extrapolation from a sample of one. This is because terrestrial organisms, from protozoans to man, are so similar in their biochemical details as to make it virtually certain that all of them have evolved from a single instance of the origin of life. A variety of observations support the hypothesis that the entire organic world has descended lineally from primordial life, the most impressive fact being the ubiquity of the molecule DNA. The genetic material of all known organisms on earth is composed largely of the nucleic acids DNA and RNA that contain in their structures information that is reproductively transmitted from generation to generation and that have, in addition, the capability for self-replication and mutation. In brief, the genetic code "is universal, or nearly so"; its decipherment was a stunning achievement, because it showed how "the two great polymer languages, the nucleic acid language and the protein language, are linked together" (Crick, 1966; details in Clark and Marcker, 1968). The Soviet mathematician Liapunov has further argued (1963) that all living systems transmit, through definitely prescribed channels, small quantities of energy or material containing a large volume of information that is responsible for the subsequent control of vast amounts of energy and materials. In this way, a host of biological as well as cultural phenomena can be comprehended as aspects of information handling: storage, feedback, message-channeling, and the like. Reproduction is thus seen, in the end, to be in large measure information replication, or yet another sort of communication, a kind of control that seems to be a universal property of terrestrial life, independent of form or substance.

In the early 1960s, I called attention to a vision of new and startling dimensions: the convergence of the science of genetics with the science of linguistics, remarking that both are emerging "as autonomous yet sister disciplines in the larger field of communication sciences, to which, on the molar level, zoosemiotics also contributes" (Sebeok, 1963). The terminology of genetics is replete with expressions borrowed from linguistics and from the theory of communication, as was recently pointed out by Jakobson (1974), who also emphasized the salient similarities and equally important differences between the respective structures and functions of the genetic and verbal codes. These, of course, urgently need further elucidation and precision. Yet it is amply clear even now that the genetic code must be regarded as the most fundamental of all semiotic networks and therefore as the prototype for all other signaling systems used by animals, including man. From this point of view, molecules that are quantum systems, acting as stable physical information carriers, zoosemiotic systems, and, finally, cultural systems, comprehending language, constitute a natural sequel of stages of ever more complex energy levels in a single universal evolution. It is possible, therefore, to describe language as well as living systems from a unified cybernetic standpoint. While this is perhaps no more than a useful analogy at present, hopefully providing insight if not yet new information, a mutual appreciation of genetics, animal communication studies, and linguistics may lead to a full understanding of the dynamics of semiosis, and this may, in the last analysis, turn out to be no less than the definition of life.

4

Problems in the Classification of Signs[*]

> *It will be my thesis that any linguistic entity can be described from two points of view, one internal to the language described and one external to it; further, that traditional linguistics has sought objectivity by adopting an external standard to which the language may be referred, while present-day linguistics seeks to find internal, relational standards; and finally, that while the internal . . . standards may lead to useful discoveries concerning the internal organization or structure of the language, linguistics cannot, unless it wishes to become entirely circular or mathematical, afford to reject the use of external standards to give its relational data concrete validity in the real world* (Haugen, 1951: 215).

The subject matter of semiotics – ultimately, a mode of extending our perception of the world – is the exchange of any messages whatever and of the systems of signs that underlie them; hence, alongside such fields as social anthropology (which deals with the exchange of mates), and economics (which deals with the exchange of utilities, viz., goods and services), semiotics is most commonly regarded as a branch of the communication disciplines (Lévi-Strauss, 1958: 326). Some investigators prefer, nevertheless, to emphasize the study of the systematic rather than the transactional aspects of the repertory of signs (noumena

* This article, dedicated to Einar Haugen, restates some of the issues covered in Ch. 1 of this book, but also tries to define, in a preliminary way, the outer bounds of the communication disciplines. It appeared in *Studies for Einar Haugen*, ed. by Evelyn Scherabon Firchow, *et al.* (The Hague: Mouton, 1972), pp. 511-21; this version was reprinted as No. 9 (1973) in the *Semiotic Studies* series of the Hungarian Academy of Sciences.

vs. phenomena, signification vs. communication). Whichever approach one may favor, the key concept of semiotics remains always the SIGN.

While numerous attempts have been made by philosophers and philosophically inclined linguists, throughout the history of semiotics, to classify signs or systems of signs, none of these efforts has as yet enjoyed universal and permanent acceptance. The criteria that must be taken into account in working toward a reasonably holistic categorization – surely a task to be completed in the distant future – seem to be threefold, and to yield interrelationships among the resulting classes that are clearly of a kind convertible into Euler-Venn diagrams: that is, overlapping classes. Such an approach appears unavoidable at this stage in the development of semiotic theory.

In biology, as Gerard (1957) has suggested, it is useful to conceive of a material system – an org, or, to use Koestler's (1967: 341) broader term, a holon – in one of three ways: its 'being', or STRUCTURE, that is, its enduring status in a synchronic sense; its 'behaving', or FUNCTION, 'a repetitive perturbation' along a secular trend; and its 'becoming', or HISTORY, representing cumulative changes in the longitudinal time section. A semiotic system, or a sign, can likewise be fruitfully examined from each of these three points of view; we can ask: what is a sign, how does the environment and its turbulences impinge upon it, and how did it come about? Functional classifications of the sign are empirical, extrinsic; they are based upon variations at different nodal points in an expanded communication model; in the words of Haugen's epigraph, this approach seeks "objectivity by adopting an external standard" to which the semiotic system may be referred. A structural identification of the sign is analytic, intrinsic; it utilizes types of association potentially inherent in the architecture of the sign itself; as Haugen put it, this approach "seeks to find internal, relational standards. . . " Finally, the problem of becoming introduces diachronic considerations of two sorts: we can focus on the evolution of sign systems in phylogeny (ritualization), or consider their development in ontogeny. This brief tribute will be restricted to a synchronic exploration of some of the functional aspects of signification; first, however, it might be useful to delineate the scope of semiotics (see also pp. 1ff., above).

Messages may be emitted and/or received either by inorganic objects, such as machines; or by organic substances, for instance, animals, including man, or by some of their component parts: e.g., ribonucleic acid, mRNA, which serves as an information bearing tape 'read' by particles, called ribosomes, that travel along it, carrying amino acid sequence information; there are pathways between the cells of living tissue that allow signal molecules to travel from one cell interior to the next (Loewenstein, 1970); and one may also speak of information, for instance, in cardiovascular functioning, where messages are conveyed from peripheral vessels to the brain, relayed thence to the heart and back to the brain. The interaction of organic beings with inorganic things, such as communication between a man and a computer, also can and has been treated as a semiotic problem (e.g., Gorn, 1968).

A further distinction could provisionally be drawn between terrestrial and extraterrestrial communication. Inquiries into the latter are shared by fields such as mathematics, exobiology, and radioastronomy with science fiction, but the study of cosmic message exchanges remains, for the present, a semiotic sub-discipline without a subject matter.

Message interchanges are most conveniently — if anthropocentrically — treated in two vast domains: in man, and in other living systems (as well as, of course, in their interaction, for instance, as regards semiotic processes that enter into the training, taming, and domestication of animals). By 'other living systems' usually the speechless animals are meant, but plants can also be said to be the sources and/or destinations of messages, notably in their interrelationships with certain animals; further, the biological status of such eminently communicative Protozoa as cellular slime molds is still in doubt.

Anthroposemiotics, that is, the totality of man's species-specific signaling systems, was the first domain concretely envisaged and delineated, under the designation SEMIOTIC. For most investigators, from John Locke, in 1690, to this day, both notions still remain synonymous. The second domain, zoosemiotics, which encompasses the study of animal communication in the broadest sense, was so labeled and comprehensively outlined only in 1963. It would now seem more accurate to consider anthroposemiotics and zoosemiotics, separately and conjointly, as two principal divisions of semiotics, having in common certain essential features but differing especially as to the fundamental and pervasive role that language plays in the former in contradistinction to the latter (Sebeok, 1969c). A third domain, endosemiotics — which studies cybernetic systems within the body — crosscuts both of the latter; in this field, the genetic code plays a role comparable to that of the verbal code in anthroposemiotic affairs, but "it is still broadly true that the coding and transmission of information of differences outside the body is very different from the coding and transmission inside" (Bateson, 1970: 10).

In the foregoing four paragraphs, there was an underlying pragmatic implication: attention was deliberately focused upon the origin and/or effects of signs or, more generally, the sorts of relationships that can prevail between the source of a message and its destination. The first basic functional classificatory criterion can, therefore, be constructed in terms of the nature of all possible sources of signs, for it is reasonable to begin to classify where the coding itself begins — at the input end. According to the distinctions just introduced, these could be provisionally diagrammed as in Table 3, p. 27, above. This excessively simplistic scheme becomes at once more complicated as the nature of the sign-receivers — the other end of the feedback loop in the transactional chain — is taken into additional consideration. Man's conspecific messages can, for example, be differentiated as intrapersonal (cf. the phenomenon of 'inner speech', or 'internal dialogue'), interpersonal (external dialogue), or pluripersonal, either centrifugal, i.e., one-to-many, or centripetal, i.e., many-to-one, or again, as in Eskimo oral tradition, where "the myth-teller speaks as many-to-many, not as person-to-person" (Carpenter, 1960). A human message may be directed at a machine, as by the experimenter who learned voluntarily to control his own alpha rhythm to send a Morse code by processing the resultant EEG by means of filters and computer program so that these messages are converted into typewritten outputs (Dewan, 1969). A human message may also be directed at a personified supernatural, as in an incantation or prayer addressed to a deity; and vice versa, animates may receive signs from the environment — cf. the phenomena of echolocation (Griffin, 1968) — or fancy receiving them, "as in some of the epigrams of Callimachus and of his imitators, the stone is thought of as carrying on a brief dialogue with the passerby" (Hadas, 1954), or again from the location of stars and planets, the length and intersection of lines in the hand, the entrails of sheep, the position of dregs in a teacup — in short, by those pseudo-semiotic divinatory techniques that are known as augury, astrology, palmistry, haruspication, and the like. Animal senders and receivers of signs are either conspecifics, or they belong to two or more species, one of which may be man. Complex and subtle semiotic ecosystems are sometimes formed by several interacting plant and animal species, as in the interesting community of milkweeds belonging to the family of Asclepiadiaceae, a group of insects, the Danaidae, and blue jays (Brower, Brower, and

Corvino, 1967). Most zoologists tend to classify interindividual sign systems first of all into intraspecific vs. interspecific varieties (e.g., Wenner, 1969: 237).

Contact among emitters and receivers is established and maintained by miscellaneous flow-processes that link them across space and time, and our functional classification of sign systems becomes still further refined as this operationally crucial third factor – the medium of transmission – is taken into account. In principle, any form of energy propagation or transfer of matter can serve as a sign carrier, depending on an animal's total perceptual equipment. Sign systems are thus also distinguishable in terms of the channel or channels connecting the input side with the output side. If an animal's sensory capacity allows for the parallel processing of information through multiple input channels, calculable redundancies will be found to prevail (an effect sometimes referred to as 'the law of heterogeneous summation'), and the application of the rules for switching from one subassembly to another, under particular circumstances, will yield different hierarchical arrangements that render the classification even subtler in consequence of contextual circumstances.

From a semiotic point of view – to say nothing of an evolutionary standpoint – it is very important to appreciate fully both the advantages and the disadvantages of every channel (see Table 4, p. 30, above) utilized for successful communication in and across all species. Yet the foundations for a comparative analysis of this kind have barely begun to be laid (cf. Sebeok, 1967c). For every semiotic system, it would be useful indeed to have a lucid and concise account, comparable with the following characterization of speech: "Speech is produced with the human body alone, without any tool; it is independent of light and can be used day and night; it fills the entire space around the source and does not necessitate a straight line of connection with the receiver; it can also be greatly varied from intimate whisper to long distance shouting; and it involves a very small amount of energy" (Lotz, 1950: 712).

Among the criterial design features of speech just cited, the author singled out for first mention that signs encoded in this mode can be produced by the human body alone, without recourse to any tools. The use of both ready-made objects and shaped artifacts as tools is known to occur variously throughout the animal world, ranging from moths and spiders through birds, otters, and primates. Chimpanzees of the Gombe Stream Reserve, for instance, build nests, fold selected leaves to facilitate drinking or to wipe their body, use sticks, twigs, and grasses to get termites, ants, or honey, and use them, as well, as olfactory probes; they also use stones in agonistic displays (van Lawick-Goodall, 1968: 202-10). The instrumental behavior of these chimpanzees exemplifies a twofold function of tool using in animals and man: a (presumably) primary amplifying function, and a (presumably) secondary semiotic function. When the chimpanzee uses a stone to break nuts, it draws material supplies from its environment to adaptively extend and improve, with relatively moderate expenditure of energy, the manipulatory systems necessary for its existence in its living space. When, on the other hand, it uses a stone in agonistic displays, the basic amplifying function is endowed with a superimposed sign function — the behavior has, in the parlance of the ethologists, become ritualized. (Ritualization was defined by Huxley, 1966: 250, in part, as "the adaptive formalization or canalization of emotionally motivated behaviour, under the teleonomic pressure of natural selection so as . . . to promote better and more unambiguous signal function, both intra- and interspecifically . . . . ") The instrumental — as opposed to the merely somatic — production of animal signs sometimes takes exceedingly bizarre forms, as in those "wonderful arena birds called bower birds, with their houses and ornamented gardens and their courtship displays that replace plumage with glittering natural jewelry" (Gilliard, 1963: 46).

Both human and animal sign systems can thus be classified into organismal, if they are produced by the body alone, or artifactual, produced by the body amplified. Diverse surrogates for spoken languages can be usefully contrasted in this way: for example, the transposition of speech into whistles is organismal, into drumbeats artifactual, although all three are manifested in the same acoustic substance. A secondary surrogate like braille ordinarily implies the use of a machine, the braille-writer, but signs encoded in the visual modality may now be decoded by the blind directly through the skin of the back (Bach-Y-Rita, et al., 1969). A transitional grouping of implements is constituted by detachable parts of an animal's body itself. Thus a particle of dung, or the trace of secretion on the territorial marking place, can function as a sort of synecdoche, with the animal's separated *pars* — that can continue to be efficacious even after the temporary departure or permanent extinction of the source — standing *pro toto* (Bilz, 1940). The identical semiotic process is the basis for contagious, in contrast to homeopathic, magic, where the intended victim's nail parings, or the like, act as the indexic signs, because of "the magical sympathy which is supposed to exist between a man and any severed portion of his person. . . " (Frazer, 1951: 43). Objects used for semiotic display can, moreover, be distinguished further according to whether they are randomly found objects, like a plucked flower, or matter, as precious metal, wrought into floral shape, to be worn as a brooch; prehistoric artists are said to have discovered, by a semiotic technique that is sometimes called "épouser les contours" (Giedion, 1960: 84), in natural rock formations the images of the animals that they sought.

Another important distinction, also highly relevant to the problems of functional classification, results from contrasting 'pure' with other sorts of semiotics. Let us recall that Morris (1946: 353) specified the task of pure semiotics to be the elaboration of "a language to talk about signs". Since it is obviously necessary to use signs for referring to signs in discourse about signs, and since, for this purpose, a signifier, or sign vehicle, is commonly employed as an index of its own sign, such "a language to talk about signs", or a semiotic system specialized for communicating about another semiotic system, can be said to constitute a METASEMIOTIC. The OBJECT SEMIOTIC then becomes any 'other' semiotic system communicated about in metasemiotic. (Variants of this pair of terms were operationally used by Hjelmslev, 1943.) Morris assigned the study of such actual sign systems to descriptive semiotics. Confusingly, however, other scholars refer to the study of phenomena which arise when signs are actually used in the process of communication as applied semiotics (one might call this 'semiotic performance'), as against pure semiotics, which then becomes the study of the underlying rules which regulate the objective structure of signs ('semiotic competence'). Again, according to a distinction introduced in 1968 by Roman Jakobson, the object of pure semiotics is the linguistic sign, whereas applied semiotics deals with such systems of signs as may be embodied, for instance, in garments or architectural constructs — "we don't inhabit signs" (de Mauro and Grassi, 1969: 253). Still others, however, prefer to confine the latter expression to merely pedagogical applications, such as the gesture inventory of Green (1968) for the teaching of Spanish. Morris himself intended by applied semiotics to circumscribe a field that utilizes "knowledge about signs for the accomplishment of various purposes" (1946: 353-54), a definition later extended to applied zoosemiotics (Sebeok, 1967a: 95), in a trichotomous model that has proved especially useful in heuristic comparisons of human with animal communication.

Higher organisms are so constructed, both centrally and peripherally, that they are able to – although they need not – draw simultaneously upon two or more repertories of sign systems. This capability, notably characteristic of man, allows for a high number and many kinds of admixtures of expressions. It also provides another criterion for classifying sign systems, as ranging from 'simple', homogenous structures to syncretic formations of varying degrees of complexity, the components of which, furthermore, may or may not be patterned symmetrically. This last point can be illustrated as follows: if I assert 'yes', and, at the same time, nod my head affirmatively, my verbal sign is symmetrical – as well as mutually redundant – with my kinesic sign. (For a striking illustration of asymmetry between an acoustic and a visual message component, see Ch. 1, fn. 61, above.)

What Lotz (1950: 717) has called a 'ribbon concept' of communication – a notion which overlaps, but is not identical, with what Birdwhistell (1968a) has called 'multichannel' communication – seems to characterize most of normal human signaling behavior; thus Bar-Hillel (1970b: 3) insists "on the fact that, in general, human communication proceeds in more than one channel at a time, that each channel has its own specific properties, and that their interaction creates possibilities whose number is greater than the sum of the possibilities of each channel taken separately, a fact which, of course, also raises questions as to the precise implications of this unusual situation". Were this imaginary ribbon to be sectioned at any point in time it would, much more often than not, reveal verbal, paraphonetic, kinesic, proxemic, olfactory, and perhaps other strands mixed together, but stacked in a hierarchy suited to the requirements of the global message involved. Signs are combined in appropriate – linguists would say 'grammatical' – ways to yield a compound designatum. The emotional attitude of a speaker towards his verbal message can be conveyed either by features – emotive, expressive – coded in the language itself, or by accompanying nonverbal features – paraphonetic, kinesic, etc., – that serve to support or belie it (contributing to effects like irony or sarcasm). The semiotic systems called macrostructures (Sebeok, 1970b) – that is, those that imply, by definition, a natural linguistic infrastructure – all constitute elevated cases of syncretism, including those with a predominantly folkloristic and artistic function. Here belong all genres of discourse composed of prefabricated text components, such as myths and the other products of oral tradition; the verbal arts in general and poetry in particular; such hybrid formations – doubly labeled with transitional awareness – as vocal music, circus acts, dramatic performances, sound film; and blended constructs of the highest intricacy, as opera. To illustrate in brief: a sound film can partake of four sign systems, one visual and three auditory – language, music, and other sound-effects (*bruit*) (Metz, 1968a: 113-14). An acrobatic act partakes of five or more, to wit, the performer's socio-dynamic behavior, his costume and other accessories, the linguistic accompaniment (oral as well as written), the lighting effects, and the musical accompaniment (Bouissac, 1971). As to the art of the opera, which, in Stender-Petersen's formulation, irreversibly presupposes the literary, the musical, and the scenic arts in all their rich variety, it is a semiotic product that has indeed achieved "un degré très élevé d'independence raffinée" (1949: 278). Take as an example a production of *Don Giovanni*, which is, to begin with, sung in a natural language, say, Italian. The secondary subcode is the libretto, the drama Lorenzo da Ponte built, in turn, out of the old Spanish *Leyenda de Don Juan* (cf. Thompson's motif C13). In the third place, there is the score, the way in which Mozart enhanced the drama musically. Then, in performance, there are the visual effects, partially controlled by the lighting, involving the scenery and a host of subtle costuming devices, helping to keep apart in appearance the distinct personalities, for example, of the bourgeois Donna Anna from the self-sacrificing Donna Elvira, and both of them from the peasant girl Zerlina. There is the cunning culinary effect of the banquet scene, and, if you are sitting close enough to the stage, there are olfactory effects caused by the smell of the greasepaint. The genius of Mozart finally orchestrated this entire masterpiece into an eloquently tight and unified macrostructure.

Secondary modeling systems constitute still another sort of macro-structure, currently much discussed by some Soviet semioticians, following the publication of a seminal article by A.A. Zaliznjak, V.V. Ivanov, and V. N. Toporov (Zaliznjak, *et al.*, 1962). This notion, in the broad sense, refers to an ideological model of the world where the environment stands in reciprocal relationship with some other system, such as an individual organism, a collectivity, a computer, or the like, and where its reflection functions as a control of this system's total mode of communication. A model of the world thus constitutes a program, as it were, for the behavior of the individual, the collectivity, the machine, etc., since it defines its choice of operations, as well as the rules and motivations underlying them. A model of the world can be actualized in the various forms of human behavior and its products, including linguistic texts – hence the emphasis of Soviet semioticians on the verbal arts – social institutions, movements of civilization, and so forth. In short, the notion of a secondary modeling system is akin to the thematic principle that some American and other anthropologists have sensed by empathy, and referred to as the ethos, the integrating or summative pattern of a culture. It is the ideal value system which gathers the 'actual culture' into a whole and fits it into patterns. However, when Northrop asserts that "norms express the ethos of a culture" (1953: 668), we have at last reached the outer bounds of the communication disciplines. In the sphere of political systems, in particular, the prevalence of the modalities of exchange may be reaffirmed precisely by their being negated. Mates, utilities, and messages are at once deprived of their signification and the elements of exchange are precipitated and apprehended as values pure and simple, because communication has ceased to be their goal: "Dans la mesure où, refusant l'idée d'un échange des femmes du groupe contre les biens et les messages du chef", we learn in an account of the chief's lack of power in some South American Indian societies, "on examine par conséquent le mouvement de chaque 'signe' selon son circuit propre, on découvre que ce triple mouvement présente une dimension négative commune qui assigne à ces trois types de 'signes' un destin identique: ils n'apparaissent plus comme des valeurs d'échange, la réciprocité cesse de régler leur circulation, et chacun d'eux tombe dès lors à l'extérieur de l'univers de la communication" (Clastres, 1962: 61-62). Such societies have succeeded in neutralizing the virulence of political authority by placing the chieftainship beyond the bounds of communication, and thus provide a forceful illustration of an institution where direct action serves as the transform of a secondary modeling system.

Wells has observed that "Semiotic has two groups of affinities. It is connected, on the one hand, with communication, and, on the other, with meaning" (1967: 103). In this essay, I have dealt only with a few phenomena of usage as these pertain to miscellaneous transactional relationships, neglecting, among other relevant factors, the entangled and controversial problem of intention, or, more accurately, goal-orientation, the concept of objective teleology (Hofstadter, 1941-42) that is not only appropriate but indispensable for the study of communication in all organisms. More importantly, I have eschewed the jungle of meaning, although I want to explicitly recognize that the pragmatic dimension of semiotics always presupposes the semantic (as well as the syntactic), and that the nature of the coupling between the

moieties — one perceptible, the other intelligible — that are traditionally and universally taken to be the minimal components of any sign
whatever must be understood as a prerequisite even for their mere
classification. Were such an analysis of aspects of signs, and of the
co-occurrence of aspects in a definite hierarchy, to be carried out here
(as in Chs. 1 and 8, this book), the following attributes would be found
criterial for the classification of the some half a dozen terms
most commonly employed in current studies of human and animal communication: the denotation of a SYMPTOM is tantamount
to its cause within the emitter, whereas that of a SIGNAL causes an
alteration in the behavior of the receiver; an ICON entails similarity
between signifier and signified, whereas the components of an INDEX
are in a status of contiguity; a SYMBOL requires the concept of an
intensional class, whereas a NAME requires that of an extensional class;
finally, an EMBLEM is opposed to a symbol as a category marked by
the channel in which it is manifested.

5

Zoosemiotics: At the Intersection
of Nature and Culture*

When, at the end of the 17th century, John Locke injected a Hellenic variant of the term *semiotics* into English philosophical discourse, reshaping and expanding the field as the 'doctrine of signs' (for he adapted *séméiotikè* from a context where it meant merely the art of musical notation), he characterized it as that branch of his tripartite division of the sciences "the business whereof is to consider the nature of signs the mind makes use of for the understanding of things, or conveying its knowledge to others". While his prime concern was with those signs of our ideas "which men have found most convenient, and therefore generally make use of", that is, "articulate sounds" or verbal signs, Locke was fully aware that other creatures, such as birds, also have perception, "retain ideas in their memories, and use them for patterns", in brief, that they are comparably served by signs. That giant among philosophers, the American C. S. Peirce, convinced that many passages in Locke's 1690 *Essay* "make the first steps in profound analyses which are not further developed", took the term with his definition over from him, then devoted a lifelong study to "the doctrine of the essential nature and fundamental varieties of possible semiosis", contending that "the entire universe is perfused with signs, if

* This essay was commissioned by *The Times Literary Supplement* where it appeared, under the title "Between Animal and Animal", in No. 3, 735 (October 5, 1973). It was reprinted, in somewhat expanded form, under the title originally given, in *The Tell-Tale Sign: A Survey of Semiotics*, ed. by Thomas A. Sebeok (Lisse: The Peter de Ridder Press, 1975), pp. 85-95; also, a slightly abridged version appeared in *The Review* 17 (1975), pp. 1-10, 20.

it is not composed exclusively of signs". Consistently, Peirce refused to draw a sharp distinction between animal and human sign-processes. His heir, Charles Morris, cast his net equally widely. However, neither Peirce nor Morris was equipped to carry out detailed investigations of animal communication or signification, although both of their intellectual armatures not merely allowed for but actually seemed to invite applications in those domains. Eventually, a succession of animal behaviorists found Morris' model and terminology at least of heuristic value: incidental works of R. M. Yerkes and H. W. Nissen (1939), P. Marler (1961), S.A. Altmann (1967), and W.J. Smith (1968, 1969a and b) constitute a scattering of outstanding examples of zoological attempts to gain some special insight into the vocalizations of a chimpanzee or that of chaffinches, or to clarify outstanding theoretical concerns within a recognized semiotic framework.

In an independent but parallel tradition, amplified by F. de Saussure's heritage, semiotics, alias *sémiologie*, has remained steadfastly anthropocentric, intertwined with language, *le patron général* of Saussure's programmatic science. Many linguists later tended to more or less agree: thus L. Bloomfield asserted that "Linguistics is the chief contributor to semiotic", and U. Weinreich called natural languages "the semiotic phenomenon *par excellence*". But it was the prominent French critic Roland Barthes who – like W. H. Auden's "linguist who is never at home in Nature's grammar" – carried this glottocentricity to its preposterous (but perhaps playfully conceived) conclusion by turning Saussure's formulation topsy-turvy with his declaration that "linguistics is not a part of the general science of signs, even a privileged part, it is semiology which is a part of linguistics . . . . " The validity of this paradoxical inversion of the customary order of things can be contemplated only, if at all, at the price of throwing all of comparative semiotics overboard by dividing the animate world into two unequal classes – speechless vs. language-endowed – and then consigning the sign behavior of well over two million extant species of animals beyond the semiotic pale. Yet such is the practical focus of most of Gallic-oriented semiotic preoccupations. To be sure, there are certain noteworthy exceptions, such as the bioacoustic researches of R.-G. Busnel, the information theoretical writings of the polymath A. Moles, and especially the inspired work of Paul Bouissac, a rare specialist in the semiotic aspect of spectacles – though hardly a prophet in his own country of France ("parce que ce n'est pas sérieux", as a fountainhead of *Tel Quel* once confided to me) – whose subtle and knowing preoccupation with animal acts in circuses (e.g., bears, the big cats, horses) has, in important respects, converged with the surpassing scientific observations carried on, since 1935, by the farsighted Swiss comparative psychologist, H. Hediger. As for the best of Soviet scholarship, this, too, has hitherto chiefly focused on the fruitful concept of secondary modeling systems, or macrosemiotic structures, which, by definition, imply a linguistic infrastructure; yet N. Žinkin has cast his studies on communication in baboons in an explicit semiotic setting, V. V. Ivanov is known to share Eisenstein's predilection for circus acts, and leaders of a recently formed team of young biologists in Moscow have privately avowed their semiotic perspective to henceforth guide their investigations of fundamental problems of animal communication.

While generations of philosophers and some linguists were prefiguring a shadowy science of signs (of which Saussure reportedly remarked, "Puisqu'elle n'existe pas encore, on ne peut dire ce qu'elle sera . . ."), seldom paying more than perfunctory heed to sign systems other than man's species-specific codes, an entirely different breed of scholars was at work developing, or, rather, redirecting, *ethology*, focusing it upon certain processes and the progress of mental evolution, largely on the basis of naturalistic observations. Although ethology (a term that can be traced back, with something like its present connotations, to the brilliant early 19th century evolutionist Étienne Geoffroy-Saint-Hilaire, and his son, Isidore) is perhaps nowadays most comprehensively yet simply defined as the biological study of behavior, a careful analysis of the literature since Darwin — especially beginning with *The Descent of Man* (1871), with its emphasis on displays and other sign stimuli — fully supports the remark of a prominent specialist in arthropods, R. D. Alexander, that "data on animal communication have contributed a thread of continuity that . . . has seemed to be the principal axis of synthesis in the entire field of animal behavior".

The semiotic concerns of ethology have crystallized around the principle of *ritualization*, a term coined by Julian Huxley, in 1914, to explain how the so-called penguin dance, climaxing the courtship ceremony of great crested grebes, has evolved from a simple locomotory movement by which this bird approaches the edge of its nest; or, interpreted more generally, how a minimally ambiguous sign function is elaborated from movements that are initially devoid of discernible semiotic motivation. This very fertile ethological concept has already opened up vast perspectives for a diachronic semiotics, but

its potential implications for the phylogenetic analysis of the components of human communication have as yet barely been touched upon,
e.g., by R. J. Andrew, Ian Vine, and others in England, by J. A. R. A.
M. van Hooff in The Netherlands, in E. Eibl-Eibesfeldt's capital 'human
ethology' workshop in Bavaria, or in the course of a disappointingly
inconclusive multidisciplinary conference of the Royal Society, volumi-
nous transactions of which were published nine years ago.

Those biologists who, somewhat in the manner of M. Jourdain, have
pursued their semiotic inquiries, "il y a plus de quarante ans", without
being aware of so doing, had the connection first made explicit in 1963,
summed up by yet another coinage, *zoosemiotics*, intended as a
mediating concept for reconciling these two seemingly antithetical
spheres of discourse, ethology and semiotics: the former, anchored in
the realm of Nature, embracing the totality of the multifarious
phenomena of animal behavior on the one hand, the second, rooted in
the matrix of Culture, traditionally held by many to comprise
exclusively man's signifying competence on the other. This new
formation was evidently welcome, for it not only diffused with great
rapidity through appropriate scientific writings, but also, more aston-
ishingly, cropped up in a 1965 novel by Pamela Hansford Johnson, not
to mention a cartoon, co-featuring Snoopy, in a March, 1973, issue of
the Milanese *Corriere della Sera*. At any rate, in the 1970s, it no longer
seems strange to find the director of a major European zoo insisting
that theoretical questions of animal communication be resolved "unter
dem Gesichtspunkt moderner Kommunikationslehren, besonders auch
der Semiotik . . . "

Ethologists refer to the behavioral dossier of a species as its
ethogram, and, like N. Tinbergen, would place a special emphasis on the
importance of amassing a complete inventory of patterns for each. In
semiotic terms, this concept encompasses an animal's species-specific
communicative code, in confrontation with which the human observer's
role necessarily becomes that of a cryptanalyst, of someone who
receives messages not destined for him and is initially ignorant of the
applicable transformation rules. The code underlying any system of
animal communication differs crucially from any language insofar as
the former is simply tantamount to the total repertoire of messages at
the disposal of the species, whereas a true language is always imbued by
the structural principle that linguists have called 'double articulation' or
'duality of patterning', involving a rule governed device for constructing
a potentially infinite array of larger units (e.g., sentences, in the

so-called natural languages) out of a finite, indeed, very small and stable assembly of smaller ones (viz., the uniformly binary distinctive features). This enormously powerful and productive hierarchic arrangement – obviously recognized by Darwin in his keen observation that "The lower animals differ from man solely in his almost infinitely larger power of associating together the most diversified sounds and ideas . . . " – seems to have emerged but twice in terrestrial evolution, both times with stupendous consequences: the same structural principle informs the genetic code (the Beadles' 'language of life') and the verbal code (our own faculty of language). It has, however, so far, not been identified in any other animal communciation system studied (including, incidentally, that of captive chimpanzees in the Western United States, who have recently enjoyed publicity of the sort previously accorded only to bottle-nosed dolphins, those fading stars of fact and fiction of yesteryear). It is therefore scientifically inaccurate, as well as, even metaphorically, highly misleading, to speak of a 'language' of animals.

As for the pious goal of a perfect ethogram, unfortunately this still remains just that, for, despite the fact that the literature of animal behavior is now enormous, and still rapidly ramifying, none of the several millions of codes still in use is entirely understood by man. This is true even of the best researched code, namely, the one that regulates the remarkable communication system evolved in *Apis mellifera*, the honeybee. While the fact that these bees perform intricate movements – their famous 'dances' – in directing hive-mates to a source of food supply, or to new quarters, has been widely reported and is now a familiar story, it is less well known that these insects transmit information by acoustic means as well. Investigators in several laboratories, working independently of one another, have been attempting to complete an account of this facet of the apiarian ethogram, in spite of the prejudgment of some major scholars that the ancient ideas of acoustic communication among the bees "belong in the realm of fantasy". Communication by sounds does occur in bees, and is probably even more elaborate and significant than has been anticipated. As K. von Frisch himself once remarked, "the life of bees is like a magic well. The more you draw from it, the more there is to draw." The same is undoubtedly true of the life of all the other speechless creatures, while our knowledge of their communicative capacities and means remains even more rudimentary.

The word *display* is another commonplace in the vocabulary of ethology, as featured, for instance, in the title of E. A. Armstrong's erudite conspectus, *Bird Display* (1942; in later editions, expanded to *Bird Display and Behaviour*). Thus a rhesus monkey's simple stare is considered a low-intensity display of hostility. This term, however, remains a seldom defined or refined zoosemiotic prime, vaguely understood by everyone to refer to such behavior patterns, of sometimes bizarre complexity, that are deemed by an expert observer to have a predominantly communicative function: indisputably, for instance, the intricate courtship activities of bower birds, that use 'display-objects' of certain specified color combinations which they have collected with great discrimination to decorate their avenue- or maypole-type houses and ornamented gardens with, substituting, as it were, glittering natural jewelry for drab plumage, are likewise characterized as displays. In brief, the ethologist's 'display' is synonymous, or substantially overlaps, with the semiotician's master concept, the 'sign', whether simple or compound, which, by all accounts – from the Stoic distinction of *sēmainon* vs. *sēmainomenon* to multiform recent and contemporary formulations – is conceived of as a bifacial construct, i.e., as constituted of two indispensable moieties: the *signifier*, an appreciable impact on at least one of the interpreter's sense organs, and the content *signified*. 'Sign', however, is a generic term: recognition of the manifold potential relations between the two parts of the sign, what Peirce has called the "fundamental varieties of possible semiosis", has led to the realization of many different sign processes. Peirce himself, in his memorable 1867 paper in *The Proceedings of the American Academy of Arts and Sciences*, introduced three, but, by the end of the century, his initial trichotomy yielded ten classes of signs, which later grew into sixty-six, including intermediate and hybrid forms, and what he called 'degenerate' signs.

A fair sample of the most commonly acknowledged and utilized signs – notably including signal, symptom and syndrome, icon, index, symbol, and name – were subjected to detailed scrutiny, particularly in the light of recently accumulated data on nonverbal communication, with the unexpected result that every type of sign thus analyzed has been found to occur in the animal kingdom as well as in human affairs, so that it is feasible now to separate, say, an iconic display from an indexic display or a symbolic display, or to comprehend thoroughly what is meant by the assertion that vertebrates seem universally to incorporate their own 'names' into all of their messages. The rather imprecise ethological notion of *imprinting* refers to a learning process responsible for restricting the filial behavior of young vertebrates, and hinges on a decisive early sensitivity to a conspicuous, familiar object, in short, a sign, the nature of which can now also be specified. The fondly cherished mythic characterization of man, adhered to by E. Cassirer's epigones and many others, as a unique *animal symbolicum* can be sustained only if the definition of 'symbol' is impermissibly ensnared with the concept of natural language, which G. G. Simpson quite aptly characterized as "the most diagnostic single trait of man". By every other definition – invoking the principle of arbitrariness, the idea of a conventional link between a signifier and its denotata, Peirce's 'imputed character', or the notion of an intensional class for the designatum – animals demonstrably employ symbols. Space limitations permit only two brief examples here, both deliberately chosen from the world of insects: in a species of dipterans of the carnivorous family Empididae, the male offers the female an empty balloon prior to copulation. The evolutionary origins, that is, the increasing ritualiza-tion, of this gesture have been unravelled, step by step, by biologists, but this story is irrelevant in a synchronic perspective: the fact remains that the gift of the balloon features a wholly arbitrary symbol, the transfer of which merely reduces the probability that the male himself will fall prey to his female partner. For the second example, consider again the honeybee. It is common knowledge that if its food source is farther away than 100 m., the bee's tail-wagging dance conveys, among other bits of information, the direction of the goal, the sun being used as a reference point. Now if the bee dances on a horizontal surface, von Frisch tells us that "the direction of a waggling run points directly to the goal", that is to say, the display is indexic (the rhythm, incidentally, depicts the distance iconically, since the farther away the goal, the fewer cycles of the dance occur in a given period). If, however, the dance takes place on a vertical comb surface – as is the case, normally, in the dark hive – then "the dancer transposes the solar angle into the gravitational angle", according to von Frisch. In other words, if a vertical honeycomb is involved, when an angle with respect to gravity is substituted as the orientation cue, the indexical aspect of the display attenuates to the extent that, temporarily, its symbolic aspect comes to rank predominant.

The essential unity of a zoosemiotic event may be decomposed, for the field observer's or laboratory experimenter's convenience, into six aspects, and the sphere of animal communication studies has, in practice, tended to divide roughly in accordance with these, the factors actually emphasized depending on each investigator's training and bias. Two of these factors – code and message – I have already mentioned; their study belongs to zoosyntactics, which deals with combinations of signs abstracted from their specific significations or their ecological setting. Zoosemantics is devoted to the signification of signs, and must take account of the context referred to by the source and apprehensible by the destination; this is the least well understood dimension of animal communication studies.

Zoopragmatics may be said to deal with the origin of signs in the source, or sender, the propagation of signs through a medium, or channel, and the effect of signs on the destination, or receiver. Contact among emitters and receivers of messages is established and maintained by an impressive variety of flow processes that link them across space and time. In principle, of course, any form of energy propagation or transfer of matter can serve as a sign vehicle, depending on an animal's total perceptual equipment. In part because of their immediate appeal to the imagination of men, and in part stimulated by technological refinements of the last three decades, the study of mechanical vibrations by which some species communicate – the field of bio-acoustics, operating across the medium of air, under water, or even through solids – constitutes one of the most advanced branches of zoosemiotics. Classical ethology was more concerned with optical systems, on the basis of which it was able to generalize such more or less fruitful concepts as the 'intention' and 'displacement' movements, and that of 'autonomic effects'; and invertebrate zoology concentrated primarily on the transfer of information by relatively stereotyped chemical substances (pheromones). One of the most fascinating channels to 'open up' lately gives access to a busy world of electrocommunication, where several kinds of discharge alterations have now been clearly shown to correlate with social situations, having to do with food, threat, attack, submission, mating, and the like, in a high number of electroreceptive species of fish surveyed. If an animal's sensory capacity allows for the parallel processing of information through multiple input channels, as is the case in monkeys and apes, whose communication, Thelma Rowell recently reminded us, "is usually carried on through several modalities at the same time", calculable redundancies will be found to prevail, so that the discovery of the rules for switching from one subassembly to another should, in principle, be determinable. Such an integrated description is, unfortunately, very rarely given in animal communication studies, yet not surprisingly so, since a fully coordinated account of our verbal with our nonverbal processes is also sadly lacking: as for Hamlet's players, discretion must, therefore, still be our tutor when we "suit the action to the word, the word to the action".

Animal emitters and interpreters of strings of signs are either conspecifics or they belong to two or more species, one of which may be man. Many zoologists, like V. C. Wynne-Edwards, tend to divide interindividual sign repertoires first of all into intraspecific vs. interspecific varieties, but it is fair to say that explorations of the former, where all messages are assumed to be mapped onto a single code, have progressed much further than those concerned with situations requiring at least a partial sharing of and switching among several codes. Mimicry, as distinguished from mere imitation – for instance, of an infant macaque of its mother – almost always requires at least two species of animals or plants (or an inorganic surrogate) for its realization, as W. Wickler has shown in his handsome introduction to the subject; in its so-called Müllerian manifestation, it is exemplified by the series of black longitudinal stripes exhibited by different species of cleaner fish that wear this uniform identification pattern, or badge, allowing them all to communicate with certain larger predators by way of this common convergence feature. Even tourists on an African safari have now learned to appreciate the palpable sharing of, say, signs of alarm by representatives of mixed game visiting at the same waterhole. Moreover, subtle semiotic ecosystems are sometimes formed not only by several interdependent animal species, but also in conjunction with plants, as in the complex community achieved by a group of insects (the Danaidae) and blue jays together with milkweeds belonging to the family of Asclepiadiceae.

How man communicates with animals, and vice versa, has, so far, been of marginal concern to both semiotics and ethology (although it is an insistent theme in the pioneering works of Professor Hediger, and K. and M. Breland's excellent little book on *Animal Behavior*, written with an engineering objective in view). Yet in all arenas of life the relation between man and animal – from protozoan to primate – is now decisive. Wherever they meet, whether man is an animal's scourge or its prey (e.g., of his still biggest killer, the mosquito); whether the two are, however unequal their partnership, symbionts (as a human-host and his household pet-guest); whether one is a parasite of the other (as F. E. Zeuner characterized man's relationship vis-à-vis the reindeer); or whether one species accepts the other as a conspecific (witness

London's late panda, which was alleged to have been imprinted upon its
keeper), or, to the contrary, as an inanimate object (e.g., man as a part
of a vehicle in a wild-life park), the liaison implies that each must,
perforce, learn, if not totally master, the essential elements of the
reciprocal's code. After establishing loose contacts with an animal, man,
if he so wills it, can follow up by taming it, a process that can be
defined as a systematic reduction of flight distance achieved by
conscious manipulation of the animal's code. A tame animal can then be
subjected to the purely synchronic process of training, and that in one
of two complementary ways: *apprentissage* or *dressage*, i.e., for scientific testing or for performing in exhibitions, the two being polar
opposites – as E. Kuckuk already emphasized in his 1936 disquisition
on a couple of young brown bears: "Die Zirkusdressur ist . . . das
genaue Gegenteil eines tierpsychologischen Versuchs." The two proce-
dures are distinguishable in at least two respects: the semiotic character
of the sign which initiates the requisite action (unmarked vs. marked),
and the degree of emotional intensity coupling the interactants
(minimal vs. maximal). Next, if economic circumstances dictate the
planned development of forms with certain properties man deems
desirable, he superposes a diachronic dimension: by selective breeding,
or alteration of the genetic code, domestication (with flight distance
approaching constant zero) will ensue. The final, alas irreversible, step
may be the cutting off of all further communication with members of
the species – the persecution, then eventual extermination, of its feral
ancestors.

   It is important to appreciate in detail how the proper methods of
semiotic analysis can illuminate the judgment of all ethological
observations and experiments – lacking which, one need only recall
that classic scandal of scientific obfuscation, known as the 'Clever Hans'
episode, that hinged on the trainer's self-delusion about the steady
stream of indexic signals, reduced to mere synecdoches scarcely
perceptible even to the acutest witnesses, that he unwittingly broadcast
to his horse, but which the animal was able to interpret swiftly and
surely; and even today, one must vigilantly be on guard to prevent the
transmogrification of clever horses (Hans was by no means the only
one) into cleverer chimpanzees! Our relationships with animals in game
preserves or zoological gardens, in the intimacy of the circus, and
comparable marine installations, or biological research laboratories, on
the farmstead or in the home, could be materially enhanced by realizing
exactly how, in all such dyadic contacts, paired systems of communica-

tion, which influence one another in exceedingly intricate ways, are juxtaposed in constant interplay.

While semiotics, at least in the vital Locke-Peirce-Morris tradition, continues to widen its horizons to comprehend the entire animal kingdom, indeed, the whole of organic existence (hence G. Tembrock's preference for a broader label, *biosemiotics*), as well as the sign functions of machines (so S. Gorn speaks of the fundamental semiotic concepts of computers), ethology is likewise moving to enlarge its scope to embrace man (a facilitative step in this direction was the recent creation of a semi-independent research group for human ethology, under the prestigious auspices of the Max Planck Institute of Behavioral Physiology; one must also single out the work of N. Blurton Jones with young children in England). By systematic application of the principles of ritualization and its corollaries to aspects of nonverbal behavior, over an impressively worldwide data base, much of it freshly collected and preserved on film, some salient facts have already been established, pertaining, for example, to the universality of certain human facial expressions and gestures previously considered culture-bound. Ethology has, of course, failed to shed any light on the evolution of man's unique faculty of language, despite Huxley's truism that it, too, is "ritualized (adaptively formalized) behaviour": ritualization works on the assumption that behavior unfolds with morphological growth and differentiation, but how can one apply the comparative method to a sample of one? The outlines of a semiotics that eschews anthropocentrism, coupled with an ethology that shuns parochialism, can already be envisaged. It seems likely that a full-fledged synthesis will be achieved before long, offering both a new paradigm and a methodology for the comparative analysis of semiosis in its full diversity, ranging from the two vast linked polymer languages at one end of the scale to the thousands of natural languages at the other, with a host of singular information coding and transmission devices, inside and outside the body of every organism, in between. Semiosis, independent of form or substance, is thus seen as a universal, criterial property of animate existence.

6
La dynamique des signes*

PRÉSENTATION

Avec l'intervention de Thomas A. Sebeok, la comparaison entre langage humain et langage animal s'enrichit d'une dimension dynamique (le devenir des signes) et d'une dimension contextuelle (transition entre codes et mise en commun des codes). Sémioticien, passé de l'étude des langues ouralo-altaïques à celle de toute forme de communication chez l'animal et chez l'homme, Sebeok représente une tendance unificatrice qui cherche les universaux de la communication non seulement à travers la phylogenèse mais même au sein des mécanismes fondamentaux de la vie. Dans un symposium organisé pendant l'été 1965 à Burg Warten-stein, Sebeok réunissait des zoologistes, des linguistes, des éthologues et des psychologues pour une mise en commun de résultats et de méthodes sur la communication des insectes à l'homme. En présentant le volume issu de cette conférence, Sebeok écrivait: "Il est clair que le code génétique doit être regardé comme le plus fondamental de tous les réseaux sémiotiques et, donc, comme le prototype de tous les autres systèmes de signalisation employés par les animaux, l'homme inclus. Dans cette perspective, aussi bien les molécules, en tant que systèmes quantiques porteurs d'une information physique stable, que les sys-

---

* These impromptu remarks were presented orally, in September, 1972, and were recorded at a Colloquium convened by the Centre Royaumont pour une science de l'homme, and are reprinted from *L'Unité de l'homme: Invariants biologiques et universaux culturels*, ed. by Edgar Morin and Massimo Piattelli-Palmarini (Paris: Seuil, 1974), pp. 61-77. Massimo Piattelli-Palmarini's prefatory remarks, and a transcription of the ensuing discussion, are included here for the sake of completeness.

tèmes zoo-sémiotiques que, finalement, les systèmes culturels, le langage inclus, s'ordonnent en une séquence naturelle d'étapes de plus en plus complexes par leurs niveaux énergétiques donnant une évolution universelle. Il est donc possible de décrire le langage et les systèmes vivants sous une même perspective cybernétique. Bien qu'il ne s'agisse à présent de rien d'autre que d'une analogie utile, susceptible à la rigueur de donner des aperçus nouveaux mais non point d'informations nouvelles, cette évaluation conjointe de la génétique, de la communication animale et de la linguistique peut nous acheminer vers une compréhension exhaustive de la dynamique sémiotique, ce qui pourrait en dernière analyse se révéler comme rien de moins que la définition de la vie (turn out to be no less than the definition of life)."[1]

Un axe heuristique privilégié, sinon unique, formé par les homologies et les analogies des phénomènes communicationnels, nous aiderait, selon Sebeok (et aussi selon Roman Jakobson), à comprendre le vivant et ses lois évolutives en partant de l'DNA et en arrivant jusqu'aux langages humains.

Cette perspective unitaire n'est pas partagée par d'autres chercheurs, lesquels y voient plutôt une perte en spécificité (donc en opérativité) qu'un gain en unité. Les biologistes moléculaires sont assez réticents quant aux extrapolations que l'on veut effectuer à partir de leur langage courant de laboratoire (pourtant lui-même emprunté à la communication humaine). L'intervention de Jacques Monod en témoigne, et son attitude fut partagée, dans le débat qui suivit l'exposé de Sebeok, par Salvador E. Luria et François Jacob. Comme il n'a été qu'esquissé, nous n'avons pas transcrit ici cet échange d'idées. Il nous faut pourtant souligner que le chemin logique et heuristique qui conduirait du code génétique aux codes culturels humains peut apparaître plus hardi qu'il n'en a l'air dans les remarques de Sebeok. Pour les généticiens et les biochimistes, le 'code génétique' est une locution utile qui désigne une chimie historicisée grâce à laquelle, pendant des millénaires, un tri opéré par les faibles énergies de liaison non covalentes a sélectionné des appariements sélectifs et récursifs. Dans son sens strict, le code génétique représenterait donc une translittération entre une séquence de nucléotides et une séquence d'acides aminés. La véritable traduction, c'est-à-dire le tribunal du sens et du non-sens, ne se situerait qu'au niveau de la stabilité structurale des produits ultimes (les protéines et leurs associations), uniquement dictée par les forces physico-chimiques.

---

[1] Sebeok, 1968b: 12.

Dans cette optique, la reproduction invariante ne serait qu'une copolymérisation ordonnée (Monod emploie l'image d'une machine à photocopier) à travers laquelle toute séquence serait redoublée au prix de rares erreurs stochastiques. La résistance que les biologistes manifestent à l'égard des jumelages analogiques serait semblable à celle des physiciens lorsqu'ils voient les forces d'attraction et de répulsion entre particules être assimilées à une 'communication' au sein de la matière. D'autres pourraient néanmoins trouver excessive cette prudence des biologistes, dont le jargon révèle de significatifs emprunts à la cybernétique, à la linguistique et à la théorie de l'information (code, message, triplettes de sens et de non sens, ponctuation, programme, etc.). Ce problème est celui de la logique d'une description anthropomorphe moderne qui a un sens précis dans le laboratoire, mais qui est souvent douteuse si elle est élargie à d'autres domaines plus complexes. Plus largement, toute tendance à unifier sur ces termes communicationnels ou informationnels les perspectives sur le vivant se heurte souvent aux mises en garde des scientifiques expérimentaux. Ainsi s'opposent d'une part une volonté d'unification théorique, qui tend à négliger les différences substantielles entre les domaines, d'autre part une optique expérimentaliste qui tend à considérer les concepts informationnels comme de simples outils manipulant la réalité étudiée et non comme constitutifs de cette réalité. Il s'agit de deux stratégies cognitives jusqu'ici considérées comme antithétiques mais qui peuvent devenir complémentaires. Quand Katz nous propose ici une vision de la sélection naturelle comme transaction informationnelle entre organisme et milieu, on peut se demander si le néo-darwinisme pourrait reformuler ses acquis dans un langage nouveau. Quand Premack nous donne sa définition clairement opératoire de ce qu'est une communication symbolique, opposée à une communication 'affective' ou 'intensive', il faut se questionner sur le manque de rigueur que ces concepts ont présenté jusqu'ici. La nécessité de concilier une lecture en profondeur du statut opératif des sciences exactes avec la rigueur qui, seule, peut transformer des analogies en modèles congrus est peut-être la nécessité même d'une nouvelle science de l'homme.

Massimo Piattelli-Palmarini

COMMENT UN SIGNAL DEVIENT SIGNE

Les linguistes disent à leurs étudiants que le domaine de la linguistique comprend l'échange de messages verbaux, lesquels sont généralement étudiés selon six aspects différents qui sont fonction de la prédilection et du penchant du chercheur. On peut centrer son étude sur le destinateur ou sur le destinataire, ce qui en gros correspond aux problèmes d'encodage et de décodage, problèmes que l'on considère parfois également comme relevant de la psycholinguistique. On peut prendre comme objet d'étude la physique de la transmission du message, les propriétés du canal et ainsi de suite, que l'on étudie en acoustique, laquelle, naturellement, est une branche de la physique. On peut prendre pour objet d'étude le contexte, lequel est surtout étudié de nos jours par les sociolinguistes et les ethno-linguistes. Et, naturellement, l'objet d'étude central, fondamental, des linguistes, c'est d'une part le code ('la langue'[2]) et, d'autre part, le message ('le discours'). Bien que je n'aie pas ici l'intention de parler de la linguistique en tant que telle, je tiens cependant à souligner un point particulier. On croit souvent que les linguistes s'intéressent exclusivement à la communication, mais je tiens à préciser que la linguistique met en réalité l'accent sur deux aspects, et que la communication ne constitue que l'un de ceux-ci, l'autre étant la signification. C'est là une distinction extrêmement importante, mais qui souvent ou bien n'est pas saisie ou bien n'est pas prise en compte par ceux qui n'appartiennent pas à la profession.

Il y a une quinzaine d'années, ce cadre m'apparut un peu trop contraignant. Autrement dit, je fus amené à considérer qu'il convenait de prêter attention non seulement à l'échange de messages verbaux, mais à tout le domaine de l'échange des messages quels qu'ils soient. C'est le domaine de la sémiotique, science vieille d'environ deux mille ans, mais qui s'est développée dernièrement et qui maintenant prospère et s'épanouit dans le monde entier. Comme je l'ai dit, la sémiotique traite essentiellement de l'échange des messages quels qu'ils soient, et des systèmes de signes qui les sous-tendent. La sémiotique comporte un grand nombre d'approches que je ne ferai qu'évoquer rapidement. On peut approcher l'étude des signes par trois avenues et, s'il m'est permis de reprendre la distinction judicieuse du célèbre physiologue Ralph Gerard, je dirai qu'on peut parler de la nature des signes (*being of signs*), du comportement des signes (*behaving of signs*) et du devenir des signes (*becoming of signs*). Tout d'abord, la nature des signes. C'est ce qu'on appelle plus communément leur *structure*, et je reviendrai sur ce point dans un moment. En second lieu, le comportement des signes, qui renvoie à la façon dont ils *fonctionnent*, par exemple à la façon dont ils sont encodés, dont ils sont transmis ou décodés. Enfin, il y a le

---

[2] En français dans le texte original.

problème du devenir des signes, qui en réalité se scinde en deux problèmes totalement distincts. L'un de ceux-ci empiète grandement sur l'objet de l'éthologie. C'est la question de savoir comment les signaux deviennent des signes au cours de l'évolution, le problème de leur phylogenèse. C'est ce qu'en éthologie on appelle généralement la ritualisation – terme que l'on doit à Julian Huxley – et qui constitue un domaine maintenant largement étudié par les collaborateurs de Eibl-Eibesfeldt en particulier et les chercheurs allemands en général. Mais, en second lieu, il y a le problème de l'ontogenèse des signes, qui lui aussi suscite à l'heure actuelle un intérêt extraordinaire. Ce problème a été évoqué par Gardner; il entre dans l'étude de l'acquisition du langage, et non seulement de l'acquisition du langage mais de celle d'autres modes de communication. Il s'ensuit qui l'on peut établir le domaine de la sémiotique en termes de structure, de fonction ou d'histoire.

Deuxièmement, comme je l'ai déjà indiqué, on peut traiter des événements sémiotiques dans une perspective de communication, et des événements sémiotiques dans une perspective de signification, mais c'est là un problème très complexe dont je ne puis parler maintenant.

Une troisième façon d'envisager la sémiotique, c'est de considérer l'espèce qui se trouve impliquée. Bien entendu, chacun suppose que le langage dit naturel se manifeste seulement chez les êtres humains. On peut toutefois faire l'hypothèse que les événements sémiotiques apparaissent dans une grande diversité d'organismes, et je suis quant à moi convaincu qu'il n'existe aucun être vivant qui n'utilise pas les signes. Si je puis m'aventurer jusque-là, j'irai même jusqu'à établir une égalité entre les processus sémiotiques et la vie elle-même. Je considère en effet que la propriété la plus fondamentale de la vie, c'est précisément le phénomène sémiotique. On peut naturellement étudier les signes chez n'importe laquelle des quelque deux millions d'espèces et plus existant sur le globe, et l'on découvrira autant de codes que d'espèces. Tout code est unique, tout code est différent de tous les autres, et pour tout code on peut, comme je l'ai déjà dit, se demander comment il fonctionne, quelle est sa structure et d'où il est venu. On peut également étudier les manifestations sémiotiques chez les êtres humains; non pas le langage en l'occurrence, mais tous les autres dispositifs de communication que possèdent les humains. Je tiens à faire remarquer, et j'insiste sur ce point, que l'on pense souvent à l'*homo loquens*, à l'être humain comme étant l'*animal qui parle*, mais je dois souligner que les dispositifs de communication dont l'homme dispose sont assurément très nombreux et très divers. Nous possédons de nombreux codes, le langage n'étant que l'un d'entre eux. Un des problèmes les plus complexes et les plus délicats est le suivant: quelle relation y a-t-il entre le langage et tous les autres répertoires dont l'homme dispose? A ce propos, une question biologiquement intéressante se pose: si le langage est aussi utile et aussi efficace que nous le supposons généralement, comment se fait-il donc que tous ces autres dispositifs de communication aient survécu, qu'ils se soient même enrichis et diversifiés dans différentes cultures comme ils l'ont fait? Ainsi, les êtres humains possèdent plus d'un système de communication, et je me suis souvent demandé comment il se faisait, si le langage est tout ce que les linguistes ont dit qu'il était, que les autres systèmes de communication n'aient pas dépéri. C'est sans doute là quelque chose qui mérite d'être débattu.

Un autre problème que je voudrais évoquer – car il se rapporte à nos discussions – est le suivant: les codes que j'ai cités, qui existent chez des êtres vivants différents, sont des codes spécifiques à l'espèce; autrement dit, chaque animal apprend vraisemblablement le code qui caractérise son espèce. Cependant, de nombreux animaux vivent dans un milieu écologique, dans un environnement où ils se trouvent en outre en contact étroit avec d'autres espèces. Et, entre une espèce et une autre, ou entre une espèce et un grand nombre d'autres, doit se développer un certain degré de partage du code (*code-sharing*). Je dirai que les mécanismes de changement de code (*code-switching*) ont à être appris et que les mécanismes de partage du code évoluent. Un des problèmes les moins étudiés de tout ce domaine est celui de savoir comment ces mécanismes se développent et quelles en sont les conditions préalables. De plus, s'il s'agit de deux ou de plusieurs espèces, et que l'homme soit l'une de celles-ci, de nouveaux problèmes apparaissent. L'expérience sur Washoe et celle sur Sarah constituent bien évidemment des problèmes de partage du code et de changement de code. En l'occurrence, nous n'avons pas uniquement dans ce cas Washoe et Sarah qui apprennent le code de l'homme, mais les Gardner et Premack qui apprennent le code des chimpanzés. Nous nous trouvons affrontés ici à un certain nombre de problèmes supplémentaires, problèmes qui, pour autant que je sache, n'ont été traités de façon vraiment sérieuse que par un seul chercheur. Je tiens à le nommer, car c'est un savant extraordinaire. Il s'agit du Pr H. Hediger, directeur du Jardin zoologique de Zurich. Hediger a soulevé la question de savoir ce qui se passe, premièrement lorsqu'on apprivoise des animaux, deuxièmement lorsqu'on entraîne des animaux, et troisièmement lorsqu'on impose une dimension diachronique à l'apprivoisement et à l'entraînement, ce qui constitue tout le problème de la domestication. Je considère que la domestication des animaux est essentiellement un problème de partage du code et de changement de code auquel on applique artificiellement une dimension diachronique. Tout ceci se retrouve également, comme l'a montré Hediger, dans les situations d'entraînement des animaux de cirque, dans les relations établies, dans les zoos, entre animaux et soigneurs. On peut encore mentionner naturellement tout le domaine de la garde d'animaux familiers et, d'une façon plus générale, toutes les interactions entre les animaux familiers et les humains. Cette interaction entre humains et animaux constitue un domaine qui reste à étudier et sur lequel on sait très peu de chose jusqu'ici.

J'aimerais maintenant parler d'un problème suggéré par une remarque de Premack. Premack parle de symboles. Bien des gens parlent des symboles de manière assez floue. Toutefois, si l'on examine de près le domaine de la sémiotique, on se rend compte, comme s'en était déjà rendu compte saint Augustin, mais comme cela a été établi de la façon la plus complète et la plus spectaculaire par le grand philosophe américain Charles Sanders Peirce, qu'il n'y a pas seulement le signe ou le symbole, mais une grande variété de signes. Sans doute sont-ils plus ou moins bien connus et plus ou moins bien nommés; en tout cas, il convient de faire porter l'investigation non sur les seuls symboles, mais sur toute la gamme et sur toutes les variétés des autres signes. Dans sa jeunesse, Peirce commença par distinguer trois sortes de signes, puis, par la suite, il en distingua dix. Devenu vieux, il en proposa soixante-six et, parvenu à ce nombre, il mourut fort à propos. Gary Sanders a récemment calculé par extrapolation que si Peirce avait encore vécu, il aurait logiquement pu arriver à 3^{10}, soit 59 049 classes.[3] J'en mentionnerai certains dont on peut facilement débattre: il y a les *signaux* naturellement, mais je ne peux vous en donner ici ni la définition formelle ni même des exemples. Il y a un catégorie de signes, bien connue des médecins (ce sont sans doute les premiers découverts), qu'on appelle les *symptômes*, avec la notion très voisine du syndrome. Il y a les trois catégories classiques de Peirce, l'*icône*, l'*indice*, et le *symbole*. Il y a une catégorie très intéressante, celle des *noms*. Apparaissent en outre un certain nombre de problèmes subsidiaires. Le 'symbole' possède de nombreuses variétés, connues sous les noms d'*emblème*, d'*insigne*, de *marque*, etc. Chacune de celles-ci à son tour possède des

---

[3] Sanders, 1970: 11.

aspects particuliers et des catégories particulières qu'il conviendrait d'étudier. J'ai étudié en détail les signes que j'ai mentionnés et depuis quinze ans j'analyse la littérature traitant de la communication animale. Il n'y a pas une seule de ces catégories que je ne rencontre dans le monde animal. Je serai donc parfaitement d'accord avec Premack pour dire que les animaux possèdent des symboles: ceci ne me surprend pas le moins du monde. Ils ont non seulement des symboles, mais ils ont des signaux et des symptômes, ils ont des icônes, des indices et des emblèmes, et ils ont des noms. Je pourrais en apporter le preuve, un chapitre de mon livre à paraître étant consacré à ce problème; mais cela demanderait beaucoup trop de temps.

Je voudrais faire encore une remarque. Nous discutons dans ce séminaire de l'unicité de l'homme et des limites de cette unicité. Ainsi posé, le problème est à mon sens légèrement faussé; en tout cas, je ne le poserais pas de cette manière. Je le formulerais plutôt ainsi: de quels systèmes sémiotiques parlons-nous, et en quoi ces systèmes sémiotiques diffèrent-ils les uns des autres? Je ne dirais pas nécessairement que l'homme est unique, mais je dirais que le langage est unique. Le langage est unique mais, strictement parlant, il n'est pas totalement unique, car, comme l'ont fait remarquer un certain nombre de chercheurs durant la dernière décennie, le code verbal et le code génétique ont certaines propriétés en commun. J'ai écrit sur ce problème pour la première fois en 1963, et il en fut discuté au cours d'un débat télévisé: François Jacob, qui se trouve parmi nous, y participait.[4] La littérature sur ce point a été récemment récapitulée par Roger Masters.[5] Toute la littérature génétique mentionne ce problème, à savoir qu'il existe des analogies frappantes et profondes entre le code génétique et le code verbal. Y a-t-il plus qu'une analogie? Peut-il s'agir d'une homologie? On l'ignore. Du moins, je l'ignore quant à moi. Je dirai donc que le problème intéressant, ce n'est pas que l'homme soit unique, mais que son langage l'est, ou qu'il l'est presque. On peut certainement dire que le code verbal est très différent des systèmes de communication des animaux ou des codes utilisés par les quelque deux millions d'autres

---

[4] Sebeok se réfère ici à un débat organisé par Michel Treguer et Gérard Chouchan et qui vit réunis François Jacob, Roman Jakobson, Claude Lévi-Strauss et Philippe L'Héritier pour débattre du thème "Vivre et parler". Deux numéros successifs des *Lettres françaises* (14 et 21 fév. 1968) ont recueilli le texte des discussions (N.d.É.).

[5] Masters, 1970: 295-320.

espèces. On pourrait préciser en quoi ils diffèrent ou de quelle façon le code génétique et le code verbal se ressemblent.

Pour terminer, je voudrais faire une dernière remarque un peu particulière. En fait, il s'agit d'une question fort embarrassante que je me suis posée et qui mérite d'être mentionnée. C'est un point qu'a également soulevé l'ornithologue et primatologue compétent qu'est Peter Marler,[6] mais qui au demeurant est une observation bien connue, à savoir: les prédispositions que manifestent quelques oiseaux à apprendre certains sons plutôt que d'autres rappellent les contraintes auxquelles est soumis l'homme lors de l'apprentissage de la langue maternelle. Or cette ressemblance est dénuée de sens du point de vue de l'évolution. On cherche toujours les racines du langage chez les alloprimates, mais, sur certains points, il y a bien plus de similitudes frappantes entre les oiseaux et les humains qu'entre n'importe quel primate et les humains. Nottebohm,[7] de l'université Rockefeller, a récemment publié dans *Science* un article très éclairant qui fournit des détails sur ce point. Si je soulève ce problème, cèst simplement par contraste avec le sens général de la discussion, mais non pas parce que j'ai une quelconque réponse à proposer, ni que quiconque soit à même de dire pourquoi il en est ainsi.

DISCUSSION[8]

Participants: Henri Altan, Solomon H. Katz, Jacques Monod, David Premack, Thomas A. Sebeok

J.M.   Sebeok partage apparemment le point de vue d'autres linguistes, et en particulier de Jakobson, je crois, selon lequel il existerait une analogie étroite entre code génétique et code linguistique, et que ceci pourrait de manière très éclairante s'interpréter en termes d'affiliation, ou d'évolution, que sais-je encore. Je pense exprimer le point de vue de nombreux biologistes en disant qu'en fait il s'agit d'une fausse analogie, qu'elle n'est pas éclairante mais bien plutôt trompeuse.

[6]   Marler, 1968: 128.
[7]   Nottebohm, 1970: 950.
[8]   Traduit par Yvonne Noizet.

D.P. Je ne veux pas tant poser une question que faire un bref
commentaire sur au moins deux types de communication dont
a parlé Sebeok. Disons que l'une est affective et l'autre
symbolique. Il est intéressant de remarquer que l'une d'elles, la
communication affective, dépend trés strictement d'une condition préalable à laquelle la communication symbolique
échappe complètement. Faisons l'hypothèse que les éléments
de base de la communication affective sont les suivants; on peut
se trouver soit dans un état positif, soit dans un état négatif;
autrement dit, on peut aimer quelque chose ou ne pas l'aimer,
et ce à des degrés différents. Disons en outre que ces états
affectifs peuvent être pris comme base de la communication.
Simplifions encore le problème, et supposons que quelque
chose d'intéressant se trouve dans la pièce d'à côté. Je peux en
revenir dans un état affectif positif, manifester mon content-
ement d'un façon ou d'une autre, ce sur quoi mon interlocuteur peut se précipiter dans la pièce d'à côté où il trouvera
peut-être des pommes mûres et les mangera. Ou bien je peux
en revenir sur le mode symbolique de communication et dire
que les pommes qui sont à côté sont mûres. Par contre, je peux
en revenir pâle, tremblant ou autre chose de ce genre, et alors
mon interlocuteur n'ira pas dans la pièce d'à côté. Ou bien je
peux en revenir et dire: "Il y a un tigre", auquel cas il n'ira pas
non plus dans la pièce d'à côté. Voilà quelques exemples de ces
états positifs ou négatifs et des différents degrés qu'ils peuvent
revêtir. On voit comment ces états motivationnels peuvent être
utilisés comme outils de communication, par opposition au
mode symbolique où l'on énonce ou décrit la situation
qui est celle de la pièce d'à côté. L'intéressant, à mon sens,
du moins dans ce cas limité, c'est que le mode affectif peut
être très efficace. Il dépend d'une condition préalable extrêmement simple à laquelle échappe totalement le mode symbolique, c'est-à-dire que, pour que le mode affectif fonctionne,
il doit y avoir concordance entre les échelles de préférences des
participants. Autrement dit, vous et moi devons attribuer les
mêmes valeurs aux objets du monde. Pour pouvoir utiliser mon
état affectif et, au premier chef, pour que je puisse prédire
votre état affectif, vous et moi devons estimer de la même
façon les choses du monde. S'il n'en est pas ainsi, si vous
n'aimez pas les pommes ou si vous n'avez pas peur des tigres,

vous ne pourrez pas utiliser mon état affectif comme base permettant de prédire votre état affectif. En revanche, la communication symbolique ne dépend nullement du fait que vous et moi attribuons les mêmes valeurs aux objets du monde; nous pouvons, vous et moi, évaluer le monde de manière très différente et néanmoins communiquer fort bien symboliquement, alors qu'il n'en est pas ainsi pour la communication affective. Du point de vue expérimental, je pense au cas où l'on place des chimpanzés (comme dans certains recherches de Menzel, fort habiles d'ailleurs) dans une cage située à l'extérieur d'une enceinte. Supposons qu'on fasse venir un chimpanzé dans l'enceinte, qu'on lui montre quelque chose, puis qu'on le ramène dans la cage, et qu'enfin on relâche tous les chimpanzés. Dans ce cas, ceux-ci trouvent beaucoup plus souvent l'objet caché que lorsqu'il n'y a pas eu d'informateur. Et je pense qu'il est juste de supposer qu'en l'occurrence nous avons affaire à un système de communication de type affectif. Or il serait intéressant de voir ce qu'il adviendrait de ce système affectif si, au laboratoire, on supprimait la concordance entre échelles de préférences. On peut par exemple faire en sorte qu'un animal soit abondamment pourvu de bananes et, de ce fait, ne leur attribue pas une grande valeur, tandis que les autres en sont privés et leur attribuent une grande valeur. La concordance se trouve ainsi supprimée. La question est alors de savoir si l'apprentissage pourrait surmonter cette difficulté. Il est naturel de penser que le rôle de l'apprentissage est de résoudre tout problème engendré par des circonstances fâcheuses, la circonstance fâcheuse étant ici cette non-concordance des préférences: les membres du groupe n'évaluent pas les choses de la même façon. Un apprentissage peut-il intervenir pour résoudre ce problème? Je pense que non. Cela n'est possible que dans des cas très particuliers où les préférences d'un organisme sont fonction de celles de l'autre, si bien que l'un ne fait que répéter l'autre; mais, s'il n'y a pas de relation fonctionnelle entre les préférences des membres du groupe, je pense que l'apprentissage ne peut jouer aucun rôle. La seule chose qui, apparemment, peut permettre de résoudre ce problème, c'est la communication symbolique ou icônique. Il est donc très intéressant de constater que le système affectif est soumis à cette condition préalable très simple qu'est la concordance des préférences chez les membres du groupe, que le système symbolique n'y est pas soumis, et qu'en fin de compte l'apprentissage ne semble pas pouvoir surmonter la difficulté dans le cas du système affectif. Il arrive très souvent que des profanes cultivés me disent: "Et comment savez-vous que les oiseaux n'ont pas de langage, ni non plus les dauphins?", ou encore: "Mon caniche et moi, nous communiquons beaucoup", et ainsi de suite. Il n'est pas du tout facile de les convaincre, faute de preuves manifestes, qu'en fait n'intervient pas de communication symbolique. Or j'ai essayé de montrer, à l'aide d'une argumentation très simple, que la communication symbolique – on pourrait utiliser d'autres termes no repose pas sur une condition préalable particulière; que la communication affective, en revanche, est soumise à la condition préalable de base d'une concordance temporelle des échelles de préférences. Tous les membres de la communauté doivent ordonner les événements du monde de la même façon et utiliser une même échelle de valeurs. Ceci constitue une condition préalable indispensable pour la communication affective. Autrement dit, si je dois utiliser votre état affectif pour prédire ma réponse à ce que je suppose être la cause de votre état affectif, la valeur que j'attribue à cette cause doit être la même que celle que vous lui attribuez. Mais ceci n'est pas une condition préalable pour la communication symbolique. Or ce qui constitue une différence de conditions préalables pour les deux formes de communication peut très facilement être converti en un test permettant de vérifier si une espèce possède ou non la communication symbolique. Pour ce faire, on observe une espèce dont les membres sont en train de communiquer (comme le font les chimpanzés de Menzel dans la situation très ingénieuse qu'il a suscitée); on prend un groupe dans lequel la communication est excellente et on induit dans les membres de ce groupe le besoin de communiquer. La procédure qu'utilise Menzel est très efficace pour induire le besoin de communiquer, mais il serait trop long d'exposer ici les raisons pour lesquelles cette procédure est particulièrement adaptée. On détruit expérimentalement la concordance des échelles de préférences et, si les animaux parviennent toujours à communiquer en dépit d'une discordance, expérimentalement établie, dans les échelles de préférences, on en conclut nécessairement qu'ils possèdent un moyen de communication symbolique. Si, en revanche, une fois qu'on a détruit la concordance dans les échelles de préférences, ils ne peuvent plus communiquer bien qu'ils éprouvent un grand besoin de le faire, et s'ils peuvent de nouveau communiquer à partir du moment où l'on a rétabli cette concordance, on peut alors, sans faire appel à des procédures plus élaborées, distinguer les espèces qui possèdent la communication symbolique et celles qui ne la possèdent pas. La méthode se ramène simplement à ceci: ces deux formes de communication sont soumises à des conditions préalables différentes, ce qui permet de tester si une espèce donnée possède ou non des moyens de communication aussi bien symboliques qu'affectifs.

J.M.   Premack a relevé à mon avis un des points principaux soulevés par Sebeok, celui de l'utilisation assez floue du concept de symbole, et de la nécessité de distinguer les classes de symboles ainsi que la relation entre les différents affects et performances de l'animal et, tout aussi bien, de l'homme.

T.A.S.   Je dirai qu'il s'agissait de ma part d'une assertion. En ce qui concerne la question, je dirai qu'il faut distinguer les classes de signes, et cela est assez difficile. Pour chaque classe, on peut donner des définitions formelles et des exemples tirés du monde animal.

S.H.K.   Je voudrais faire remarquer qu'il existe un lien entre ce que Jacques Monod et Sebeok ont dit à propos du code génétique et du code linguistique. Ce lien est à mon avis susceptible de résoudre partiellement ce problème. Ce lien se trouve au niveau du traitement de l'information. S'il n'en était pas ainsi, on pourrait envisager toute l'évolution comme une façon de collecter l'information sur un environnement particulier et sur les modifications qui se produisent dans cet environnement, ceci se produisant dans le temps. La conclusion serait que l'analogie en question — j'ignore s'il s'agit là d'une analogie formelle, je ne dis pas qu'il s'agit d'une homologie, je ne vais pas jusque-là — est à chercher avec les processus de la pensée et que l'analogie réside en ce que les processus de la pensée collectent également l'information relative à l'environnement et permettent à l'organisme – en l'occurrence, tout organisme, tout animal qui possède cette capacité – de stocker cette information. Ils permettent à cet organisme particulier de s'adapter aux modifications de l'environnement tout au long de la vie de cet individu ou de cet organisme. Dans un système unicellulaire très simple, vous trouveriez toutes les adaptations qui semblent se produire sur toute la durée du cycle de la vie de l'organisme. Ce serait ainsi la génération suivante que l'information génétique changerait en termes d'une modification de l'environnement. Cependant, dans le cas d'un cycle de vie plus long que celui-ci, dans lequel on a une certaine forme de système de contrôle, l'information peut alors être stockée tout au long de la vie de cet organisme particulier. Maintenant, y a-t-il des analogies au-delà de ce point précis, c'est-à-dire des analogies formelles concernant une éventuelle similitude des codages?A vrai dire, je ne pense pas que les codages pourraient être semblables, mais je crois qu'ils sont très sensiblement similaires en ce qui concerne cet élément fondamental.

T.A.S. Le fond du problème de l'analogie entre code génétique et code linguistique est en réalité très différent quand on le prend d'un point de vue linguistique. Le langage est un mécanisme très particulier, organisé de manière hiérarchique. Cette organisation hiérarchique est généralement désignée sous le nom de dualité, mais en réalité ce terme prête à confusion car il signifie essentiellement que l'on a un ensemble de sous-systèmes, et que le sous-système de base comporte un répertoire universel de traits binaires. C'est ce que les linguistes appellent des traits distinctifs, (*distinctive features*), traits qui sont en eux-mêmes dépourvus de signification, mais à l'aide desquels on peut fabriquer un nombre infini de phrases, lesquelles forment un autre sous-système. Pour ce qui est de l'ensemble des systèmes de communication des organismes, ceci constitue un phénomène unique, car nulle, part ailleurs dans le monde animal on ne trouve trace d'une telle organisation hiérarchique. Le code génétique, si je le comprends bien, fonctionne de manière analogue. On a quatre unités de base qui sont en elles-mêmes dépourvues de signification, mais qui se combinent en des unités plus grandes, lesquelles se combinent en unités encore plus grandes qui, finalement, donnent lieu à un nombre infini de suites. C'est là le cœur de l'analogie, mais Jakobson est allé encore plus loin et a trouvé des analogies beaucoup plus fines, et je suis un peu gêné de devoir ajouter qu'il se réfère là explicitement à Monod.

J.M. J'ai simplement commis une confusion de langage en empruntant des termes aux linguistes pour décrire ce que nous estimons être aussi mécanique qu'une machine. Dans la mesure où vous revenez sur ce point, j'ajouterai que, pour les biologistes, la mécanique du code est comparable à une machine à photocopier, et non pas à un langage. C'est là tout le problème.

H.A. Y a-t-il unicité du langage? Ne serait-il pas possible qu'une des raisons qui en font quelque chose d'unique soit l'utilisation de la mémoire, étant entendu que le terme mémoire est pris ici au sens très simple de capacité de reproduire comme le fait une machine à photocopier, et non pas au sens complet du terme? Nombre de critiques qui peuvent toujours être faites à des résultats aussi remarquables que ceux de Premack sont susceptibles d'être atténuées de cette manière, car on peut toujours critiquer ce type de résultats en disant, comme on l'a souvent fait, qu'on ne sait pas si ce qui est enregistré ce sont les catégories de l'animal ou les catégories de l'expérimentateur. Il se pourrait que la réponse à cette question vienne, comme l'a dit Premack lui-même, d'une preuve de créativité, autrement dit, de la capacité de l'animal d'inventer quelque chose qui ne lui a pas été enseigné. Cette preuve de créativité peut s'appuyer sur deux faits. D'une part sur l'invention d'un langage de même type que celui qui a été enseigné, ou tout simplement sur le fait que l'observateur déchiffre un langage spontané de l'animal, qu'il ignorait être un langage. C'est en somme le problème du partage du code dont vous parle Sebeok.
D'autre part, n'est-il pas possible qu'un simple élargissement des capacités de la mémoire soit lié à une manière à la fois nouvelle et créative d'utiliser les catégories préexistantes, un peu à la façon de ce qu'on fait avec les ordinateurs? On sait que, dans certains cas, il est possible de modifier totalement les

performances d'un ordinateur en lui ajoutant des éléments inertes et triviaux qui comportent strictement quelques blocs mnémoniques supplémentaires, ce qui accroît le nombre de 'bits'[9] de la capacité de stockage de l'ordinateur. De ce simple fait, et sans modifier l'unité centrale de traitement de l'ordinateur, on change complètement les performances de celui-ci. Il devient capable de faire des choses qu'il était incapable de faire jusque-là, simplement parce qu'on lui a ajouté un certain nombre de capacités de mémoire. Ceci se rattache également au problème évoqué par Premack au début de son intervention, lorsqu'il disait que, pour expérimenter plus commodément, il a décidé de convertir le langage parlé en langage écrit, en vue d'éviter les difficultés inhérentes à l'utilisation d'une mémoire insuffisante. Je pourrais évoquer également les problèmes posés par Schutzenberger à propos de l'itérativité des opérateurs que l'animal peut maîtriser.[10] Il est bien connu en technologie des ordinateurs que, si l'on ajoute simplement des éléments qui ne sont pas qualitativement différents de ceux que possédait déjà la machine, à savoir des capacités de mémoire, il arrive un moment où l'on change qualitativement la performance du système tout entier.

[9] Unité de mesure de la quantité d'information (N.d.É.).
[10] Voir Morin et Piattelli-Palmarini (eds.), 1974, p. 50.

7

'Dialect' from a Zoosemiotic Perspective*

... minél több részletvonalból rajzoljuk meg egy-egy nyelvjárás képét, annál hívebb lesz a rajzunk. Minél több kritériumot vonunk be vizsgálódásunk körébe, annál pontosabb eredményt várhatunk tőle. E tekintetben kétség nem is merülhet fel (Laziczius, 1932: 54).

Hungarian scholars (e.g., Horányi and Szépe, 1975: 6) occasionally allude to the explicitly semiotic preoccupations of Laziczius. Thus it is well known that several sections of his introduction to general linguistics develop consequences from the twin Saussurean notions that verbal phenomena are semiotic in character and that signs are organized into systems (Laziczius, 1942: 26ff., 69ff.). The semiotic of Laziczius hardly goes beyond that of Saussure, but it does transcend his master's conception in one important specific respect: while Saussure appears never to have envisioned the possibility of sign processes, within the broad framework of social psychology (or, in Naville's account, sociology) (Ch. 1, this book), occurring outside of human existence, Laziczius – in a remarkable digression – contrasts verbal signs with sign processes uncovered by Karl von Frisch in the honeybee (Laziczius, 1942: 31; cf. Sebeok, 1972: 11n.). Laziczius' chief inference, namely, that the bee can be the source of a message and its destination, but that this message can never denote, i.e., that it can have no cognitive function ("A méhek nyelve...az ábrázolásra már képtelen"), turned out to be erroneous: in part, because it was based on a 1923 report

* This article has not previously appeared, but a Hungarian version is being published, in 1976, in *Nyelvtudományi Közlemények* 78:2 (the Laziczius 80th Anniversary issue).

which, in the investigator's own words, "had missed the most interesting aspects" (von Frisch, 1967: vi); and, in part, because Laziczius was unduly constrained, I think, by an excessively simplistic model of the communicative act propagated by Karl Bühler (e.g., Laziczius, 1966: 16, 46, 61, 64), from whose work, one can confidently assume, he learned indirectly of the eminent Munich zoologist's experiments (cf. Bühler, 1934: vif.; Sebeok, 1972: 35f.). However, what matters to us is not that subsequent developments in zoosemiotics (Sebeok 1974a: 192) have seemingly invalidated a passing observation that Laziczius embedded in a linguistic context, but that he foreshadowed with great sensitivity what has since become a very live issue indeed· "Is a comparative semiotics possible?" (see Ch. 3, this book).

In this necessarily brief commemorative tribute, I wish to call attention to a problem area that would certainly have excited the scientific imagination of Laziczius had the relevant data been uncovered in his lifetime: given the indubitable fact that many animals, including, *inter alia*, species of insects, frogs, birds, and mammals, have developed dialects – some inherited, others learned, but environment always interacting with heredity in a highly complex fashion (Brown, 1975: 433; Wilson, 1975: 168) – how does this broaden our thinking about linguistic evolution, or, to pose two somewhat different questions, what conceivable evolutionary function can we ascribe to the diversity of human dialect patterns, and what corollaries of interest to the linguist does a consistently comparative, i.e., cross-specific, semiotic approach suggest?

Let me begin by concisely reviewing a few salient cases of dialect variation reported in the vast literature of animal communication (Sebeok 1968, 1977a), starting with an example from the social insects (one that would especially have delighted Laziczius, and to which this great cosmopolitan scholar would have instinctively tuned in), stemming from the Carniolan race of the honeybee, *Apis mellifera carnica*, upon which most of the enviably precise research by von Frisch and his students has been concentrated (von Frisch, 1962, 1967: 293-320). Comparative investigations in six races, i.e., genetic strains of *A. mellifera*, have revealed that the area indicated by a round and by a tail-wagging dance, respectively, and the dancing rhythm, differ for each, such variations having been appropriately referred to as dialects. As I have related before (Sebeok, 1972: 46f.), this dialect phenomenon was then exploited in an ingenious way, as a result of which it was found, in conformity with the von Frisch communicative hypothesis, that, for instance, the Italian (*ligustica*) race of workers underestimated from (viz., 'misunderstood') the tempo of the Austrian (*carnica*) dances, whereas, conversely, the Austrians overestimated from (viz., 'misunderstood') that of the Italian dances in a mixed colony composed of the two strains.

The second mammal, next to man, in which the phenomenon was reported, less than a decade ago, was the elephant seal, *Mirounga angustirostris*, where consistent differences in the threat vocalizations of males were observed and described. The geographical variations in their vocal behavior were explicitly said to resemble local dialects in humans; the mode of transmission, it was felt, "would account for the rapid development of dialects in separated geographical areas and their apparent perpetuation from one generation to the next", leading the investigators to suggest the conclusion "that man is not the only mammal in which normal vocalizations are learned from other species members" (Le Boeuf and Peterson, 1969: 1656). There is further evidence – ultimately, subject to interpretation that depends on the resolution of taxonomic disputes – that the pika, *Ochotona princeps*, pothead whales (several *Globicephala* species), and the squirrel monkey, *Saimiri sciureus*, show geographical variation in their calls that may most accurately be characterized as dialects.

In passing, it should be emphasized that it would be wrong, in this mammalian context, to limit the concept of 'dialect', despite the etymology or the preponderance of pertinent research, which has focused upon the acoustic modality, to regional variations in just the sound pattern. One has but to recall that in man even sign languages may clearly be divided by dialect area boundaries, a lack of uniformity which has been adumbrated for Ameslan in respect to at least two Southern and three New England states (Croneberg, 1965: 313ff.), but which obviously needs much more extensive documentation than can be accorded here.

Geographic variation in bird vocalizations – especially songs of courtship and of territorial advertisement – have been most meticulously studied, and this literature was thoroughly reviewed by Armstrong (1963: 88-111), and later by Thielcke (1969). Several inquiries have shown that the patterns may be distributed as a kind of mosaic, where each local population is characterized by a song type which distinguishes it from neighboring populations, but which may also recur elsewhere. The rain-call of the chaffinch, *Fringilla coelebs*, is a classic example of mosaic variation on the European continent; (in linguistic geography, configurations of this nature are sometimes referred to as 'lateral areas' [cf. Bonfante and Sebeok, 1944: 383f.]). Thielcke proposed to reserve the term 'dialect' only for vocalization variants with a mosaic distribution, but, as of seven years ago, the descriptive data failed to provide any explanation of "how mutually independent dialects arise within the same species or even within the same song". Although, he surmised, the "function of dialects is perhaps to reduce variability in order to increase the effectiveness of the signal", he concluded that we "know nothing about the function of dialects" (Thielcke, 1969: 322).

The occurrence of dialects, then, is widespread in birds, but their developmental basis has hitherto been analyzed in only a few species. It is important to be mindful that 'dialect' refers here to differences between demes within a species that contrast in their vocalizations from other demes: what are implied are variations in phenotype but not, of course, that these are due to learning alone (Brown, 1975: 663f.). In species where the nature and extent of the variation have been most thoroughly described – notably, the white-crowned sparrow, *Zonotrichia leucophrys*, inhabiting the San Francisco Bay area – learning and cultural transmission of the dialect features from generation to generation have been proved to be important, not genotypic (in a simple sense) but phenotypic (Marler and Tamura, 1962: 375). Extrapolating from these data, as well as from another sparrow, the chaffinch, and a parrot species, *Amazona amazonica*, Nottebohm (1970), in the course of an important overview of the study of avian vocalizations, reexamined the possible evolutionary significance inherent in the formation of vocal dialects. This far-reaching contribution immediately stimulated the thinking of several linguists concerned with the search for possible mechanisms at work in human dialect formation (e.g., Grace, 1970, esp. fn. 2; Labov, 1973: 246f.).

Nottebohm's argument proceeds from the observation that vocal learning is strongly correlated with the occurrence of dialects and complex song repertoires. In most instances, then, the evolution of plastic ontogenies – which means that some of the features of the song are acquired by learning from other members of the deme – can be assumed as subserving two fundamental purposes: "(1) mating like with like, and (2) wooing, stimulating, and retaining a partner" (Nottebohm, 1975: 79). Thus males must learn to utter the dialect of their birth area, because females develop a preference for the song dialect of the region where they are born, and will eventually express this preference in the choice of their mate. Were this not so, gene flow would occur between adjacent populations, tending to eliminate vocal differences, attenuating or doing away altogether with the effectiveness of dialect barriers. In the contrary case, "dialects acquired as vocal traditions would persist even in the presence of genetic variability" (Nottebohm, 1975: 80). It is, therefore, no longer true, as earlier investigators used to emphasize (e.g., Armstrong, 1963: 89), that bird dialects crucially differ from dialects of human speech in that the former are wholly controlled by heredity whereas the latter are culturally developed population markers, without an obvious evolutionary function.

As Labov has pointed out, "The value of Nottebohm's contribution is not in setting forth a theory or an hypothesis that we can test immediately, but rather suggesting an alternative view to broaden our thinking about linguistic evolution" (1973: 247). The question at issue is the value of language diversity for humans, providing, more generally, for relative cultural isolation and the maintenance of cultural pluralism. It is interesting to note that, in the present climate of linguistic inquiry, with its pounding reemphasis on universal grammar, both a new impetus and a model for the search for an underlying mechanism that could account for the "fantastic diversity of human tongues, often geographically proximate", in brief, for what Humboldt has called, a century and a half ago, *die Verschiedenheit des menschlichen Sprachbaues*, seem to have been pressed home to us from outside the field of linguistics: "How can such exceeding variety have arisen", Steiner continues in wonderment, "if, as transformational grammar postulates and biology hints, the underlying grid, the neuro-physiological grooves, are common to all men and, indeed, occasion their humanity? Why, as carriers of the same essential molecular information, do we not speak the same language or a small number of languages corresponding, say, to the small number of genuinely identifiable ethnic types? No one has come up with a satisfactory hypothesis. . ." (Steiner, 1971: 69).

Nottebohm's suggestion is that dialects in birds may provide a relative degree of genetic isolation by the role they play in the mating behavior, but without any "necessary irrevocable commitment to actual speciation", adding that, whereas "genetic isolation of small populations may lead to high rates of extinction and even possibly to excessive inbreeding, differences in vocalizations are probably rarely insuperable barriers to breeding, and thus the microevolutionary process is kept more flexible and open". Further, he himself raises the intriguing possibility that dialects "have played an active role in human evolution", and that these "might have influenced the emergence of local physiological adaptations" (1970: 955). Some anthropologists concerned with extant tribal societies that, at least until recently, lived in ecological balance with their environment, are beginning to examine the question of the extent to which language area patterns facilitate inter-group contact among hunters and gatherers and simple horticulturalists, allowing a flexible response to local environmental stress (Hill, forthcoming). This trend represents a truly creative synthesis of dialect geography and areal linguistics on the one hand, with ecological and evolutionary biology on the other. A further corollary of this research intimates a solution for the perennial puzzle why we all pass through the divide of linguistic puberty, that is, a stage of maturation beyond which the human individual's language learning ability is dramatically reduced: this deficit, too, must be the product of evolutionary selection, functioning, as in birds, to encourage diversity in dialect patterns. No doubt, Laziczius would have approved of this kind of multidisciplinary endeavor, utilizing zoosemiotic theories and data to illuminate anthroposemiotic conundrums, for it is in good conformity with his over-all scientific program: "A kutató munka egyre újabb matériákat igyekszik feltárni, egyre mélyebb aknákból igyekszik gyarapítani a meglévő anyagot, hogy minél teljesebb, minél többrétű legyen". It is not inconceivable that, were he writing today, a remark he once made about Schleicher could, *a fortiori*, be applied to himself: ". . .ha valaki élete végén megkérdezte volna, hogy mit tart nagyarányú és sok tekintetben értékes munkásságából a legfontosabbnak, bizonyára azt válaszolta volna: a természettudományi módszer átültetését a nyelvtudományba" (Laziczius, 1942: 107, 109f.).

8

Six Species of Signs: Some Propositions and Strictures*

0. PRELIMINARIES

0.1 The sign is bifacial. In 1305, in his unfinished treatise, *Dē vulgarī eloquentiā* (I-3, 1957: 18), Dante proffered this formulation of the concept of the (verbal) sign: "hoc equidem signum . . . sensuale quid est, in quantum sonus est; rationale vero, in quantum aliquid significare videtur ad placitum." His restatement is in good conformity with practically every model of the intrinsic structure of the sign that, with one emphasis or another, has been put forward in accounts dealing with

* *In memoriam George Ts'ereteli.* This article deals further with a complex of related problems first presented, under the title "The Structural Classification of Signs", as an informal report to the participants of the Fourth Summer School on Secondary Modeling Systems, in Tartu, Estonian S.S.R., during August of 1970 (cf. Revzina, 1972: 230f.), followed by a memorable and most instructive discussion. With this paper, I wish to pay tribute to the distinguished achievements of contemporary Soviet semiotics (cf. Segal, in Lotman and Uspenskij, 1973: 452-70), a field of international cooperative endeavor to several branches of which Academician George Ts'ereteli has made manifold contributions that are as profound as they have proved fecund.

This version is reprinted from *Semiotica* 13:3 (1975), 233-60. A French version appeared in *Degrés: Revue de synthèse à orientation sémiologique* 6 (1974); an Italian version appeared in *Versus: Quaderni di studi semiotici* 11 (1976); and for a condensed Hungarian version, see *Jelentéstan és stilisztika*, ed. by Samu Imre, István Szathmári, and László Szűts (Budapest: Akadémiai Kiadó, 1974), pp. 518-23. The article, as originally intended, will now be published, in Georgian, in a special issue dedicated to Ts'ereteli's memory – "Nišris ekvsi saxeoba: Cinadadebani da šenišvnebi", *Filologia Orientalis – Journal of the Oriental Institute* (Tbilisi, 1976). The material considerably develops ideas delineated in a tentative way on pp. 42-45 in this book.

the foundations of the doctrine of signs, ranging from Stoic philosophy to contemporary thinking. This expression implies that the sign is constituted of two indispensable moieties, one *aisthēton*, perceptible (or sensible), the other *noēton*, intelligible (or rational): the *signifier*, an appreciable impact on at least one of the interpreter's sense organs, and the content *signified*. (In medieval Latin, the corresponding pair of terms for the Stoic *sēmainon*, 'signifier', and *sēmainomenon* 'signified', was *signans* and *signatum*; rendered by Saussure as *signifiant* and *signifié*; in German, usually, as *das Signifikat* and *der Signifikant*; by Morris as *sign-vehicle* and *designatum*; by some Soviet scholars [cf. Revzina, 1972: 231] as 'thing' and 'concept', etc.)

0.2 *'Zero signs'*. In various systems of signs, notably in language, a sign vehicle can sometimes – when the contextual conditions are appropriate – signify by its very absence, occur, that is in *zero* form. Linguists who employ the expression 'zero sign' (viz., zero phoneme or allophone, zero morpheme or allomorph, or the like), must mean either 'zero signifier', or, much more rarely, 'zero signified', but never both; if taken literally, the notion of a 'zero sign' would be oxymoronic. (On the use of zero in linguistics, see Jakobson, 1966 [1939], or 1940; Frei, 1950; Godel, 1953; Haas, 1957.) The role of zero sign vehicles in communication systems other than the verbal has never been properly analyzed. Pohl (1968: 34-36), for instance, erroneously remarks that civilian clothing functions as a zero when worn in a context of uniforms; but this confounds the unmarked/marked opposition with the realized/zero opposition.

Zero sign vehicles also occur in animal communication systems. Thus Ardrey (1970: 75) claims that the African "elephant's alarm call is silence", and so, too, René-Guy Busnel that the temporal parameter between the message exchanged by two members of the species *Laniarius erythrogaster*, that is, "the rhythmic pattern of silences . . . and not the acoustic part of the signal itself" carries the information (Sebeok, 1968b: 138); but a heuristically more promising inquiry is suggested by the quasi-prosodic phenomenon that, in several types of fireflies, pulse interval is a significant element in stimulating females, and that these intervals are distinct in different species, e.g., in *Photinus consanguineus* and *macdermotti*; in the related *lineellus*, furthermore, the pulse number is variable, "which further indicates the significance of pulse interval" (Lloyd, 1966: 78).

The existence of zero forms in various systems of communication does not, therefore, vitiate the classic bipartite model of the sign.

0.3   *Token/Type, Denotation/Designation.* A particular occurrence of a sign – what Peirce labelled 'sinsign' (2.245) – is now more commonly called a *token* (4.537, which Peirce sometimes also referred to as an 'Actisign'), whereas the class of all occurrences of the sign – Peirce's legisign (earlier 'Famsign'; cf. 8.363) – is called a *type.* Paraphrasing Peirce's own illustration, one can say that if a page in a book has 250 words upon it, this is the number of word tokens, whereas the number of different words on a page is the number of word types (this distinction was recently explored afresh by Richards, 1969).

Among the principal questions that have occupied most students of the verbal sign, three have seemed basic and inescapable: how do particular sign *tokens refer*; how do sign *types* acquire and maintain their constant capacity to *mean*; and what, precisely, lies at the heart of the distinction between the relation of reference, or *denotation*, and the relation of meaning, or sense, or *designation*; (a fourth important question, about the relation of meaning and use, could be added; cf. Wells, 1954). The modern cleavage between meaning and reference has recurred in many guises since Frege's classic consideration, in 1892, of *Sinn* and *Bedeutung*: approximately, e.g., as Husserl's *Bedeutung* vs. *Bezeichnung*, Mill's *denotation* vs. *connotation*, Paul's *Bedenkung* vs. *Benutzung*, Saussure's *valeur* vs. *substance*, and the like. 'Semantics' is often, if loosely, used as a cover term encompassing both the theory of verbal reference and the theory of verbal meaning, but should, in the strict sense, be confined to the latter. Analytic philosophers, such as Carnap (1942), typically assign the theory of truth and the theory of logical deduction to semantics, on the ground that truth and logical consequence are concepts based on designation, and hence semantic concepts. The term 'zoosemantics' was provisionally coined, in 1963, to extend the theory of meaning to attempt to account for presumably corresponding designative processes among the speechless creatures (Sebeok, 1972: 80).

A noticeable discrepancy between what a sign type designates and the denotation of one of its tokens may be responsible, on various levels, for the linguistic processes known to poetics and rhetoric as 'figures of speech', as well as kindred phenomena found in animals (Bronowski, 1967). This also underlies the mechanism involved in lying, which – certain opinions notwithstanding – corresponds to various forms of deception found throughout the animal kingdom.

0.4   *Classifying aspects of signs.* Recognition of the manifold possible relations between the two parts of a sign – the signifier and the signified – has led to numerous attempts by philosophers and philosophically inclined linguists, throughout the history of semiotics, to classify signs or systems of signs. Among these, Peirce's ultimate (c. 1906) and maximal scheme – which he elaborated slowly but persistently over a period of some forty years – with sixty-six varieties, including intermediates and hybrids, was surely the most comprehensive, far-reaching, and subtle (Weiss and Burks, 1945; but cf. Sanders, 1970, who considers their attempt at extrapolation 'ill-advised'). In the verbal field, one of the more thoughtful and suggestive efforts of recent times was Bally's (1939), while Jakobson's special study (1970) devoted to the classification of human signs in general once again widens the horizons of current semiotic inquiry. Spang-Hanssen's survey (1954, but actually completed in 1948) provides a convenient overview of 'modern' psychological approaches by Ogden and Richards, Karl Britton, Bertrand Russell, Charles Morris, as well as of linguistic ones, by scholars as heterogeneous as Ferdinand de Saussure, Leo Weisgerber, Alan H. Gardiner, Karl Bühler, Eric Buyssens, Leonard Bloomfield, and Louis Hjelmslev. Today, only some half a dozen species of signs – often with several more or less vaguely sensed subspecies – are regularly identified and commonly employed, with but roughly comparable definitions; however, in virtually all cases, these are considered only over the domain of language and man's other species-specific systems, say, the secondary modeling systems of the Russian semiotic tradition that imply a verbal infrastructure, or music, or the like (Sebeok, 1972: 162-77). In what follows, the six species of signs that seem to occur most frequently in contemporary semiotics will be taken up anew, provisionally redefined, discussed briefly, and illustrated not only from anthroposemiotic systems (that is, those that are species-specific to man), but also zoosemiotic systems, in order to show that none of the signs dealt with here is criterial of or unique to man (7.4; this argument, and its implications, will be developed much further in Sebeok, 1977d).

It should be clearly understood, finally, that it is not signs that are actually being classified, but, more precisely, aspects of signs: in other words, a given sign may – and more often than not does – exhibit more than one aspect, so that one must recognize differences in gradation. Eco (1972a: 201) insists that "Ein ikonisches Zeichen ist der bezeichnete Sache *in einigen Aspekten* ähnlich", as Charles Morris has before him, but it is equally important to grasp that the hierarchic principle is inherent in the architectonic of any species of sign. For instance, a verbal symbol, such as an imperative, is commonly also endowed with a signal value (cf. 1.3). An emblem (which is a subspecies of symbol; 5.4) may be partly iconic, such as the flag of the United States, since its seven red, horizontal stripes alternating with six white ones stand one for each founding colony, whereas its fifty white stars in the single blue canton correspond one to each State in the present Union. A primarily indexic sign, as a clock, acquires a discernible symbolic content in addition if the timepiece happens to be Big Ben. In the designs of the central Australian Walbiri, the iconic bond between the forms of the sign vehicles and the referents assigned is said to be central, "for there is no systematic subordination of the iconic element to a second abstract ordering system", in contrast to heraldry, where, as in a pictorial writing system, "the iconic qualities linking the visual forms to their meanings tend to be attenuated", that is, to become stepwise symbolic, "because of the over-all adjustment of the visual forms to another underlying socio-cultural system for which the former constitutes a communication code" (Munn, 1973: 177f.); (for the process of 'deiconization' in general, and the more uncommon reverse transformation, see Wallis, 1975: 7f.). Morris' dictum, "Iconicity is . . . a matter of degree" (1971: 191), coupled with Count's comparably terse formula, "Symbolization . . . is supposable as a matter of a continuous (qualitative) degree" (1969: 102), seem to sum the matter up adequately.

To recapitulate, aspects of a sign necessarily co-occur in an environment-sensitive hierarchy. Since all signs, of course, enter into complex syntagmatic as well as paradigmatic contrasts and oppositions, it is their place both in the web of a concrete text and the network of an abstract system that is decisive as to which aspect will predominate in a given context at a particular moment, a fact which leads directly to the problem of levels, so familiar to linguistics – being an absolute prerequisite for any typology – but as yet far from developed in the other branches of semiotics. This important issue, of which Soviet colleagues, too, are keenly aware (e.g., Lotman and Uspenskij, 1973: xxi; cf. also Meletinsky and Segal, 1971), cannot be dealt with here, beyond underlining it, and making an ancillary terminological assertion: that a sign is legitimately, if loosely, labeled after the aspect that ranks predominant.

1. SIGNAL

1.1 *When a sign token mechanically or conventionally triggers some reaction on the part of a receiver, it is said to function as a signal.*

1.2 Note the specification that the reaction may be provoked either mechanically (i.e., naturally) or conventionally (i.e., artificially); this is in accordance with the view that "Signals may ... be provided by 'nature' ", but that they may also be produced artificially (Kecskemeti, 1952: 36). Note also that the receiver can be either a machine or an organism, or, conceivably, even a personified supernatural (cf. p. 74, above).

1.3 A most interesting and productive reexamination of the concept of signal is to be found in a recent essay by Pazukhin (1972). His argument, and resultant definition, which resembles but is not identical with the one given above, rest on the development of a series of oppositions, stemming from the need to distinguish the physical, or technological, notion of signal from the one prevalent in the humanities and social sciences – briefly, from a purely semiotic conception; and the need to separate physical phenomena which are signals from the class of non-signals, while, on the other hand, to discriminate signals from signs. A defect of this article is that Bühler's well-known thesis is wrenched out of its context and dismissed out of hand as having given "rise to numerous improper interpretations, which conceive Bühlerian 'signals' as *species of signs* (Zeichen, after Bühler), conveying commands, requests and other kinds of imperative messages" (Pazukhin, 1972: 28). There are two fallacies involved here: one is the neglect of Bühler's so-called 'organon model' as a whole, in which the concept of signal takes its logical place along with the concepts of symptom and symbol, and that cannot therefore be understood in isolation. A more serious error is to forget that one must constantly deal with *aspects* of signs: to repeat, a verbal command is very likely to have both a symbol-aspect and a signal-aspect, and the sign in question will oscillate between the two poles according to the context of its delivery.

1.4 It may be well to recall what Bühler did say about the signal, within the framework of his model. In Bühler's view, the signal appeals to the destination, whose interior or exterior behavior it governs, i.e., it acts, as it were, like a traffic regulator, which elicits or inhibits reaction; by contrast, the symptom (Section 2) has to do with the source, whose inner behavior it expresses; and the symbol (Section 5) relates to the designation.[1]

---

[1] "Es ist *Symbol* Kraft seiner Zuordnung zu Gegenständen und Sachverhalten, *Symptom* (Anzeichen, Indicium) Kraft seiner Abhängigkeit vom Sender, dessen

1.5 Pazukhin rightly emphasizes the necessity "to achieve a substantial discrimination of signals and signs", then analyzes "a few most promising tentatives" (1972: 29f.), including the hypotheses of such Soviet philosophers or linguists as L. Abramian, A.A. Brudny, and A. Zalizniak, but finds fault with them all, chiefly owing to his conviction that none of them offer "adequate criteria for a realistic opposition of signals to other media of interaction" (1972: 30). In our opinion, it is first essential to realize that the relation of signal to sign is that of a marked category to an unmarked one, that is, precisely that of a species to the genus to which it belongs (7.2), as Bühler has also claimed. Secondly, Pazukhin introduces and discusses in detail what he calls two modes of control, both of which are interactions based on the idea of causal relationship: direct control, and block-and-release control. Control by signaling is a special case of the latter, which naturally leads to the conclusion, implied by Pazukhin's definition of signal, that "There is only an occasional relationship between signal and reactions produced by it" (1972: 41). This, however, is merely a weak echo of Peirce's explicit coupling of all sign-processes — hence signaling as well — with processes involving mediation or 'thirdness'. Witness the following passage:

It is important to understand what I mean by *semiosis*. All dynamical action, or action by brute force, physical or psychical, either takes place between two subjects . . . or at any rate is a resultant of such actions between pairs. But by 'semiosis' I mean, on the contrary, an action, or influence, which is, or involves, a co-operation of *three* subjects, such as a sign, its object, and its interpretant, this tri-relative influence not being in any way resolvable into actions between pairs . . . my definition confers on anything that so acts the title of a 'sign' (Peirce, 5.484).

1.6 Consider the following: C.R. Carpenter, a prominent student of animal behavior, writing in connection with alloprimates, takes that occasion to define signaling behavior generally, in many qualities, forms, and patterns, as "a condensed stimulus event, a part of a longer whole, which may arouse extended actions. Signaling activity, in its simplest form, is produced by an individual organism; it represents

---

Innerlichkeit es ausdrückt, und *Signal* Kraft seines Appels an den Hörer, dessen äusseres oder inneres Verhalten es steuert wie andere Verkehrszeichen" (Bühler, 1934: 28 and *passim*).

information; it is mediated by a physical carrier, and it is perceived and responded to by one or more individuals. Like the stimulus event, of which signaling behavior is a special case, this kind of behavior *RELEASES* more energy than is used in signaling" (1969: 44). Now Pazukhin rejects three criteria that have been variously proposed for defining signals, on the ground that they "cannot be considered essential" (1972: 41). These criteria – all of them used by Carpenter – are: the presence of a certain amount of energy; the delivery of information about something; and being dispatched by an animal. We endorse completely the elimination of all three factors from a viable definition of signal.

1.7 Examples of signals are: the exclamation, 'Go!' or, alternatively, the discharge of a pistol to start a footrace (a conventional releaser vs. a mechanical trigger, as in 1.2). The term is commonplace in studies of animal communication – see Burkhardt, *et al.* (1967), Sebeok (1968b, 1977a), and the literature cited by Sebeok (1972: 135-61) – where it is often used interchangeably with a seldom defined zoosemiotic prime, *display* (e.g., Smith, 1965: 405).

2. SYMPTOM

2.1 *A symptom is a compulsive, automatic, nonarbitrary sign, such that the signifier is coupled with the signified in the manner of a natural link.* (A *syndrome* is a rule-governed configuration of symptoms with a stable designatum.)

2.2 Both terms have strong, but not exclusively, medical connotations (cf. Ostwald, 1968); thus one can say, by metaphoric extension, 'the rise of modern anthropology was a symptom of colonialism', and the like; (see also 2.7).

2.3 It is a peculiarity of symptoms that their denotata are generally different for the addresser, viz., the patient ('subjective symptoms') than for the addressee, viz., the physician ('objective symptoms') – in a felicitous phrase of Barthes (1972: 38), "le symptôme, ce serait le réel apparent ou l'apparent réel". For some Freudian implications of this observation, cf. Brown (1958: 313; see also Kecskemeti, 1952: 61); and for admirable work in this classic area of semiotics, see the representative books of Ruesch (most recently, 1972) and Shands (especially 1970).

2.4   It is interesting to note that the subtle Port-Royal logicians drew a distinction between 'ordinary' symptoms and what physicians would call 'vital signs', on the basis of an essentially quantitative criterion. Thus they observed that "il y a des signes certains . . . comme la respiration l'est de la vie des animaux; et il y en a qui ne sont que probables . . . comme la pâleur n'est qu'un signe probable de grossesse dans les femmes . . . " (Arnauld and Nicole, 1662 [1816]). In other words, the specification, 'compulsive, automatic', in the above definition, is subject to a probabilistic refinement, for, although the denotation of a symptom is always equivalent to its cause in the source, some symptoms are effectively connected with an antecedent condition 'for sure', whereas the link of other symptoms with the foregoing state of affairs is merely assumed with varying degrees of likelihood.[2]

2.5   Semiotics – referring in earliest usage to medical concerns with the sensible indications of changes in the condition of the human body – constituted one of the three branches of Greek medicine. Since symptoms were among the earliest signs identified, they constitute a historically important category for any inquiry into the beginnings of the theory of signs, for instance, the thinking of such physicians as the Alexandrian physiologist Erasistratus (310-250 B.C.) and anatomist Herophilus (335-280 B.C.), and the Epicurean Asclepiades by Bithynia (fl. 110 B.C.), mentioned, among others, by Sextus Empiricus. Symptomatology, or semeiology (see pp. 53f., above), eventually developed into a branch of medicine with a specialized threefold preoccupation with diagnostics, focusing on the here and now, and its twin temporal projections into the anamnestic past and the prognostic future (or as Galen [130-ca. 200] used to teach, "Semeiotice in tres partes dirimitur, in praeteritorum cognitionem, in praesentium inspectionem et futu-

---

[2]   Arnauld and Nicole, moreover, evidently recognized the emblem (5.0): "Il y a des signes joints aux choses, . . . comme l'arche, signe de l'église, étoit jointe à Noé et a ses enfants . . ."; and, at least in our reading, the icon (3.0) and perhaps the index (4.0) as well, as in the following remarkable passage: "La troisième division des signes est, qu'il y en a de naturels qui ne dépendent pas de la fantaisie des hommes, comme une image qui paroit dans un miroir est un signe naturel de celui qu'elle représente et qu'il y en a d'autres qui ne sont que d'institution et d'établissement, soit qu'ils aient quelque rapport éloigné avec la chose figurée, soit qu'ils n'en aient point du tout . . ." (1662[1816]). The contributions of Port-Royal to semiotics, including a study of the specific effects of the *Grammar* and the *Logic* on John Locke, still await proper historical appraisal; Brekle's judgment (1964), that "Für die Zeichentheorie . . . ist diese Gattung nicht interessant", must, therefore, be regarded as premature.

rorum providentiam"). A rapprochement between the general theory of signs and the medical praxis involving signs is rather recent, in no small part stimulated by the distinguished work of Michel Foucault (Barthes, 1972: 38); but it was, in some measure, remarkably anticipated by Kleinpaul, in 1888, who paid homage to Hippocrates (460-377 B.C.) as "der Vater und Meister aller Semiotik" (1972: 103) in tracing this nexus out in its Saussurean prefigurements; and emphatically so by Crookshank (1923: 337-55).

2.6   Barthes, following Foucault, deems it wise to distinguish symptom from sign, and chooses to oppose the two within the well-known schema of Hjelmslev, whose elaboration on the bifacial character of the sign into form and substance, expression and content, seems to continue to fascinate Romance semioticians. Barthes assigns the symptom to the category that Hjlemslev called the substance of the signifier, and then goes on to argue that a symptom turns into a sign only when it enters in the context of clinical discourse, just when this transformation is wrought by the physician, in brief, solely "par la médiation du langage" (1972: 39). However, such a view is tenable, if at all, only in such special cases when the destination of a symptomatic message is a physician, or, by extension, a veterinarian, or at least a computer repairman. In fact, the destination need be none of these; it could, for example, be a speechless creature. Autonomic effects, that is, symptomatic displays, were acutely observed and described by Darwin, and virtually all modern research in both interspecific and intraspecific animal communication ultimately rests on passages such as his remark that the erection of the dermal appendages, in a variety of vertebrates, "is a reflex action, independent of the will; and this action must be looked at, when occurring under the influence of anger or fear, not as a power acquired for the sake of some advantage, but as an incidental result, at least to a large extent, of the sensorium being affected. The result, in as far as it is incidental, may be compared with the profuse sweating from an agony of pain or terror" in man (Darwin, 1872: 101f.). Human symptoms such as these, and a host of others, can easily be perceived and acted upon by, e.g., such domesticated animals as dogs and horses (as the notorious 'Clever Hans' episode in the history of psychology amply bears out; see Hediger, 1967), and in a variety of other situations in which language does not, indeed, cannot, play any sort of mediating role. In this global semiotic perspective, then, it remains our thesis that the opposition of symptom to sign parallels that of signal to sign (1.5), namely, of a marked category (species) to an unmarked one (genus) (7.2).

2.7 It is likewise fallacious to assume that the function of a symptom is invariably morbific: as Kleinpaul has astutely remarked, there must also exist a semiotic of 'radiant' good health, a condition where the organism may be observed, as it were, 'beaming' symptoms of well-being (cf. 1972: 106). Thus the exclusive identification of symptomatology with nosology can be quite misleading (see also 2.2).

2.8 Note that Bühler (1934; see also fn. 1, this Chapter) amplified his term 'Symptom' with two quasi-synonymous words, 'Anzeichen, Indicium', and that others would actually classify all symptoms as a subspecies of indexes (Section 4), often with such qualifications as 'unwitting indexes', or 'mere unintended indexes' (e.g., Jakobson, 1970: 10). The difficulty with this suggestion is that the place of 'intention' – or, more broadly, goal-orientation – in a communication model remains an entangled and controversial problem (Meiland, 1970). In the sense of self-awareness – so-called 'subjective teleology' – the notion may be criterial in the definition of all anthroposemiotic systems, and notably characterizes language, but it is hardly pertinent to zoosemiotic analysis, where introducing it may have stultifying effects. A more detailed discussion of intention lies beyond the scope of this paper (but see Ch. 1 above, fn. 65; and Sebeok, 1977d).

2.9 Like all signs (0.4), symptoms may figure in both paradigmatic systems and syntagmatic chains. Investigation of the former has hitherto been rudimentary, but has become promising with the growing application of computer technology to the art of diagnosis. A syntagmatic concatenation of symptoms can be of two sorts: let us call them topical and temporal. A topical syntagm is made up of a bundle of symptoms manifested simultaneously, say, along different regions of a human body. Thus the basic operative parameters in a surgical procedure may involve an electrocardiogram, an electroencephalogram, cardiac output, central venous pressure, peripheral arterial pressure, rectal temperature, respirations, all monitored and interpreted synchronously by the attendant medical team. A temporal syntagm implies input information from the same source, but at successive intervals set along the time axis. Thus Hediger (1968: 144f.) relates that the excrement of giraffes is kept under auditory observation in zoos as a continuing guide to the animal's state of health: "normally, the falling of faeces should give a typical rustling sound", he reports, but "if the excrement is voided in shapeless, pattering portions", the keeper is alerted to the possible existence of a pathological condition.

It might prove quite instructive to explore in much more depth such fruitful ideas as the interplay of paradigm and syntagm and of the axis of simultaneity with that of successivity, of substitution vs. combination, and the like, in a field as different from linguistics as (at first blush) symptomatology appears to be (see especially Celan and Marcus, 1973). Barthes' essay (1972) is suggestive, but essentially this task must await the considerable advancement of semiotics on a much broader front.

3. ICON

3.1 *A sign is said to be iconic when there is a topological similarity between a signifier and its denotata.*

3.2 It was in 1867, in his paper "On a New List of Categories", that Peirce first published his now famous fundamental triad, and initially asserted that there were three kinds of signs (or, as he then called them, 'representations'): (a) *likenesses* (a term he soon abandoned in favor of *icons*), or "those whose relation to their objects is a mere community in some quality"; (b) *indices*, or "those whose relation to their objects consists in a correspondence in fact"; and (c) *symbols* (which are the same as *general signs*), or "those the ground of whose relation to their objects is an imputed character", which he later called 'laws', meaning conventions, habits, or natural dispositions of its interpretant or of the field of its interpretant. (We shall return to the index in Section 4, and the symbol in Section 5.)

3.3 Peirce (2.277) later distinguished three sub-classes of icons: *images, diagrams,* and *metaphors.* The notion of the icon – that is ultimately related to the Platonic process of *mimesis,* which Aristotle then broadened (in the *Poetics* IV) from a chiefly visual representation to embrace all cognitive and epistemological experience – has been subjected to much analysis in its several varieties and manifestations, yet some seemingly intractable theoretical questions remain (3.4). Images (which are still sometimes simplistically equated with all icons, or, worse, are naively assumed to be confined solely to the visual sphere) were recently studied in two exceptionally thoughtful inquiries, by Eco (1972b) and by M. Wallis (1975: Ch. 1), respectively. As for the theory of diagrams, this loomed very large in Peirce's own semiotic researches, and has now been carefully reviewed by Zeman (1964), Roberts (1973), and Thibaud (1975), in some of its far-reaching ramifications, which include modern graph theory. Peirce did not himself much pursue the ancient rhetorical device of metaphor, beyond correctly (notwithstanding Todorov's stricture[3]) assigning this, in his list of categories, to the icon. The iconic functions of language have also undergone a good deal of reexamination lately, e.g., by Jakobson (1965), Valesio (1969), and Wescott (1971).

3.4 Despite the vast, ever multiplying, and by and large helpful literature advancing our understanding of the icon, several serious theoretical problems persist (cf. Sebeok, 1975c). Two among these — let us call them the issue of symmetry and the issue of regression — are worth at least a brief pause here; some others are discussed by Eco (1972b and 1976: 190-217), in a consistently interesting albeit still inconclusive way.

    3.4.1 Wallis, for one, following custom, asserts, *ex cathedra*, that "The relation of representation is nonsymmetrical: an iconic sign or an independent conventional sign represents its representatum but not vice versa" (1975: 2). Now let a snapshot of a reproduction of a famous painting — say, *La Gioconda* — be an iconic sign, or image, for the copy, which thus becomes the denotatum (or representatum), but which is itself an iconic sign for the original portrait hanging at the Louvre, its denotatum; but this painting, too, is an iconic sign for Leonardo's model, the lady known as Mona Lisa, *its* denotatum. In this diachronic sequence, Mona Lisa came first, her portrait next, then its reproduction, finally a photograph of that. Note, however, that there is nothing in either of the definitions above (3.3 or 3.2) requiring the imposition of any kind of chronological priority: Peirce's definition speaks of "a mere community in some quality", and ours only of "a

---

[3]   Todorov says that "the icon is a synecdoche rather than a metaphor — it can't be said for instance that the black spot resembles the colour black" (1973: 17). However, a synecdoche, as any other metonym, belongs clearly to the category of indexical signs, falling well within its definition (Section 4) — thus a black spot can be said to constitute a sample of the color black.

topological similarity", which would both apply backwards just as well as forwards. Is it merely an unmotivated convention to assign a progressive temporal sequence to the relation between signifier and signified? The difficulty can perhaps be driven home by way of the following: suppose a renowned contemporary personage, such as the Pope, is known to me – as he is to most Catholics – only through his photograph, or some other pictorial representation, but that, one day, I get to see him in the flesh: on that occasion, the living Pope would become for me the 'iconic sign' for his long-familiar image, its photographic or lithographic denotatum (Peirce, of course, saw nothing strange in a human being himself being a sign; cf. 5.314, and 6.344). The problem is not unfamiliar to ethologists either. Thus Konrad Lorenz alluded to it in his remark, "The form of the horse's hoof is just as much an image of the steppe it treads as the impression it leaves is an image of the hoof" (Introduction to Wickler, 1973: xi). If this attribute of reflexivity can be shown to be an indispensably characteristic property of icons, then surely time's arrow must be incorporated in revisions of extant definitions.

3.4.2 As for the vertiginous problem of regression, let it be illustrated by the following: An infant daughter can be said to be an iconic sign for her mother, if there is a topological similarity between her, as signifier, and her mother, its denotatum. However, the little girl can likewise, though doubtless to a lesser degree, stand as an iconic sign for her father, every one of her siblings, all of her kinfolk, and, further, for all members of the human race, but also for all primates, and, further still, all mammals, all vertebrates, and so forth, and so on, in unending retrogression to ever more generalized denotata. This peculiarity of iconic signs deserves much more careful consideration than can be accorded to it here, partly for reasons of logic, partly to illuminate the psychological bases of their considerable, if vicarious, evocative and magical powers, a few implications of which for conduct and culture history are alluded to by Wallis (1975: 15-17).

3.5 There are many instances of iconicity in animal discourse (for a discussion of genotypic icons, see Gregory Bateson, in Sebeok, 1968b: 614ff.), involving virtually all of the available channels, e.g., chemical, auditory, or visual. The iconic function of a chemical sign is well illustrated by the alarm substance of the ant *Pogonomyrmex badius*: if the danger to the colony is momentary, the signal – a quantum of released pheromone – quickly fades and leaves the bulk of the colony undisturbed; conversely, if it persists, the substance spreads, involving an ever increasing number of workers. The sign is iconic inasmuch as it varies in analogous proportion to the waxing or waning of the danger stimuli (Sebeok, 1972: 95f.).

The behavior of certain vespine audio-mimics illustrates the iconic function of an auditory sign. Thus the fly *Spilomyia hamifera* Lw., displays a wingbeat rate of 147 strokes per second while hovering near the wasp *Dolichovespula arenaria* F. (which it also closely resembles in color pattern). Since this wasp flies with 150 wing strokes per second, the two flight sounds are presumed to be indistinguishable to predators, and fly-catching birds are thus deceived (Sebeok, 1972: 86f.).

Finally, an elegant (if sometimes disputed) example of a complex piece of behavior that evolved, as it were, to function as a visual iconic sign, is graphically described by Kloft (1959): the hind end of an aphid's abdomen, and the kicking of its hind legs, constitute, for an ant worker, a compound sign vehicle, signifying the head of another ant together with its antennal movement. In other words, the ant is alleged to identify the likeness (the rear end of the aphid) with its denotatum (the front end of an ant), and act on this information, viz., treat the aphid in the manner of an *effigy* (a subspecies of icon).[4]

4. INDEX

4.1 *A sign is said to be indexic insofar as its signifier is contiguous with its signified, or is a sample of it.*

4.2 The term *contiguous* is not to be interpreted literally in this definition as necessarily meaning 'adjoining' or 'adjacent': thus the Polaris may be considered an index of the North celestial pole to any earthling, in spite of the immense distances involved. Rather, contiguity should be thought of in classical juxtaposition to the key principle in the definition of the icon, to wit, similarity. 'Contiguous' was chosen because of its pervasive use, when paired with 'similar', in many fields of intellectual endeavor, ranging from homeopathic vs. contagious

---

[4] A special study by the author, with particular reference to the continuing international debate between 'iconophiles' and 'iconoclasts', is in preparation just as this book reached page proof stage. Emphasizing the biological foundations of the subject, and to appear under the title "Iconicity: Evolutionary and Systematic Implications", the study is a substantial elaboration of Sebeok, 1975c.

magic (Frazer; cf. pp. 76f., above) to poetics and rhetoric (system vs. text, metaphor vs. metonym), *Gestalt* psychology (factor of similarity vs. factor of proximity, Wertheimer, 1923: 304-11), neurology (hypothesis of the polar types of aphasia by Jakobson and Luria), and, of course, linguistics in the Saussurean tradition (paradigmatic axis vs. syntagmatic axis, opposition vs. contrast), etc.

4.3 Peirce's notion of the index was at once novel and fruitful, as Wells has rightly emphasized (1967: # 2b). Peirce's indexical signs have received close study on the part of some of the most prominent philosophers of our time, whether they tagged them egocentric particulars (Russell, 1940), token-reflexive words (Reichenbach, 1948), indexical expressions (Bar-Hillel, 1954), or whatever (Gale, 1967). At the same time, Peirce's ideas now inform the revisionist views of some of our most thoughtful contemporary linguists, to the effect that "Grammatical theory ... must take into its scope ... a theory of conversation, and [that] certain understandings about deixis and pronominal reference make up part of that theory" (Fillmore, 1972: 275). Of course, the process of deixis was also recognized by linguists in the past (e.g., Frei, 1944; Bursill-Hall, 1963), notably in the guise of the 'shifter' – a *mot juste* coined by Jespersen in 1922 (1964: 123f.), whose idea was later extended, among others, by Sturtevant (1947: 135f.), and then significantly amplified by Jakobson (1963: Ch. 9),[5] but it is currently being studied most sensitively and in full awareness of its basic theoretical implications for and beyond grammatical theory by Fillmore (1973), in his admirable series of papers devoted to the spatial, temporal, discourse-oriented, and social deictic anchoring of utterances in 'the real world'. His rigorous investigations seem, at present, to offer the most hopeful approach toward solving some of the knottiest theoretical issues of sociolinguistics, and may even, ultimately, turn out to have been the most constructive first approximation to the far more refractory salmagundi of topics usually labeled 'pragmatics' (Carnap, 1942; Staal, 1971). (Cf. also Peirce, 2.289.)

4.4 In one of his most memorable examples, Peirce recalls that the

---

[5] According to Jacques Lacan's powerful metaphor, the unconscious is structured like language; one might say that his abolition of the consciousness-unconsciousness dichotomy turns consciousness into something very much like our shifter, and hence that it, too, tends to function in the manner of an indexic sign.

footprint Robinson Crusoe found in the sand "was an Index to him of some creature". In like fashion, "a vast map of such records" is printed overnight by animals of all sorts, all over the countryside, leaving "tracks and traces of immense variety, often of wonderful clarity". These "stories written in footprint code" compel "countryside detection", and are beautifully deciphered by such experienced field naturalists as Ennion and Tinbergen (1967: 5); their meticulous track photographs and prints indeed depict an astonishing array of indexical signs in the most literal and immediate sense. (For further vivid details, see Bang and Dahlstrom, 1974.)

The pointed lip gesture in use among the Cuna Indians of Panama, as analyzed by Sherzer (1973), provides a neat instance of cultural integration into a single unified arrangement of a verbal index with a nonverbal index. His description also shows that, whereas the index constitutes a marked category in opposition to the sign, the Cuna lip work stays unmarked in its focal indexical function in opposition to those accretive forms that have acquired peripheral meanings.

A small family of cerophagous picarian birds, a common species of which bears the scientific name *Indicator indicator* (*nomen est omen?*), are the celebrated honey-guides. These birds have developed a remarkable symbiotic relationship with certain mammals – ratels, baboons, and men – by employment of a purely indexic link: they guide their symbionts to the vicinity of wild bees' nests. The leading is preponderantly delophonic, but delotropic elements enter into it too: that is, a would-be guiding bird will come to, say, a person, and chatter until followed, but keep out of sight of the pursuer most of the time. Although its dipping flight is conspicuous, with the bird's white tail feathers widely spread, the honey-guide 'indicates' mainly by means of a repetitive series of chirring notes that subside only when it sees or hears flying, buzzing bees whose nest, of course, is the target (Friedmann, 1955).

The theory of honeybee (*Apis mellifera*) exploitation of food sources has been described (von Frisch, 1967) and pondered by many scientists, including semioticians and linguists (Sebeok, 1972: 34-53). It is common knowledge that if the food source is farther away than 100 m., the tailwagging dance conveys, among other bits of information, the direction of the goal, the sun being used as the reference point. Now if the bee dances on a horizontal surface, "the direction of a waggling run points directly to the goal", that is to say, the sign is indexic (the rhythm 'indicates' the distance in analog fashion: the farther away the goal, the fewer cycles of the dance in a given time). If, however, the dance takes place on a vertical comb surface — as is the case, as a rule, in the dark hive — then "the dancer transposes the solar angle into the gravitational angle" (if the run is pointed upward, this indicates that the food source lies in the direction of the sun, if downward, opposite the sun, if 60° left of straight up, 60° to the left of the sun, and so forth) (data reported by von Frisch, 1967: 230f.). If a vertical honeycomb is involved, in other words, when an angle with respect to gravity is used as the orientation cue, the sign ceases to be an index: its symbolic aspect now ranks predominant.

5. SYMBOL

5.1 *A sign* without either similarity or contiguity, but only *with a conventional link between its signifier and its denotata, and with an intensional class for its designatum, is called a symbol.*

5.2 The feature 'conventional link' — Peirce's 'imputed character' — is introduced, of course, to distinguish the symbol from both the icon (3.1) and the index (4.1). The feature 'intension', on the other hand, is required to distinguish it from the name (6.1), as we shall see. The logical opposition between intension (sometimes also called 'objective intension', and often 'comprehension') and extension has been drawn in a bewildering number and variety of ways: some 220 of them — ranging from 530 B.C. to 1966 — are enumerated by Frisch alone (1969: 183-214). "The use of 'intension' varies still more than that of 'extension' ", according to the standard treatise on the subject (Carnap, 1956: 18), although by no means the last word (Stanosz, 1970). For our present purposes, an intensionally defined class is one defined by the use of a propositional function; the denotata of the designation are defined in terms of properties shared by all, and only by, the members of that class (whether these properties are known or not) (Reichenbach, 1948: 193). In the terminology of Lewis, intension refers to "the conjunction of all terms each of which must be applicable to anything to which the given term would be applicable" (1946: 39).

5.3 Admittedly, 'symbol' is the most abused term of those under consideration here. In consequence, it has either tended to be grotesquely overburdened (.1.), or, to the contrary, reduced to more

general kinds of behavioral phenomena (.2.), or even to absurd nullity
(.3.). A few brief illustrative instances of both tendencies must suffice
here; they are merely intended to underline the need for further
conceptual clarification.

   5.3.1   An unjustifiably excessive generalization and overly broad
application of the concept of symbolic forms marks the writings of
many of Ernst Cassirer's epigones or of those indirectly influenced by
his philosophy (see p. 36, above and fn. 66). In cultural anthropology, a
case in point is Leslie White, who once wrote: "Human behavior is
symbolic behavior; symbolic behavior is human behavior. The symbol is
the universe of humanity . . . the key to this world and means of
participation in it is – the symbol" (1940). The hyperbole is reflected,
essentially, in the viewpoint espoused by the founder of the International Society for the Study of Symbols and so advocated by him
(Kahn, 1969).

   5.3.2   According to the psychologist Kantor, ". . . the term symbol
is made to do duty for everything the psychologist calls a stimulus"
(1936: 63). One may well ask, how widespread is this redundancy
among behavioral scientists?

   5.3.3   Although the term is included in Cherry's otherwise helpful
glossary, it is immediately followed by this odd disclaimer: "We avoid
the term *symbol* as far as possible in this book . . . " (1966: 309). As a
matter of fact, in many widely-used linguistics books sampled, the term
is never mentioned at all (save perhaps in the special combination,
'phonetic symbol'), but there are a few judicious exceptions (notably,
Landar, 1966, and Chao, 1968).

5.4   A number of important symbol subspecies – whose semiotic
import, however, has seldom been properly analyzed – is in more or
less common use, at least in contemporary English. Such subordinate
terms, with increasing intension, include, among other signs: *allegory,
badge, brand, device* (in heraldry), *emblem, insignia, mark,* and *stigma*
(when not embodied as a symptom, as in the expression *venous
stigmata*, suggesting alcoholic excess).[6]

___

[6]   "The Greeks . . . originated the term *stigma* to refer to bodily signs designed to
expose something unusual and bad about the moral status of the signifier. The
signs were cut or burnt into the body and advertised that the bearer was a slave, a
criminal, or a traitor – a blemished person, ritually polluted, to be avoided,
especially in public places. Later, in Christian times, two layers of metaphor were
added to the term: the first referred to bodily signs of holy grace that took the

Let us take a brief look at only one of these, the *emblem*. It is clear, from the outset, that its distribution must be narrower than that of its immediate superordinate: thus one can say that the hammer and sickle is either the symbol or the emblem of the Communist Party, or the Eiffel Tower of Paris, but one cannot say that H_2O is a **chemical emblem*, or [ə] a **phonetic emblem*.

Following a proposal put forward by David Efron in 1941 (1972), Ekman and Friesen (1969b) reintroduced and sharpened the notion of the emblem:

Emblems differ from most other nonverbal behaviors primarily in usage, and in particular in their relationship to verbal behavior, awareness and intentionality. Emblems are those nonverbal acts which have a direct verbal translation, or dictionary definition, usually consisting of a word or two, or perhaps a phrase. This verbal definition or translation of the emblem is well known by all members of a group, class or culture . . . . People are almost always aware of their use of emblems; that is, they know when they are using an emblem, can repeat it if asked to do so, and will take communicational responsibility for it.

They have in mind here nonverbal emblems only, and it is, indeed, the case that an emblem is most often conceived of as a highly formalized symbol in the visual modality. However, this need not always be so. Thus Lévi-Strauss has suggested (in a personal communication) that recited genealogies of notable individuals, say, of African ancestor chiefs, may well be regarded as being emblematic; such verbal acts could readily be accommodated within the scope of the foregoing formulation, as perhaps could Hollander's (1959) decidedly more idiosyncratic usage in connection with metrics.[7]

---

form of eruptive blossoms on the skin; the second, a medical allusion to this religious allusion, referred to bodily signs of physical disorder. Today the term is widely used in something like the original literal sense, but is applied more to the disgrace itself than to the bodily evidence of it" (Goffman, 1963: 1-2). For an illuminating discussion of *status symbol* or *prestige symbol* vs. *stigma symbol*, and of these in opposition to 'fugitive signs' which Goffman calls points, see pp. 43-48.

[7] For a delightful book devoted to chiefly emblems and devices as kindred literary genres of the 17th century, see Praz. "The emblem", he says, "combined the 'mute picture' of the plate, the 'talking picture' of the literary description, and the 'picture of signification', or transposition into moral and mystical meanings" (1964: 171).

It should be obvious, even from these sparse paragraphs, that the *Wortfeld* of the symbol is a very complex one indeed, and that the emblem and its congeners must await a fully correct lexicographic interpretation in conjunction with the unfolding of the lexical domain of the immediately dominant term, symbol, as a whole (7.3).

5.5 Symbols are often asserted to be the exclusive property of man, the *animal symbolicum*, but the capacity of organisms to form intensional class concepts obtains far down in phylogenesis,[8] and this ability for constructing universals from particulars was provided with a solid mathematical-neurological rationalization over a quarter of a century ago (Pitts and McCulloch, 1947; cf. Arbib, 1971). Both according to the definition of the symbol offered in 5.1, and the more common Aristotelian definitions resting on the doctrine of arbitrariness that were promoted in linguistics especially by William Dwight Whitney and, after him, Saussure (Engler, 1962; Coseriu, 1967), animals undoubtedly do have symbols. We have previously commented on the arbitrariness of tail work in dogs, cats, and horses (Haldane, 1955: 387; p. 44, above), a set of examples that could easily be amplified: thus a fearful rhesus monkey carries its tail stiffly out behind, whereas, in baboons, fear is conveyed by a vertical tail. However, the converse is not necessarily true: "a mother of a young infant [baboon] may hold her tail vertical not in fear but to help her infant balance on her back; and the tail may also be held vertical while its owner is being groomed in the tail region" (Rowell, 1972: 87). According to Altmann, "With few exceptions, the semantic social signals that have been studied in primates so far are arbitrary representations" (1967: 339); and, more generally, according to Bronowski, "It might be thought that because only human beings think with arbitrary symbols, they are also alone in speaking with them. But once again, this is not so" (1967: 376); and Lévi-Strauss has recently remarked that "Les animaux sont privés de langage, au sens ou nous l'entendons chez l'homme, mais ils communi-quent tout de méme au moyen de signaux, donc d'un système symbolique" (Malson, 1973: 20). Even Manfred Lurker, a foremost chronicler of human symbolic processes, is convinced that "Sicher gibt

---

[8] "The structure of the genetic message . . . imposes the structure of animal communities. But with mammals the rigidity of the programme of heredity becomes less and less strict . . . . One even sees the appearance of a new property: the ability to do without objects and interpose a kind of filter between the organism and its environment: the ability to symbolize" (Jacob, 1974: 319).

es Symbolerscheinungen im Reich der Tiere" (1968: 4). (On biological symbolism in intercellular communication, and a brilliant discussion of metabolic symbols and their representation of unique states of the environment, see Tomkins, 1975.)

For a conclusive example of a symbol in animal behavior, we turn to the insects, of the carnivorous family Empididae. In a species of dipterans of this family, the male offers the female an empty balloon prior to copulation. The evolutionary origins, that is, the increasing ritualization (Huxley, 1966), of this seemingly bizarre gesture has been unravelled, step by step, by biologists, but this story is irrelevant in synchronic perspective: the fact is that the gift of an empty balloon is a wholly arbitrary sign, the transfer of which simply reduces the probability that the male himself will fall prey to his female partner.

6. NAME

6.1 *A sign which has an extensional class for its designatum is called a name.*

6.2 In accordance with this definition, individuals denoted by a proper name as *Veronica* have no common property attributed to them save the fact that they all 'answer to Veronica'. An extensional definition of a class is one that is given "by listing the names of the members, or by pointing to every member successively" (Reichenbach, 1948: 193), or, as Kecskemeti put it, "Considered in terms of its intension . . . a name is simply a blank, unless and until a description referring to the same object is supplied" (1952: 130), say, 'Veronica with the handkerchief', Saint Veronica, or the like. (For a semantic analysis of proper names, cf. the thorough study by Sφrensen, 1963; see also the thoughtful essay by Buyssens, 1973.)

6.3 When the signification of a sign permits only one denotatum, it is said to be singular. Singular signs, including proper names, belong to a mode of signifying that Morris has labeled *namors*, "which are language symbols". Namors are members of the same family of signs, called 'identifiors', to which two other subcategories belong: *indicators* — the non-linguistic pendant to namors; and *descriptors*, "identifiors which describe a location" (Morris, 1971: 76f.). In the parlance of Husserl (1970: 341f.), the name of a person, which "bezeichnet, aber

charakterisiert . . . nicht", is also normally univocal ('eindeutig'), although it may, by chance, be plurivocal ('mehrdeutig'), "wenn mehrere
Personen gleichen Namens sich finden". Human individuals are identified by verbally attestable namors, say, a personal name or (in the U.S.,
since 1935), a unique Social Security registration number; and by a
host of nonverbal indicators, "the means by which a person, or dead
body, may be definitely recognized, even in cases where the person
purposely attempts to mislead . . . " (Wilder and Wentworth, 1918: 5,
and see *passim*, for an impressive array of positive identity markers).

6.4 It is well known that all animals broadcast a steady stream of
'identifiors', that is, displays identifying their source in one or more
ways: as to its species, reproductive status, location in space or time,
rank in a social hierarchy, momentary mood, and the like (Sebeok,
1972: 130). In addition, "the best organized societies of vertebrates
can be distinguished by a single trait so overriding in its consequences
that the other characteristics seem to flow from it", Wilson
(1971: 402) remarks as he draws a pivotal distinction between the
'impersonal' societies formed by the insects on the one hand, and the
'personal' societies found in birds and mammals on the other: this
attribute is the recognition of individual identity, a feature of relatively
small circles with long term socialization in the young, that presupposes
play and has as its corollary a high degree of mutual cooperation among
the adults. Each member of such a society "bears some particular
relationship to every other member" (*ibid.*), and thereby comes to be
known to all others as unique. Coupled to efforts to establish and
maintain the requisite network of multifarious 'personal' bonds is the
development of an intimate form of communication, which necessarily
involves the use of appropriate supportive signs: thus the notion of
'uniqueness' implies the manifestation of indicators, or, in Goffman's
terminology, 'identity pegs' (1963: 56f.).

The literature of vertebrate communication takes it for granted — at
least, *ex hypothesi* — that indicators, viz., their own names, are
universally incorporated into all messages of birds and mammals
(Smith, 1969a, b). Witness the following explicit passages by an
eminent ornithologist: " . . . when the partners were absent, the
remaining bird would use the sounds normally reserved for his partner,
with the result that the said partner would return as quickly as possible
as if *called by name* . . . Field observations suggest at times that one
bird is *calling* its partner back '*by name*' " (Thorpe, 1967; emphasis

supplied). Specific examples can be multiplied from a large variety of vertebrates, including canines and felines, primates (van Lawick-Goodall, 1968: 270; Rowell, 1972: 23), and marine mammals as well – individual whale click trains are even referred to as 'signatures' (Backus and Schevill, 1966), apparently by analogy with the so-called 'signature-tunes' of birds.

7. CONCLUSIONS

7.1 *On the being, behaving, and becoming of signs.* This essay has dealt with some half a dozen possible relationships that are empirically found to prevail between the signifier and the signified components of signs, and certain problems attendant to the definitions offered, in particular as these may have a bearing on their classification. Borrowing the alliterative triad employed by Ralph Gerard as a first approach to his classification of a material system, the org – roughly the same as Arthur Koestler's holon (see further pp. 26f. and 72f., above) – we can say that our foregoing discussion was concerned with the *being* of a sign, or its structure, that is, its enduring status in a synchronic sense; the focus of the inquiry fell within the realm of signification. A structural definition of the sign is analytic, intrinsic, and static; it utilizes types of associations inherent, in fact or virtually, in the architecture of the sign itself.

It should, however, be supplemented with a searching examination of its *behaving*, or its function, a repetitive perturbation along a secular trend. A functional definition of the sign is pragmatic, extrinsic, but dynamic; it is based upon variations at different nodal points of an expanded model of the communicative process, as depicted, for instance, by a Morley triangle (Sebeok, 1972: 14). Wells has aptly stated that "Semiotics has two groups of affinities. It is connected, on the one hand, with communication, and, on the other, with meaning" (1967: 103). We have attempted, on another recent occasion (see Ch. 4, this book), to explore a few phenomena of usage as these pertain to miscellaneous transactional relationships; accordingly, this paper should be regarded as a companion piece to the former. Both of these endeavors are strictly synchronic exercises.

The question of *becoming*, or history, representing cumulative changes in the longitudinal time section, introduces manifold dia-chronic considerations. These are of two rather different sorts: those having to do with the evolution of signs in phylogeny, in a word, their ritualization (Huxley, 1966); and those having to do with their elaboration in ontogeny. Study of the former requires the collaboration of ethology with semiotics; research of the latter belongs to the advancing field of psycholinguistics (which might as well be renamed 'psychosemiotics').

In sum, although semiotics is, especially nowadays, most commonly regarded as a branch of the communication disciplines, the criteria that must be integrated when working toward even a reasonably holistic comprehension of signs derive from studies of both signification and communication (*noumena* and *phenomena*), and they must also be in good conformity with research findings in ethology and developmental psychology.

7.2 *Applying the law of inverse variation.* The terms 'sign', 'symbol', 'emblem', 'insignia' are here arranged in the order of their subordination, each term to the left being a genus of its subclass to the right, and each term to the right being a species of its genus to the left. Thus the denotation of these terms decreases: e.g., the extension of 'symbol' includes the extension of 'emblem', but not conversely. On the other hand, the conventional intension of each term increases: the intension of 'emblem' includes the intension of 'symbol'. Sometimes, however, variation in the intension is accompanied by no change in the extension: thus, in the sequence 'sign', 'symbol', 'omen', 'augury' and 'portent', the extension of the last pair of terms is, within the semiotic universe of discourse, materially the same. This implies that if a series of semiotic categories is arranged in order of their increasing intension, the denotation of the terms will either diminish or will remain the same.

7.3 *A lexical domain.* Besides the six species of signs announced in the title of this article, allusion was made to a wide variety of others, including allegory, badge, brand, descriptor, device, diagram, display, effigy, emblem, identifior, identity peg, image, indicator, insignia, mark, metaphor, namor, signature, stigma, and syndrome. No doubt, these and a high number of cognate terms — especially those introduced by Peirce (e.g., 2.254-263) and, after him, by Morris (1971: 20-23) — would make a capital subject for an impressive monograph on the *Wortfeld of SIGN*, in its multiple ramifications, and not only in English but also in all those other languages in which the literature of semiotics, or semiology (Sebeok, 1973), is efflorescing. Despite Revzina's remark that 'it would evidently be more natural to treat those definitions of signs given [in Tartu, four summers ago] as an attempt at a lexicographical interpretation of corresponding language concepts" (1972: 231), such was but incidental to our principal purpose, namely, to work towards the ultimate goal of establishing a unified basis for a holistic categorization of signs, noumenal and phenomenal, static and dynamic, synchronic and diachronic (7.1), and, most importantly, valid as well in a cross-specific perspective (7.4). The doctrine of signs is, after all, as John Locke reminded us in 1690, that branch of knowledge "the business whereof is to consider the nature of signs . . . "

7.4   *The ubiquity of signs.* As the English zoologist R.J. Pumphrey has observed, there are two schools of thought in regard to the theory of language development: "All are agreed that human speech differs in material particulars from the speech of other animals. There are those who, like Darwin, believe in gradual evolution, but there have been others who have believed that speech is specifically a human attribute, a function *de novo*, different in kind from anything of which other animals are capable" (Sebeok, 1972: 88). Without wishing to embrace and attempt to justify here either some version of the continuity theory of language evolution or, conversely, some version of the discontinuity theory (as, for example, advocated by Eric H. Lenneberg, in Sebeok, 1968b: 592-613), one thing must, above all else, be emphasized: the research strategy pursued by us calls for an undeviatingly comparative standpoint, relying upon an entire range of biosemiotic data, from man and animals alike (cf. Sebeok, 1972: 106-21, 162-77). When looked at from this strictly comparative perspective, the distribution of at least the signs considered in this article fails to conveniently coincide with the division of animates into two unequal classes, one speechless and the other language endowed.[9]

[9]   An important article by Thom (1973), bearing on several of the topics discussed above, appeared too late to take into account here.

9

Notes on Lying and Prevarication*

L'animal ne peut émettre ni mots, ni phrases.... Ce qui manque à l'animal pour pouvoir parler, c'est le cerveau (Rosetti, 1965 13).

Among the so-called communication disciplines, the science of linguistics, being confined to the study of verbal messages exchanges, constitutes a marked category in contradistinction to the unmarked branch of knowledge we call semiotics, the subject matter of which is the transmission of any messages whatever and the systems of signs that underlie such transactions (see Ch. 1, above). Academician Alexandru Rosetti — to whom this essay is affectionately dedicated — has succinctly anticipated (as evoked in the epigraph above) the preponderance of contemporary opinion concerning man's species-specific *faculté du langage*, and perhaps even its probable locus (cf. Lenneberg, 1971). In the necessarily brief inquiry that follows, I wish to argue the ancillary point that, given that the propensity for language is indeed a uniquely human endowment, the phenomenon of 'lying' presupposes, as has not infrequently been claimed (cf. Kainz, 1961: 141-48), the use of verbal signs and the governing principle of combinatorial productivity informing them; but further to insist that there is a broader underlying mechanism that can be observed to operate over the expanse of the semiotic domain, particularly in the communicative repertoires of other animals. One linguist, Sturtevant (1947: 48), has speculated that "language must have been invented for the purpose of lying", an extreme claim the obverse of which was delineated in better balance by

* This article is reprinted from *Revue Roumaine de Linguistique* (October 20, 1975): *Festschrift in Honor of A. Rosetti.*

the philosopher Caws (1969: 1380), when he insisted that "truth . . . is a comparative latecomer on the linguistic scene, and it is certainly a mistake to suppose that language was invented for the purpose of telling it."

To avoid terminological confusion, let mendacity in language here be consistently labeled LYING, which thereby becomes a marked concept too; its unmarked pair, potentially involving any sort of sign, will generically be termed PREVARICATION (following the usage of Hockett, 1966: 12f., adapted and extended by the primatologist Altmann, 1967: 353ff.). The linguists' task thus manifestly includes accounting for this use, or misuse, of verbal resources, whereas the functions of semiosis will be understood to comprehend prevarication in general, such as lying, all human deception by nonverbal means (e.g., Ekman and Friesen, 1974), as well as the multifarious forms of sign forgery, mimicry, 'protean displays', misdirection, misinformation, and misrepresentation found in other species; indeed, "nearly all animals resort to deception" (Hinton, 1973: 97). The first approximation to a strictly linguistic exploration of the Augustinian *magna quaestio . . . de mendacio*, considered earlier, in the main, in theological contexts, remains the suggestive if scarcely systematic attempt by Weinrich (1966) that opened up a host of interesting possibilities: "Lügt man mit Wörtern? Lügt man mit Sätzen?", he asked; ought, that is, lying be assigned to semantics (and, one hastens to add, logic), or to syntax, or apportioned in what measure to each? There are, however, other important problems upon which this pioneer investigator barely touched, or not at all: the crucial dependence of the lie on double deictic anchorage, namely, the question how, precisely, a false utterance is integrated both in its linguistic context and extra-linguistic cotext; the subtle distinctions between lying and ambiguity, figures of speech, delusions, errors, fiction, especially drama, the notion of playing, the performance of ritual, the formulation of hypotheses, the wielding of models; and, furthermore, the developmental, or ontogenetic, dimension of all of the aforementioned. (Lying on an international scale, by actors representing states, in its various surprising ramifications was discussed by Jervis [1970: 66-112], in awareness of the implications of the theory of signs.)

A lie is, of course, itself a complex sign, whether homogeneous or syncretic (cf. p. 33, above), and therefore for any statement to be a lie it is a requisite that it be understood to be one. Nothing is a lie in itself. To become one, the minimal requirement is that the sign be manifested in the behavior of an organism that treats the statement as a sign of its associate in a triadic relationship (as explicated by Peirce). The vexing issue of intentionality (see p. 35, fn. 65, above) may have marginal utility when man is at least one of the interlocutors, or when the exchange involves a tamed animal, one whose character has been, as David Katz once picturesquely put it, "tainted by man's fall from grace" (cited in Hediger, 1955: 150). This emphasis is in good conformity with a distinction drawn by Morris (1971: 200) between lying, "the deliberate use of signs to misinform someone", and what I have dubbed a kind of prevarication, "the mere making of false statements". An elucidation of the range of topics alluded to still awaits expert semiotic analysis and eventual synthesis, but a parochial linguistic approach will no longer do, for such reports as are summarized below must fruitfully be integrated into a unified frame with what may be known about human verbal deception.

The power of a man's most ancient companion to lie to him was denied by the poet: "Buy a pup and your money will buy / Love unflinching that cannot lie . . . . " Yet Rüppell's (1969) remarkable observations in Diabasodden (West Spitsbergen, Svalbard) have clearly demonstrated a dramatic episode of prevarication in the feral Arctic fox, a species of the same subfamily of Canidae to which Kipling's domesticated dog also belongs. On this unpopulated island, Rüppell kept in view a pair of polar foxes with four cubs. The shy vixen visited the tenting place on the cliff, and carried off bits of cheese and other nourishment; especially large chunks were fetched toward the lair, some 500 m. away. En route, however, the hungry cubs jumped their elder, barking and biting, and snatched the choice morsel away. A young animal positioned himself by the food. Turning hindquarters toward the parent, the cub lifted its tail, urinated in her direction, then began to eat. The deprived vixen ran a few steps toward the cub, stared, then, suddenly lifting up her muzzle, repeatedly issued her high-pitched warning cry. The cub dropped the morsel at once, scurrying off among the rocks. The mother now ran to what was left of the cheese and devoured it. She successfully repeated this ruse over the next few days, in the absence of any manifest danger, but eventually the young caught on and, thereafter, in spite of the parental warning signal, would no longer abandon the food. What is especially noteworthy about this deceitful behavior is that no second instance has even been observed in any other family of Arctic foxes, which were studied under essentially identical circumstances, leading to the conclusion that what is involved is evidently other than innate (although how the vixen invented or otherwise acquired the practice in the family described is unknown). Pfeiffer's assertion (1969: 265) that this sort of behavior, "call it pretense or deceit, is peculiarly primate behavior; it is seen in no other species", is therefore thoroughly mistaken. Parallel examples have, for instance, been recorded in blackbirds and song thrushes by Thielcke (1964). Summing up his commentary on cases as these, Wickler (1971: 135) concluded: "Es besteht kein Zweifel dass sowohl die Drosseln wie der Eisfuchs ein unter ihresgleichen übliches akustiches Verständigungssignal gezielt missbrauchten und sich dadurch einen individuellen Vorteil auf Kosten der anderen verschafften. Damit ist die Behauptung widerlegt, dass nur der Mensch zur Lüge fähig sei und dass bei Tieren die Lüge ausscheide weil ihnen die Sprache fehlt." The misuse of intraspecific warning signs, which evolved to maximize genetic fitness of individuals in defined environments, cannot, of course, be habitually condoned in any social group precisely because they would tend to become devalued to the point where they may cease to function when danger really threatens. This surely is the lesson of Aesop's shepherd who cried – to stick with the Canids – "Wolf!" once too often, and the rationale for this tale (Type 1333) doubtless has its ultimate roots in phylogeny.

Interspecific instances of sign forgery are numberless. The interactants might include plants, e.g., orchids of the genus *Ophrys* (Wickler, 1968: 206ff.); humans deceived, e.g., by a lonesome gorilla or an Airedale terrier (Hediger, 1955: 150ff.), or deceiving some other animal, say, by manipulating normal releasers with superoptimal models or interfering with the natural rhythm of biological clocks; or variously related animal species, a single example of which (after Lloyd, 1965 and 1975) will have to suffice. Many American fireflies communicate with each other by means of a species-specific succession of light impulses, or a prosodic 'blink-code'. Now carnivorous females of the genus *Photuris* are able to copy the flash-responses of *Photinus* females. If a courting male of the latter species approaches a predatory female of the former, she mendaciously displays the signs of *his* species, thus luring him only to be eaten as soon as he settles in the vicinity. In other words, *Photuris femmes fatales* inherit a semiotic repertoire with coexistent sub-codes, at least one of which is reserved to directly perpetuate the species, and at least a second of which serves effectively the same end by misinforming, seizing, and deriving vital nourishment from a member of another.

To summarize: prevarication is seen as a pattern of semiosis prevalent among living creatures (plants and animals, including man in his nonverbal behavior). The underlying mechanism may be exclusively under genetic control (e.g., in mimicry), or be, as in the higher animals, increasingly subject to willful regulation. A distinction must be drawn between deceptive maneuvers by animals in captivity (tame or domesticated), and those in the wild. Lying is a category of prevarication criterial of language; its semiotic attributes, however, still remain very imperfectly understood.

10

The Semiotic Web: A Chronicle
of Prejudices*

0. PROLOGUE

Five years ago, Eric Hamp graciously invited me to review for the *International Journal of American Linguistics* Pierre Guiraud's latest contribution to the "Que sais-je" series, *La sémiologie* (1971). Then, several months ago, the editor of *Language Sciences* asked me to review the English translation of the same work for our own periodical. I resisted both temptations, for two principal reasons: precisely five years ago, I had myself completed a monograph-sized account (see Ch. 1, this book) – to be sure, I view it as a first approximation – of the field as it appeared to me then, and I did not feel that, within the brief confines of a review, I could immediately add anything useful to my friend's argument or, what seemed much more important, say anything about semiotics in general that would usefully amplify my observations that had just gone off to be recorded in print. Secondly, there was the matter of potential conflict of interest: I am now about a year away from submitting a new handbook dealing with the theory of signs, recontracted for by Penguin some months back (Sebeok, 1977d). Although Guiraud's treatment and mine differ substantially in scope as well as point of view, and both are, in fact, dissimilar in virtually every detail, even stemming from two discrepant traditions – neatly epito- mized by our respective titles, *Semiotics* vs. *Semiology* (explained in Ch. 2, above) – I thought that it would be indelicate for me to indulge in public discussions, let alone excoriations, of comparable efforts by

*   This article is reprinted, with essential corrections and additions, from the *Bulletin of Literary Semiotics* 2 (1975), 1-63. French, Hebrew, Polish, and (Brazilian) Portuguese versions are currently in preparation.

respected colleagues in a heat in which Guiraud's and mine are but two of several entrants, with yet other finalists lined up at the gate (see 3., below).

Nevertheless, I was stimulated to respond by compiling the record that follows – a highly personal, and hence selective, chronicle of publications and other major events, including especially curricular developments and news of pivotal meetings that have recently occurred or are about to take place – of the field of semiotics. There is a considerable, pressing demand for an accounting of this sort, getting more insistent as this province of knowledge, variously cultivated in Antiquity, thoughtfully reexamined in the Middle Ages, scrutinized afresh during the Renaissance, elaborated into something like its contemporary forms under the impetus of the model of Saussure (1857-1913) and, above all, that of Peirce (1839-1914), begins to spread like wildfire, penetrating national borders and, at the same time, invading, like an infection, a range of human endeavor from anthropophagy (Clerk, 1975) to more respectable culinary practices (Barthes, 1967a: 27f.), or from geomancy (Jaulin, 1970) and fortunetelling by tarot (Corti, 1973) to abstract ideology (e.g., Verón, 1971; Rastier, 1972; Veltsos, 1975), many of the crafts, such as those of the comic strip (Fresnault-Deruelle, 1975) and the animated cartoon (Horányi and Pléh, 1975), all of the arts, a host of traditional academic disciplines, and not only a wide array of the nomothetic sciences of man (in the usage of Windelband [1894] and Huxley [1963: 7f.]) but, though to a lesser extent so far, certain natural sciences (notably, ethology and genetics) as well. As written contributions and conferences multiply at a bewildering rate, we may well ask: Is the amount of semiotic information increasing, or is entropy about to engulf us? Will the wildfire, perhaps a consequence of the tempo and impact of modern communications, and our fascination with the underlying mechanisms, prove luminous, or a mere will-o'-the-wisp? And when Kristeva (1963b: 31) tells us that "la sémiotique ne peut se faire que comme une *critique de la sémiotique*", is she not teetering on the edge of paralipsis?

1. TOWARD A HISTORY OF SEMIOTICS

As I had previously remarked at the outset of my diachronic delineation of semiotics (see pp. 3-26 and fn. 8, above), "A full history of this field is yet to be written". Nonetheless, some progress in that direction is being made (see also Walther, 1974: 9-43), notably instigated by a well-conceived and serviceable biennial Polish periodical (*Studia* 1971, 1973) entirely devoted to the publication of primary text materials supplemented by secondary studies, with bibliographic guides bearing on historical matters. Although Vol. 1 was entirely in Polish, and is, moreover, out of print, Vol. 2 contains an English or French abstract of each of the six articles included, thus increasing its usefulness abroad; (Vol. 3 is announced for 1976, but no further volumes have, alas, been authorized).

Prominent mention should be made here of a truly outstanding, even indispensable, collection of readings (Rey, 1973), distilling a panorama of breathtaking reach and dazzling amplitude of semiotic ruminations throughout the ages, held together by the erudite compiler's always accurate, revealing, and insightful running commentary on the textlets featured. This first volume is divided into two quantitatively and qualitatively unequal parts, with the initial three-fourths emphasizing the philosophical tradition of the West, from Plato to Comte (cf. Rey, 1971), with a valuable excursus to India, and an imaginative indulgence drawing on the marvelous *Cahiers* of Valéry; and three less satisfactory concluding chapters devoted to semiotics in universal grammars, extracts from Humboldt, Whitney, and John Stuart Mill, with a wrapup from Bréal and the inevitable Saussure. A particularly welcome feature of Rey's book is its thorough index of forms and concepts. Anyone wishing to dig around seriously among the roots or later divarications of semiotics could do no better than to begin with this *vade mecum*, the second volume of which will cover the busy decades of 20th century semiotics that 'really' began with Peirce. (Vol. 2 of Rey's book should be out in 1976. Very well conceived, it is, in fact, divided into two major sections, the first on foundations, the second dealing with epistemological considerations.)

As Charles Morris implied in his cursory note on "The History of Semiotic" (Morris, 1971: 335-37), would-be historians ought to launch their searches either via the best pertinent secondary sources, such as standard histories of logic (e.g., Bocheński, 1956, or Schenk, 1973), or of other particular disciplines, such as linguistics (Sebeok, 1975d) or medicine (Garrison, 1929: 884f.); but if their intentions are truly honorable, they must, of course, revert directly to the primary sources themselves, as elegantly exemplified by the 'lost' Epicurean treatise of *Philodemus* (De Lacy and De Lacy, 1941). A most remarkable piece of historical reconstruction, which is certain to decisively affect our over-all perspective of semiotic development, is the establishment by John Deely of an autonomous edition of the text of the *Treatise on*

Signs by Jean Poinsot (1589-1644), which "occupies a virtually independent and entirely privileged position" in this Iberian cleric's huge *Cursus Philosophicus* (Deely, 1974: 850 1975; Poinsot, forthcoming). Poinsot, commonly known as Joannis a Sancto Thoma (Maritain, 1943; Herculano de Carvalho, 1969; Coseriu, 1969: 135f.), appears, in retrospect, to have forged the most solid, lasting link between the Scholastic semioticians – an intellectual milieu in which this keen thinker was still profoundly at home – and the emergent doctrine of signs envisaged, labelled, and foreshadowed by John Locke half a century later, in 1690 (Land, 1974: 15; Parret, 1975; Kelemen, 1976).

An important essay, intended to highlight the achievement of Locke and several milestones in the subsequent development of semiotics, has recently appeared by Roman Jakobson (1975), who, more than anyone else, has attempted to reconcile competing semiotic traditions, all the while insisting that variations be also clearly and critically recognized within what is enduring and invariant (on Jakobson and semiotics, cf. Eco, in van Schooneveld and Armstrong, 1976). His review touches on the semiotic activities of Jean Henri Lambert (in connection with which Karl Söder's dissertation, available on microfilm, should also be consulted), Joseph Marie Hoene-Wroński, Bernard Bolzano, Edmund Husserl on Husserl, especially in relation to Jakobson, see now Holenstein, 1976: 13-55), Charles Sanders Peirce, and Ferdinand de Saussure. It is precisely in the writings of Jakobson that the two principal modern semiotic traditions – what I referred to elsewhere (see Ch. 2, above), in shorthand fashion, as the 'Locke-Peirce–Morris pattern' vs. the 'Saussure pattern' – have creatively coalesced. By contrast, the astonishing insights of the Greeks (Weltring, 1910) and of the Scholastics are perceived by us but dimly (cf. Kretzmann, 1967), as a disjointed mosaic with occasional tantalizing flashes of brilliant color (for the medieval period, see, e.g., Bursill-Hall, 1971; Pinborg, 1972); and even the attainments of such Olympian figures as St. Augustine (354-430) (Simone, 1972), or Leibniz (1646-1716), rightly identified as "one of the major figures in the history of semiotic, and of syntactics in particular" (Morris, 1971: 336; Dascal, 1972, 1975), have barely begun to be assessed for their own sake, let alone in relation to their intellectual predecessors (on Augustinian dialectic in relation to Stoic semiotics, see, however, Pinborg, 1962), contemporaries, or successors in the long unfolding tapestry of the theory of signs.

Perversely, however, a veritable orgy of Saussurean exegesis continues to inundate us. Considering that, compared, for instance, with that of Peirce, "La contribution apportée par Ferdinand de Saussure au progrès des études sémiotiques est évidemment plus modeste et plus restreinte" (Jakobson, 1975: VII), this thickening chorus of adulation is not only embarrassing but a downright distortion of true historical equilibrium (cf. de Mauro's notes 73 and 139, in Saussure, 1972). My guess is that the great Swiss linguist would have been astonished to find himself thrust into the role "d'initiateur et du précurseur" of semiology (Mounin, 1968: 33), and utterly disconcerted by the gaffe, locked into a major French reference work, claiming that "Le premier à concevoir cette science semble avoir été F. de Saussure..." (Prieto, 1968: 93). Benveniste (1969) knew better, and it is to be hoped that the book of Culler (forthcoming) will redress the balance of historical judgment, as Calvet (1975) also tried to do.

Ogden and Richards were perhaps the earliest (1923) to note that "By far the most elaborate and determined attempt to give an account of signs and their meaning is that of... C. S. Peirce" (Ogden and Richards, 1938: 279). About Peirce's work in semiotics Morris later (1946) observed that "His classification of signs, his refusal to separate completely animal and human sign-processes, his often penetrating remarks on linguistic categories, his application of semiotic to the problems of logic and philosophy, and the general acumen of his observations and distinctions, make his work in semiotic a source of stimulation that has few equals in the history of this field" (Morris, 1971: 340). Peirce, a thinker of visionary penetration, remains thus far the most genial force in the history of semiotics. There is, moreover, a growing consensus the world over, among historians of ideas in general, "that no thinker since Leibniz in the 17th century has exhibited Peirce's mastery over so many diverse disciplines, or possessed his wealth of seminal ideas for cultivating them" (Nagel, 1959: 185; on ranking with Leibniz, cf. Fisch, 1972). However, because of the misfortunes of his biographical circumstances (intimated in various standard notices [e.g., Nagel, 1959]), partly grounded in problems arising from his nature, register, life-style, his name and accomplishments are still relatively unknown and, incredibly, only about one half of his copious written legacy, endowed with a density that may be unique in the modern context, has hitherto been published (Peirce, 1965-66). Largely on the basis of the misleadingly titled *Collected Papers*, a secondary literature of some fifty scholarly books – a few of them specifically concerned with his semiotic (e.g., Greenlee,

1973, Savan, forthcoming) – and of perhaps a thousand or more articles have been produced, a fair number of such items appearing in the first decade's run of the *Transactions of the Charles S. Peirce Society*.

This chronicle is hardly the place to expatiate on the entangled story of Peirce and his philosophical bequeathments, save to report that their scandalous neglect is, happily, about to be set aright within the framework of the newly established Center for American Studies of Indiana University in Indianapolis; (the Institute for Studies in Pragmaticism, which has been active at Texas Tech University for several years, will, no doubt, continue to contribute to the advancement of knowledge of Peirce, by collaboration with the Indiana University Center in several concrete ways). Foremost on the Center's program is the preparation of a comprehensive fifteen-volume chronological edition, fully annotated and indexed, of Peirce's writings, the entire opus then to be published, including his biography with other secondary literature, under the imprint of the Indiana University Press. Max H. Fisch, Peirce's uniquely qualified biographer, is the Editor-in-Chief, and Edward C. Moore, a distinguished specialist on Pragmatism, is the Associate Editor. The prospectus is explicit in its commitment semiotics: "The new edition will make available still unpublished work of his in that field, from the beginning to the end of his lifelong devotion to it." A national disgrace will thus slowly begin to be atoned for in the guise of a major contribution of ours to the Bicentennial celebration, punctuated by other diverse ceremonies of respect – and, it is to be hoped, the advancement of semiotic learning – at The Johns Hopkins University (where Peirce had been an instructor for five years), and followed by a different kind of international happening (Congress on Pragmatism and Semiotic, June, 1976, Amsterdam).

If Peirce was the fountainhead of today's semiotics, its most globally influential and revered living giant – yet one whose achievements are already integrated as a peerless episode in the history of the subject – is Charles Morris. His pertinent writings are all at last readily available in a single volume (Morris, 1971), and a veritable multinational industry has now sprung up laboring to produce critical explication or analysis of his theory of signs (e.g., Apel, 1973, beside Rossi-Landi's latest book [1975a] and article [1975b], and a spate of dissertations, among which I found Eakins [1972] and Fiordo [1976] the most useful). Interesting problems waiting to be tackled will certainly focus upon the profound involvement of Morris with George Herbert Mead (1863-1931) (Miller,

1973; Kang, forthcoming), whose social psychology itself had a manifestly semiotic orientation, palpably resonant in, for example, Erving Goffman's masterful books; and, to the contrary, Morris' surprising intellective independence from, although eventual terminological and otherwise surface reconciliation with, Peirce (cf. Dewey, 1946; and Morris' 1971: 444-48 rebuttal).

This being a very personal reckoning, I would like to seize this occasion to publicly avow my good fortune at having first encountered semiotic notions in a University of Chicago seminar of Morris' in the early 1940s – precisely midway, that is, between his *Foundations of the Theory of Signs* (1938) and *Signs, Language and Behavior* (1946). I have thus had the singular, and very likely unique, privilege of having studied with both Morris and, not long afterwards, Jakobson, the two having cross-pollinated in the intervening years.

It is obvious that the semiotic tidal wave that has washed over the several arts and sciences in the past decade affected them unevenly, each to a different degree. I have heard it said, for instance, that the potential for applying the theory of signs to the cinema (cf. p. 35, fn. 63, above; Bellour and Metz, 1971; Metz, 1974) is already exhausted; (indeed, the vacuousness of Michelangelo Antonioni's latest film, *The Passenger*, has even been partly – but, as the facts bear out, because of an absurd misunderstanding of the true sequence of events – blamed on a scriptwriter "crazed with semeiology, the science of signs" [cf. Simon, 1975: 16]). On the other hand, Kowzan has noted in his prize-winning book (1975: 173) that "Le seul genre de spectacle qui . . . a été abordé scientifiquement du point de vue sémiologique, est l'art du cinéma", which confirms "en même temps le besoin d'une ouverture sémiologique sur l'art théâtral, la nécessité de considérer le spectacle du point de vue de la sémiologie". Although Kowzan's assumption exaggerates – he is evidently unaware of Bouissac's pioneering studies (1976), or of Rector's (1975) altogether different spectacles – and even the semiotics of the theater is far from virgin territory (Todorov, 1971; Helbo, 1974 [*nota bene* the asterisked fn. on p. 359], 1975; De Marinis and Magli, 1975; and of a work that will be of incalculable consequence when translated, Osolsobě, 1974), his point is a telling one. What it means to me is that 'historical' judgments about the success or failure of semiotic praxis in most branches of conduct and learning are altogether premature. How do physicians appraise a fellow M.D.'s contention for "the necessity to Medicine of a Theory of Signs" (Crookshank, 1923: 354; cf. Lewis, 1970)? How do social scientists react when one of the world's most sober and esteemed anthropologists announces that the concept of culture he espouses and whose utility he attempts to demonstrate "is essentially a semiotic one" (Geertz, 1973: 5), and when one of its giants classifies anthropology as "the bona fide occupant of the domain of semiotics" (Lévi-Strauss, 1973: 18)? What do logicians make of Carnap's uncompromising assertion (1942: 250) that *the task of philosophy is semiotical analysis*? How are ethologists affected by the urgent plea of a great animal psychologist that crucial experiments be repeated "unter dem Gesichtspunkt moderner Kommunikationslehren, besonders auch der Semiotik" (Hediger, 1970: 178; cf. Hediger, 1974: 29, 37), or arguments that their object of study is, in the end, hardly more than a special case of diachronic semiotics (Sebeok, 1975a: 85-95)? And, finally, do linguists appreciate the truth and devastating implications for the future of the language sciences of Nida's strategic remarks (1975: 13) about the importance "that language be viewed in the broader perspective of semiotics, since only as language could be seen as a symbolic system could the role of meaning within language be fully appreciated", and that "the fundamental insights of Peirce" be more fully cherished, since some of his concepts are "basic to the understanding of language as a semiotic system capable of explicating its own symbolization"? (See also Sebeok, 1977c.) Such questions are intended to give a foretaste of the shape of debates to come within semiotics, as well as when considering the logical filiation of the subject and its placement in the hierarchical order prevailing among the sciences of man. Movement towards the definition of semiotic thinking in the biological and the anthropological framework of a theory of evolution represents, however, at least in my view, the only genuinely novel and significantly holistic trend in the 20th century development in this field; by far the greatest forward steps in this direction have come from the awesome imagination of the French topologist, René Thom (1974, esp. Ch. XI), but will require much detailed elaboration and implementation, along several fronts, as I have adumbrated elsewhere (Sebeok, 1977b).

2. OF THE RECTIFICATION OF TERMS

Semiotics must surely be one of the rare provinces of knowledge the very practitioners of which have failed to reach a consensus even about what to call their own discipline.[1] That there are sound historical

[1] An instructive parallel is, however, reported by Stent (1969: 35-36) from the

reasons for this state of affairs, which I have attempted to trace and, in some measure, to explain (cf. Ch. 2, above; and Arrivé, 1974: 28), is cold comfort to the uninitiated and perplexing even to the professional. The problem, however, neither begins nor ends there. In Jakobson's scheme of things, as in many others (see p. 1, above; Prieto, 1975: 125-41, etc.), semiotics is wholly or at least partially assigned a place "within the total science of communication" (Jakobson, 1974: 36) – but then 'communication' usually stays an undefined prime. This, in turn, leads to further grave difficulties, which have upset both some psychologists (e.g., Burghardt, 1970) and some zoologists (e.g., Tavolga, 1974), working in the subfield of 'zoosemiotics' (itself a relatively recent coinage, for which see Sebeok, 1972: 178-81). For this reason, several recent efforts have been made to clarify what counts as 'communication', and it is no accident that the two most productive analyses that I know of appeared in the context of animal behavior studies (MacKay, 1972; Glasersfeld, 1974).

The terminological confusion deepens the closer one looks at the customary divisions and subdivisions of semiotics. For instance, as regards the once familiar and seemingly well-defined Syntactics-Semantics-Pragmatics trichotomy (Carnap, 1942: 8-11; Morris,

---

natural sciences: "To designate his approach to the understanding of life processes, Astbury coined the term *molecular biology*. Though for the next decade Astbury made vigorous propaganda in its favor, this neologism was very slow to find wide acceptance. Throughout the romantic period, for instance, no member of the Phage Group thought of or referred to himself as a 'molecular biologist,' for the very good reason that structure then played as peripheral a role in his preoccupations as did genetics in the preoccupations of the structural analysts. In fact, the Phage Group had *no* generic designation at all to describe its activity. Its members were most reluctant to call themselves, as might have seemed natural, 'biophysicists.' For, as was explicit in my earlier quotation from Delbrück's 1949 speech, 'A Physicist Looks at Biology,' they considered *that* term to have been 'ill-used.' More precisely, in the eyes of the Phage Group, two kinds of people were then wont to refer to themselves as 'biophysicists': physiologists who were able to repair their own electronic equipment, and second-rate physicists who sought to convince biologists that they were first-rate. It was only in the wake of the confluence of structure and genetic analysis produced by subsequent developments ... that the veterans of the romantic period and their disciples suddenly realized, like Monsieur Jourdain, that what they had been doing all along was molecular biology. Their pressing need for adopting *some* satisfactory cognomen for their line of work was later explained by Francis Crick: 'I myself was forced to call myself a molecular biologist because when inquiring clergymen asked me what I did, I got tired of explaining that I was a mixture of crystallographer, biophysicist, biochemist and geneticist, an explanation which in any case they found too hard to grasp.' "

1971: 23-54), what emerged in the course of an International Symposium on Pragmatics of Natural Languages (Jerusalem, June 22-27, 1970) was the very elusiveness of pragmatics and the fact that the participants could come to no agreement about the nature of this beast, real or mythical; Max Black's canny proposal "to save at least one allegedly tangible feature of pragmatics, viz., 'contextics' " came to naught (Staal, 1971: 29). In Montague grammar, pragmatics is hardly distinguishable from semantics, or, at least, the borderline appears, for the present, gossamer-thin (Montague, 1974: 64, 96, 120).

Let me make a stab at exploring, at some length but not exhaustively, just one other example, the wide ramifications of which obtruded upon me as I sat down to prepare the plenary address on the topic assigned to me by the organizers of the First Congress of the International Association for Semiotic Studies (eventually delivered, in Milan, on June 6, 1974): "Nonverbal communication" (Nelson, 1975: 315f.). It soon dawned on me that this deceptively simple phrase, widely bandied about and incorporated in a large miscellany of book titles (among others, Bosmajian, 1971; Davis, 1971; Eisenberg and Smith, 1971; Hinde, 1972; Knapp, 1972; Mehrabian, 1972; Ruesch and Kees, 1956; Scherer, 1970; Weitz, 1974; see also the entries under MacKay [1972] and Tavolga [1974]), is well-nigh devoid of meaning or, at best, susceptible to so many interpretations as to be nearly useless. Mehrabian (1972: 1f.) naively distinguishes a "narrow and more accurate sense", declared to refer "to actions as distinct from speech", i.e., "hand and arm gestures, postures, positions, and various movements of the body or the legs and feet", from a broader but supposedly traditional sense, by which he seems to mean what Crystal (1969: 293) had once labelled 'content-free speech', intended to cover, among kindred phenomena, those called by some investigators para-linguistic events. When we next ask what paralinguistics may possibly comprehend, Crystal relates that all of the following were suggested in response to an inquiry of his: "animal vocalization (or some aspect of it), memory restrictions on language, recall ability for language, utterance length, literary analysis, environmental restrictions on language use..., glossolalia, and emotional expression in general language disturbance — in effect, a fair proportion of sociolinguistics and psycholinguistics" (1974: 269).

Supposing, however, for the sake of simplicity, that we return to Mehrabian's first, and evidently preferred, sense of 'nonverbal': we are at once confronted by a further morass of nomenclature — a host of terms that "themselves offer variety without clear distinction" (Stokoe, 1974: 118), to wit:

(*a*) The term 'nonverbal', or 'non-verbal' (or, more rarely, 'extra-verbal' – cf. Graham and Argyle, 1975), is objectionable because it includes far too much, and, moreover, what it does comprehend varies according to each investigator's whim (Harrison, *et al.*, 1972). Also, it wrongly implies the independence, indeed, usually the primacy, in some implicit synchronic way, of the verbal component in humans. The formula, "communication minus language = nonverbal communication" is clumsily negative, simplistic, and obscurantist.[2] In other words, "It makes no sense to speak of 'verbal communication' and 'nonverbal communication'. There is only communication, a system of behavior patterns by which people are related to one another" (Kendon, 1972b: 443), in brief, the subject of the holistic field of interaction ethology (alias semiotics), adumbrated in a conference (Amsterdam, August 31 - September 4, 1970), organized by Goffman and me for the Wenner-Gren Foundation (Sherzer, 1971). Yet another hare, which I don't care to run with here, lurks in the careless way in which 'communication' is confounded with 'behavior', especially in the context of the nonverbal. This confidently assumes that all behavior (Scheflen, 1972, 1974; Hinde, 1974) neatly bifurcates into a kind that communicates and a kind that does not communicate – which is, in fact, a matter of controversy even among animal behaviorists, and hardly helped by the introduction of qualifying weasel words such as 'social', 'goal-directed', or the like.

(*b*) The term 'pantomime', to be sure, denotes significant gesture without speech, or dumb show, but has a heavy overlay connoting Roman and English dramatic entertainment, sometimes designated as a prose ballet (see the *OED*). For most, the associations are bound to be less semiotic than histrionic.

(*c*) Gesture, "the most familiar term, begs the question we want to ask. Why should facial and corporeal movement take on a unique quality if being performed by our species and not by any other" (Stokoe, 1974: 118)? One could, of course, as I have done (Sebeok, 1972: 163ff.), set apart 'anthroposemiotic' gestures, i.e., such as are species-specific in man (Efron's category of arbitrarily-coded, hence culture bound, emblems comes immediately to mind; see Ekman and

---

[2]   In this research area, a negativistic tendency seems to prevail since at least 1888, when Kleinpaul paradoxically designated the topic of his classic compilation as *Sprache ohne Worte*, that is, 'speech devoid of words' (Kleinpaul, 1972).

Friesen, 1969b: 63-68), and 'zoosemiotic' gestures found in humans, i.e., such devices that we demonstrably share with some other form of animal life (a very nice example being the evolution of laughter and smiling; see van Hooff, 1972). This distinction is, however, both awkward and hard to maintain in practice. Another difficulty with this term is that its extension fluctuates widely according to the user's predilection; thus, for Ruesch, for example, in his sensitive classificatory scheme, gestures (Ruesch and Kees, 1956: 37) belong with the numerous "varieties of nonverbal language", one subdivision of which he named 'action languages', among which gestures are singled out as only one category in about a dozen. Furthermore, Ruesch follows Critchley (1939) in closely tying gestures to speech.

(d) Kendon, on the other hand, prefers to reserve 'gesticulation' for "those complex movements of the hands and arm and head" (1972a: 178f.) that actually accompany the flow of speech. This, however, would require another term, or set of terms, unspecified (also by others, e.g., Jakobson 1974: 31), for movements which do *not* co-occur with, or are disjointed from, speech.

(e) Stokoe (1974: 118) cites 'motor signs' as "Jakobson's term. . .and it is characteristically exact". I think that it is neither. Franz Boas, in his 1941 introduction to Efron's book (1972: 19), carried over the word 'motor' into this context (although he coupled it with 'habits' instead of 'signs'), but, to most linguists, the phrase will rather evoke an expression especially propagated by Stetson, 'motor phonetics', which he defined as "the study of the skilled movements involved in the process of handling articulatory signals" (1951: 6). It is not at all uncommon to find statements to the effect that "In Phonetics, the motor processes are the center of consideration" (Meader and Muyskens, 1962: 20). What all this means is that 'motor signs' can be equally of a verbal and a nonverbal character, unless one distinctly specifies what part of the body is at play, viz., the so-called organs of speech, or, as in the Jakobson piece (1972) referred to by Stokoe (but which, in any case, was a translation from a Russian article of 1970), the whole head as a *Gestalt*, plus, as the author explicitly enumerates, the pupils (cf. now Hess, 1975), eyeballs, eyebrows, and the facial musculature separately as well as in concert (for research on facial expressions in general, cf. Ekman and Friesen, 1975).

(f) The expression 'body language', perhaps suited for use in Sunday supplements (Davis, 1970), became popular in this country through the title of a best seller (Fast, 1970) with a conception of unmatched vulgarity, and yet it also recurs as the operative part of the title of a book with, presumably, earnest intentions (Scheflen, 1972); (for an early, sophisticated use, in an unmistakably semiotic context, see Latif [1934: 76f.]). Such kindred labels as 'bodily communication' (Argyle, 1975), 'body talk' (Poiret, 1970), or 'face language' (Whiteside, 1974; cf. Mar, 1974) are also found, but more sporadically. These terms clearly imply a phenomenal dualism postulating a body language opposed to – what? A 'mind language'? (I really doubt that this view is in good conformity with the ideas about language as a direct 'mirror of mind' that Chomsky imagined in his 1967 Beekman lectures [Chomsky, 1972]!)

(g) When all else fails, semioticians revert to their ancestral source in searching for more or less exact terms with a safely antique vibrancy, as I myself have done (Sebeok, 1972). The splendid periodical of our colleagues in Russia was, with great deliberation, entitled *Semeiotikè* (1965-75), after which the title of Kristeva's collection of papers (1969b) acquired a doubly sympathetic Graeco-Soviet resonance (Coquet and Kristeva, 1972: 324). In the field under scrutiny here, there is also a plenitude of quasi-classical coinages: 'kinesics' (Bird-whistell, 1970), 'coenetics', with a superabundance of subsidiary terms like 'haptics', 'geustics', and 'strepitistics' (Wescott, 1966: 350), 'proxemics' (Hall, 1968; Watson, 1970; Baldassare and Feller, 1975), 'tacesics' (Kauffman, 1971), and so forth and so on. Lexical innovations of this ilk may conceivably be of heuristic value; unfortunately, they also tend to map out crazy quilts of territory which then compact into exclusive feeding grounds for budding students, as well as fiercely defended fortalices against strange intruders, bristling with aggression and escalating counter-aggression. The recent history of 'kinesics' can be looked at as a case study in territorial behavior or misbehavior, spoiling whatever utility the label may once have enjoyed. Wescott's pullulating vocabulary has totally misfired. 'Proxemics', despite the well-deserved popularity of Hall's two main books (in the second, 1966, the key word is introduced and defined in the second sentence), has hardly become a byword, and is not even mentioned by the 'other' leading student of spatial behavior, Sommer (1969). Kauffman's portmanteau, approximately blended from 'tactile proxemics', just missed a chance to be picked up in the, up to now, chief book on human tactile communication (Montagu, 1971).

(h) The latest, and in some ways the most attractive, proposal, introduced and, in some measure, developed by Stokoe (1974: 118), is 'gSign', where *g* stands for any 'gestural manifestation', and *sign* for 'sign-vehicle in a semiotic system'. I can think of all sorts of ways of integrating 'gSign' into semiotic theory and practice. Stokoe, who, more than anyone else in America, has clearly perceived the place of sign languages in semiotics (cf. his 1972 book), and who is the founding editor of *Sign Language Studies* (1972-), is in an excellent position to vigorously promote it.

The foregoing sample exercise,[3] which could be replicated from almost any corner of the field, was merely intended to demonstrate the urgent need for a concerted effort to regulate semiotic terminology in reasonably orderly fashion. Solo attempts are not altogether lacking since Maldonado's innovative venture in 'Präzisierung der Terminologie' (1961). His unpublished lemmata are, however, reported to outnumber by far those that appeared in his diminutive but trailblazing booklet, which was even partially multilingual. Another modest mini-dictionary of high quality, in five languages including Russian, was published in Israel (Hrushovski and Even-Zohar, 1972), and, quite recently, a monolingual (Portuguese) glossary has appeared, this one in Brazil (Rector, 1974). The most ambitious printed work of this sort (Bense and Walther, 1973) thus far is also the most disappointing, for several reasons, some of them detailed in Ketner and Kloesel's (1975) searching review article in *Semiotica*.

On June 3, 1974, I proposed, during the First Congress of the International Association for Semiotic Studies, to a convocation of over fifty interested scholars from many countries, a plan – subsequently ratified by the General Assembly – for an *Encyclopedic Dictionary of Semiotics*. This *EDS* would contain three categories of entries:

I. Articles tracing the history of all terms used in semiotics, with suggestions for standardizing current usage, for, as noted by Nelson (1975: 317f.), the editors "will succeed at their task most surely if they clarify all the seemingly exotic equivalences among languages in technical terms, establish primacy or origin within the original context and system and simply list even the *hapax legomena* or nonce terms".

II. Evaluative biographies of leading figures in semiotic studies. Each author would be required to relate his subject to his intellectual

---

[3] Critchley's (1975) titular adoption of Hall's (1959) title, with a quite different scope and intent, simply won't do either. Critchley aims "to write about gesture, and with it gesticulation, pantomime and the like," but he himself goes on to remark that gesture "may sometimes be audible though still unvoiced" (Critchley, 1975: i).

antecedents, show wherein lies his unique contribution to the advancement of semiotics, and trace his influence on later semioticians and his
role in intellectual history in general. An example might be Gottlob
Frege (1848-1925), who both vastly extended the early semiotics of the
Stoics and their successors through the ages, and initiated the modern
period in the study of logic in the form in which it is able to give an
account of sentences involving multiple generality (cf. Dummett,
1973).

III. Detailed descriptions of the impact of semiotics on other fields
of inquiry, say, at random, anthropology (Firth, 1973; Geertz, 1973;
Sperber, 1974; Turner, 1975), economics (Fedorenko, 1970 or 1972;
Rossi-Landi, 1974: 1915-19), psychiatry (Bär, 1975) and psycho-
analysis (Verdiglione, 1975), still photography (Lindekens, 1971),
visual art (Schapiro, 1969); and upon certain delimited, objective
copora, such as prayerful gestures in and outside of Christianity (Ohm,
1948), Nevada cattle brands (Watt, 1967), American cigarette advertise-
ments (Sparti, 1975; for other kinds of advertising, cf. Nöth, 1975),
Slovakian popular costumes (Bogatyrev, 1971), or verbal transforms of
Parisian fashions (Barthes, 1967b).

The *EDS* would be published in a single volume, in English, but
matching glossaries in other languages would also be supplied. An
exhaustive bibliography would be incorporated, keyed to the entries.
The number, scope, and relative length of the entries and the names of
the scholars who would be invited to contribute them will be
determined by an international editorial board to be appointed by the
IASS. I envisage a manual of up to 500,000 words, and estimate two
years for its preparation. The project can commence as soon as full
funding has been secured.

Simultaneously, a project at McGill, in Canada, overlapping in coverage
with that of our first category, but with a further extension into
esthetics, is also in the planning stage. It differs, too, in that it would be
produced mainly, so to speak, in-house, that is, by the principal
investigators (Peter Ohlin and Irena Bellert) themselves.

It is heartening to note that so many colleagues feel the need for
taking steps to dispel the clouds of obfuscation which have threatened
to permanently befog semiotics. We, of all people, must be ever mindful
of Peirce's "Ethics of Terminology" (2.219-226), where he teaches
"that the woof and warp of all thought and science is the life inherent
in symbols. . . Yet the scientific and philosophical worlds are infested
with pedants and pedagogues who are continually endeavoring to set up

a sort of magistrature over thoughts and other symbols. It thus becomes one of the first duties of one who sees what the situation is, energetically to resist everything like arbitrary dictation in scientific affairs, and above all, as to the use of terms and notations. At the same time, a general agreement concerning the use of terms and of notations – not too rigid, yet prevailing, with most of the co-workers in regard to most of the symbols, to such a degree that there shall be some small number of different systems of expression that have to be mastered – is indispensable" (2.220).

3. INTRODUCING SEMIOTICS

In my biased judgment, there were two – and only two – general semiotic treatises written during the interwar period, one produced on each side of the Atlantic, that deserve the appellation of miniature classics: Morris' *Foundations of the Theory of Signs* (1938 = 1971: 13-71), in the generation following Peirce, "whose work," Morris remarked there (1971: 44) "is second to none in the history of semiotic"; and Buyssens' *Les langages et le discours* (1943 = 1967: 9-74), in the generation following Saussure, whose 'voeu' he intended to carry out in this essay (1943: 6, §6). These two slender masterpieces had rather dissimilar fates. The Morris monograph achieved well-deserved international recognition and influence (cf. Rossi-Landi, 1953, 1975a; Eakins, 1972; Fiordo, 1976), which continue to flourish. On the contrary, the Buyssens pamphlet, perhaps because of the ill-starred date of its first publication in Belgium (see pp. 17f., above), received hardly any attention, although Hjelmslev did once refer to it as "A comprehensive attempt at a general semiology" (1953: 69, fn. 1). It has eventually had a limited, though plainly salutary, effect on scattered Francophone writings in the field (e.g., Pohl, 1968); and my high estimation of it is significantly shared – as are some other judgments expressed in these pages – by that incomparable Italian literary critic (who is also the President of our International Association for Semiotic Studies), Cesare Segre (cf. 1973: 33-37). Whenever I am asked by neophytes desirous of entry how to gain immediate access to semiotics, I direct them to these indispensable twin keys – Morris and Buyssens, each marked by a simplicity of approach, limpidity of style, critical discernment, and captivating devotion to their subject matter.

Apart from Morris' own *Signs, Language and Behavior* (1946 = 1971: 73-397), neither an introductory nor an advanced synthesis has yet been produced by any single American or other Anglophone semiotician in the postwar era to date. Restraints on the semiotic floodgates began at first to be lifted, with the onset of the 1960s, both here and abroad, less by dint of the creative efforts of individual scholars than through the common academic collaborative instrumentality of a host of colloquia, conferences, seminars, and all sorts of other meetings, many of them international and multidisciplinary, initially culminating in the 1974 Congress, but continuing beyond, seemingly into eternity (see 6., below).

In the West, Roland Barthes' extended, fascinating essay (1964, 1967a), perceptive as it was radical, set in motion a new inquiry and debate in a personal idiom, or, if you will, reopened Pandora's box of semiotic tricks. Barthes, after he read Saussure in 1956, launched on what he has since denominated 'L'aventure sémiologique' (1974: 28), not in a loose metaphoric sense but in full etymological awareness of adventure, and for explicitly 'political' reasons (cf. Calvet, 1973, 1974), namely, as an ideological maneuver. Although Calvet claims (1973: 116) that the manual was intended to be an "ouvrage pratique, ouvrage d'initiation, clefs en quelque sorte", it obviously goes much further than that. The author rightly wants to know why the science of signs has made so little headway since Saussure. The search for an answer leads him to his notorious paradoxical inversion of Saussure's formula, and to the conclusion that semiotics is a part of linguistics, to be specific, "that part covering the *great signifying unities* of discourse" (Barthes, 1967a: 11). By this reversal of the customary hierarchy of entities, Barthes gains an instrument – the concept of signification – for bringing to light the unity of the research being carried out in a number of disciplines, an aim he shares, *inter alia*, with Morris (1971: 17f.). Traditional Saussureans have variously condemned Barthes' inferences and conclusions (e.g., Buyssens, 1967: 13f.; Mounin, 1970: 12f.; Prieto, 1975: 132-41), though I happen to think on trivial grounds; my own objections continue to derive from his absolute exclusion of sign processes among the speechless creatures from the semiotic universe, an anthropocentrism that, for me, detracts seriously from the brilliance of his book (cf. pp. 12 and 84f., above; and Segre, 1973: *passim*).

The 1960s also witnessed the rise of a self-designated 'Marxist semiotics', an uneasy synthesis the most curious aspect of which was its well-nigh complete rout by other schools within the Soviet Union,[4] and its silent treatment throughout most of Eastern Europe, with the notable exception of the German Democratic Republic. The most popular books in this vein, with an announced epistemological goal, were written by Klaus (1963), Resnikow (1964 in Russian, 1968 in German), and Albrecht (1967). Klaus was also widely acclaimed by radical students of that decade in the German Federal Republic, and Resnikow was even translated for Italian consumption (1967). Generally speaking, conflations such as these are bound to be flawed, and burdened by their understandably requisite but still irritating quota of slogans. However, I have always derived consolation, not to say vast amusement, from a claim Klaus made, in the opening paragraph of his Foreword, according to which semiotics became, after World War II, "in breiten Schichten der Bürgertums der USA, vor allem aber bei der Intelligenz", a "Modewort", or fashionable catchword. Let me hereby solemnly assure Herr Klaus that my experience has been precisely the opposite: to this day, in the ruling circles of America, throughout our bourgeoisie, sadly inclusive of our intelligentsia, semiotics is emphatically still not a word to conjure with.

From the end of the last decade onwards, Continental textbooks of semiotics, or collections intended to serve as such, began to appear in profusion, and I would single out from this period the following works that all tyros should be acquainted with:

In English – Eco (1976), Guiraud (1975), and the two Sebeok anthologies (1974b: 209-626, and 1975a);

In French – Prieto (1966), the Mounin collection (1970), Guiraud (1971), and Martinet (1973);

In German – Bense (1967), Eco (1972), Walther (1974), Nöth (1975), and Trabant (1976);

[4] For representative writings by the celebrated Soviet – sometimes, eponymously, "Tartu" – School on Secondary Modeling Systems, consult all of Semeiotikè (1965-75), Revzina (1972), and the references given on pp. 22ff., above, esp. in fns. 36-38. Lotman, et al. (1975) set forth an authoritative, if programmatic, statement about the semiotic-typological nature of the concept of culture, as envisaged by five leaders of the group, many of whose most important writings have been variously reprinted, translated, and/or anthologized in the West, a few short pieces in the pages of Semiotica. Two especially useful collections, both published in Italy, are by Faccani and Eco (1969), and Lotman and Uspenskij (1973), the latter containing a valuable survey, by D. M. Segal, of "ricerche sovietiche nel campo della semiotica negli ultimi anni" (452-70), rounding out Meletinsky's and his own earlier (1971) conspectus. Cf. also Eimermacher (1971, 1974), and Fokkema (1974).

In Hungarian – Stepanov (1976);
In Italian – Eco (1968, 1973, 1975);
In Russian – Stepanov (1971);
In Spanish – Gutiérrez López (1975);
In Swedish – Malmberg (1973).
Some of the works cited were also published in other languages or, as Malmberg's very readable and ingeniously illustrated paperback, are about to be. These references are, of course, intended to supplement other basic works already mentioned, especially in 3., and ought further to be rounded out by a welter of treatments of the subject, or of aspects of it, in a recent outpouring of relevant encyclopedias and handbooks of a similar character, and certain special collections. A sampling from this kind of literature will be found in the following chronological listing: 1968 – Martinet, Prieto, Weinreich; 1969 – Meetham/Hudson; 1971 – Kristeva/Rey-Debove/Umiker, Moles; 1972 – Ducrot/Todorov; 1973 – Dubois, Pottier; 1974 – Koch; 1975 – Stammerjohann.[5]

Of all the aforementioned, I have a decided preference for Eco (1976). To my taste, this book of his is the most sophisticated, comprehensive, readable account of semiotics now on the market, with a proper historical perspective as well as a critical but entirely fair regard for contemporary scholarship. In the jargon of the Italian left, the author has been identified as an 'idealist'; if so, I admire the company he keeps. (Incidentally, Eco's elegant little book on signs [1973] is altogether splendid too; regrettably, it is, so far, available in Italian only.)

4. CATALOGUING SEMIOTICS

Bibliographies bore me, but I am prepared to concede their limited utility, if carried out well. The trouble is that, in general, they are not: often, they are a farrago of unread chunks of redundant learning

[5] There are numerous reference works devoted to 'symbols', often restricted to the graphic sense. A sampling of the best recent source books of this genre includes: Bertin (1967), Brun (1969), Massin (1970), Shepherd (1971), Dreyfuss (1972), and de Vries (1974). For a recent account of theoretical and experimental work in graphics, see Krampen (1965). Among general dictionaries on symbols, I found the four volumes compiled by Chevalier and Gheerbrant (1973-74) by far the most useful. An absorbing periodical pertaining to graphics is *Visible Language: The Journal for Research on the Visual Media of Language Expression*, now in its 10th volume.

churned out in amorphous lumps by dilettantes rather than experts properly trained in bibliographic methodology.[6] I have, myself, amateurishly dabbled at the art, applying it to the subfield of zoosemiotics, although I did insist on at least one absolute criterion for the inclusion of any items in my annotated guides: first-hand acquaintanceship with each entry (Sebeok, 1968a, 1972: 134-61, 1975b). (In my editorial capacity, I have, furthermore, encouraged the publication of such unique tools as Hewes' multidisciplinary bibliography of some 11,000 items that deal with the origins of language [1975].)

I know of only one bibliography that purports to cover semiotics as a whole: Eschbach (1974); (a follow-up volume has been announced). As such, it is perhaps commendable for its ambitiousness, or, at any rate, as a first approximation to a synthesis. However, it attempts too much while it achieves too little; in the end, it leaves one limp, with a chaotic impression of the scope and content of semiotics. Too, the compiler was seriously mistaken to try to incorporate the unedited lists of publications of fifteen quite arbitrarily chosen individual scholars, some alive and, presumably, still productive, others deceased yet far from exhaustively catalogued (the coverage of Peirce is, e.g., particularly dreadful). One also wonders, among similar reservations, why on earth 126 of John Dewey's publications, most of them not even marginally relevant to the subject, were allotted space?

There exist, of course, numberless bibliographies – annotated or otherwise, frankly select or declared to aim towards comprehensiveness – of this or that aspect or branch of semiotics. Thus Lotz (1972) is typically idiosyncratic, containing merely what he considered "the most significant contributions in Western scholarship dealing with the problem of script" – only fourteen items in all. By contrast, it is hard to fathom the principles of selection that governed the make-up of Huggins and Entwisle (1974), an annotated bibliography of iconic communication, neatly prepared by a computer according to a uniform

---

[6] I suppose it behooves me to furnish here at least one example of a work that I would regard as a model bibliography of some semiotic topic, in this case, in linguistics. Such a work, of immense authority and professional competence, from a narrow segment of the field, is Paul Rivet and Georges de Créqui-Montfort's *Bibliographie des langues Aymará et Kičua* (1540-1955, in 4 vols.), which I had the pleasure of reviewing some twenty years ago (Sebeok, 1953, 1958). The entries and layout of Russell (1973), in a kindred genre, constitute another attractive pattern deserving of the attention of would-be bibliographers of semiotics; (cf. *Semiotica* 11, 385f.).

plan; (as it happens, I am concurrently writing a speech on "Iconicity" [Sebeok, 1975c], but, unaccountably, have failed thus far to locate, among the approximately 350 entries listed in this book, even a single reference I needed to look up by way of documentation).

Let me drive my aversion to bibliographies home, reverting, by way of documentation, to the field of 'nonverbal communication', some terminological predicaments of which I mentioned above, in Section 2. A respectable scholarly working bibliography, usefully annotated in part, was published by Hayes (1957) although in a hardly accessible regional journal. Over the ensuing decades, several serious efforts of a similar nature followed, the most carefully wrought among them being M. Davis' annotated and indexed listing of some 931 titles (1972) (claiming [88] not to duplicate most of the references included by Hayes). The compiler explains the purpose, scope, and criteria for selecting her entries. Yet she nowhere alludes to the fact – which I find shocking – that solely English-language items are to be found in her book. Again, Davis does explicitly tell her readers: "Books and articles on . . . expressive movement . . . are cited" (vii). This notwithstanding, one searches in vain for mention of the most important book of the century on this subject, Bühler (1968) – or references to the works of Johann Jakob Engel, Th. Piderit, Guillaume Benjamin Duchenne, Louis Pierre Gratiolet, Wilhelm Wundt (cf. 1973), Ludwig Klages, to name only some contributors to the topic discussed by Bühler. How can any such bibliography omit naming Kleinpaul, whose book (1888[1], 1972[2]) has, to this day, no peer? Or the Canon Andrea de Jorio's magnificent study (1832) of gesture in ancient art and literature compared with gestures in common use in the Naples of his time? Or Brilliant's examination (1963) of postures found in Roman statuary by reference to the known use of gesture as a code system, as set out in the ancient manuals of rhetoric? Understandably, she could hardly have known Bouissac's penetrating 1973 treatise on the measurement of gestures; but his sources – Arcange Tuccaro, P. J. Barthez, G. Strehly, Eadweard Muybridge (sometimes dubbed "the father of the motion picture", cf. Hendricks, 1975), E.J. Marey, N. Oseretzky, and others – are ignored as well. The coverage of the so-called 'natural' sign language systems – i.e., those used by Indians of the Great Plains and surrounding regions, and by many Australian aborigines – is shamefully spotty (cf. Mallery, 1972; Sebeok and Umiker-Sebeok, forthcoming), to say nothing of monastic gestural systems (cf. e.g., van Rijnberk, 1953; Buyssens, 1956).

After these censures, I do apologize to Miss Davis for venting my spleen on her book and making it my scapegoat, especially since I regard her bibliography as the *best* of its kind. Later checklists (Key, 1974; Ciolek, 1975) are not nearly up to her standards of accuracy, and have an even woollier definition of their focal topic. (Labeling one's bibliography as 'provisional' is, to me, merely a cop-out.)

Umberto Eco has recently observed that "a bibliography of works which may be defined as 'semiotic' is still missing". Because of this felt need, he decided to allocate a good deal of space in his journal, *Versus*, to remedy this situation. Accordingly, last year, a double issue of it (Nos. 8/9) was wholly devoted to the publication of nineteen bibliographies, with eight others announced for issues to come soon. Some of these center on a country or region, say Poland or Scandinavia; others on a topic, say zoosemiotics; still others on works in a specific language, say Spanish; while some, of course, are a medley. "Although we are perfectly aware of the inevitable limits of this work," Eco remarks in his Foreword to the series, "we think in any case that this repertory may be considered as one of the most complete at present and we sincerely trust that it may be of some help to many scholars" (Nos. 8/9: 5). The quality of these bibliographies ranges from truly excellent to absolutely wretched, but even these are (I think) better than none, and I see no harm in bringing all of them to the attention of students who might find them serviceable, if used with caution. Accordingly, I list them in what follows, in appropriate categories (with fascicle numbers given if published in *Versus* No. 8/9):

Semiotic studies in Belgium (2), Brazil (3), Bulgaria, Canada (4), Czechoslovakia (5), France (parochially limited, 7), Germany, Great Britain (8), Greece, Hungary, Israel (10), Italy (with a supplementary section on the semiotics of the cinema, 11), Poland (12), Romania, Scandinavia (13), Soviet Union (15), Switzerland (14), United States (very restricted, but varied, 16). Semiotic studies in Spanish (6). "On the Meaning of the Built Environment" (English only, 9). Zoosemiotics (Sebeok, 1975b); semiotics of the theater; architectural semiotics (in Spanish).

Bibliographies tend to reflect their compilers' cultural myopia in subtle ways. Those dedicated to nonverbal communication (like most recent general monographic accounts of the subject, including, surprisingly enough, the few — like Scherer, 1970[7] — published abroad)

---

[7] Not, however, Strehle (1974), which appears to have made precisely the contrary assumption.

seem tacitly to assume that this is a strictly American game (or, sometimes, perhaps an Anglo-Saxon one, with Charles Darwin as its ritually cited godhead). Others suffer from a generation gap: they cannot see back beyond the early 1950s. Moreover, there is now a hazy but uneasy association of nonverbal communication studies with the clinical or social trend known as sensitivity training or encounter movements, and their off-shoots (Back, 1972), embarrassing skeletons seldom paraded by scientific researchers in public, though obtrusive enough in their bibliographic closets. If examined with care, each of the Eco-located country bibliographies displays national chauvinism to a degree, which may, indeed, be unavoidable at this stage. But I personally care little whether a piece on, say, architectural semiotics came out in Buenos Aires or London: what matters is how that fragment fits into the semiotic tapestry as a whole. Partial knowledge misleads us, as St. Paul (the great apostle to the Gentiles who was so preoccupied with perennial semiotic questions of code-switching) cautioned in one of his Epistles to the Corinthians, from incorrect assumptions to inaccurate conclusions: "For we know in part, and we prophesy in part" (I.xiii.9) – hence the dense tangle of the *web* as the controlling metaphor for the many logically interacting circumstances suggested in this paper.

5. CONFERRING ABOUT SEMIOTICS

As Stankiewicz has recently pointed out, the connection of poetics with semiotics was clearly formulated in 1929, in one of the *Theses* of the Linguistic Circle of Prague, which proclaimed that "Everything in the work of art and its relation to the outside world. . .can be discussed in terms of sign and meaning; in this sense aesthetics can be regarded as a part of the modern science of signs, of semiotics" (Stankiewicz, 1974: 630). In 1958, I organized a conference on verbal style my scholarly contribution to which considered 'the semiotic system' of a text in its interrelation with its phonic organization (Sebeok, 1960: 231), and where a main theme developed by Jakobson, in his epochal closing statement on "Linguistics and Poetics", stemmed from an observation that "many poetic features belong not only to the science of language but to the whole theory of signs, that is, to general semiotics" (*ibid.*, 351). This Bloomington meeting was doubtless the initial one in a series of get-togethers, nominally devoted more or less to the verbal arts, but distinctly tinged with a trace of already perceptible semiotic coloring. In the 1960s, such conferences rapidly expanded in two directions: they became international as to participants, and turned increasingly pansemiotic as to subject matter. Both extensions resulted directly from initiatives taken by Polish semioticians, the origins of whose lively interest in this area "are to be found in the intensive development of the Polish school of logic during the last fifty years. Following the Second World War Polish scholars displayed growing interest in problems common to the theory of literature and linguistics. This led to a series of international work-groups on poetics in Poland, which can also boast of having become a tradition . . . . The natural development of the disciplines mentioned. . .eventually leads to a discipline which would encompass all systems of signs and man, as their author and receiver, that is, to semiotics" (Greimas, *et al.*, 1970: vf.). The first "International Conference of Work-in-Progress devoted to Problems of Poetics" (*Poetics*. . .1961) was held in Warsaw in 1960, the second in 1961 (*id.*, 1966). These were followed by two successive meetings in Poland on semiotics at large, the first in 1965, the second held under the auspices of UNESCO, in the town of Kazimierz, in 1966 (Griemas, *et al.*, 1970; magisterially examined by Osolsobĕ, 1973a; cf. p. 24, above). Finally – and I use the word both advisedly and pessimistically – a third meeting was convened in Warsaw for 1968, "at which time an international political crisis prevented the holding of more than a rump session" (p. 24, above); nonetheless, most of the papers read or intended for presentation were, in due course, published in full, or at least in abstract (Rey-Debove, 1973). All those who care about the amazing progress and spread of semiotics during the previous decade – which, as is well known, culminated in the foundation, in Paris, on January 21, 1969, of the International Association for Semiotic Studies (IASS) – must become familiar with the bulky contents of the four aforementioned tomes of conference transactions, and be ever mindful of the historic efforts of our Polish confreres on behalf of the entire worldwide community of semioticians.

In another place (see pp. 21ff., above), I have described the pioneering U.S. interdisciplinary conference on semiotics that took place in Bloomington in the Spring of 1962 (the proceedings of which were later embodied in Sebeok, Bateson, and Hayes, 1972[2]). A rather differently styled North American Semiotics Colloquium was held in Tampa, July 28-30, 1975 (the proceedings of which will appear in the *Advances in Semiotics* series of the Indiana University Press, in 1977;

cf. Sebeok, 1977b). This Colloquium – the Honorary Chairman of which was Charles Morris – was particularly interesting because it was closely interlinked, in fact, formed an organic part of the 1975 Linguistic Institute of the Linguistic Society of America, co-sponsored by the entire State University System of Florida through the University of South Florida; (a wide selection of semiotics courses, for the first time ever, made up one of the main focus areas of the summer-long program of the Linguistic Institute, with a multinational visiting faculty and a large corps of students in attendance from many countries – see also 6.). Second, the dozen or so invited Colloquium speakers were deliberately chosen from among prominent semioticians resident in either Canada or the United States. One principal aim was to wind up with the foundation of a viable North American semiotics association of some sort, having several specific tasks and responsibilities, including eventual affiliation with the IASS.[8] Third, support for the Colloquium

[8] The Program of the Colloquium, held July 28-30, was as follows: Rulon Wells, Yale University, "Philosophy of Language and Semiotics"; J. Jay Zeman, University of Florida, "Peirce's Theory of Signs"; Henry Hiż, University of Pennsylvania, "Logical Basis of Semiotics"; Edward Stankiewicz, Yale University, "Semiotics and the Verbal Arts"; Harley C. Shands, The Roosevelt Hospital, "Clinical Semiotics"; Louis Marin, The Johns Hopkins University, "Semiotics and the Visual Arts"; Özséb Horányi, Hungarian Academy of Sciences, "Theoretical Possibilities for the Description of Pictures"; Diana Agrest, Princeton University, and Mario Gandelsonas, The Institute for Architecture and Urban Studies, "Semiotics and Architecture"; Jean-Jacques Nattiez, University of Montreal, "Semiotics and Music"; Paul Bouissac, University of Toronto, "Semiotics and Spectacles: The Circus"; Solomon Marcus, University of Bucharest, "Semiotics and Spectacles: Theatre"; Erik Schwimmer, University of Toronto, "Semiotics and Culture"; Thomas A. Sebeok, Indiana University, "Summation: Semiotics in Nature and in Culture". Also in attendance, and vigorously participating in the debates, were Thomas V. Gamkrelidze, of the U.S.S.R., and more than a dozen prominent semioticians from Poland (led by Jerzy Pelc), Czechoslovakia (Ivo Osolsobě), Hungary, Romania, and Yugoslavia.

At the concluding Business Meeting, two principal items were discussed by the assembled participants. The first of these resulted in the creation of a Semiotic Society of America. Three officers were provisionally elected: Henry Hiż, of the University of Pennsylvania, *President*; Eugen Bär, Hobart and William Smith Colleges, *Vice-President*; and Thomas A. Sebeok, Indiana University, *Secretary-Treasurer*. The aforementioned are collectively charged with responsibility for formally incorporating the new Society, and drafting its Constitution, which is to be ratified at the next meeting, when regular elections will also be held. It is intended that the Society will, in due course, affiliate with the International Association for Semiotic Studies.

The second item centered on the organization of semioticians in Canada. It

was provided, over and above the local sources, through the munficence of the American Council of Learned Societies as well as the International Research and Exchanges Board; the latter provided generously for the unprecedented added participation of scholars from centers of semiotic researches in Czechoslovakia, Hungary, Poland, Romania, the U.S.S.R., and Yugoslavia.

In the U.S.S.R., the first formal meeting on semiotics was held, in Moscow, in the Summer of 1962. The resulting book (*Simpozium* 1962) opens with a short paper by V. V. Ivanov, who defines the meaning and scope of semiotics in a most valuable way. The last of the world-renowned series of semiotic colloquia, held in Estonia, appears to have been the sixth (*Semeiotikè* 1975). Whether or not these creative seminars will be allowed to formally continue, their literary impact has already been massive (cf. p. 166, fn. 4, above), and the seeds carried abroad by a handful of young participants from the group have begun to germinate in foreign soil. Their exertions will not have been in vain, for the rich crops are beginning to be harvested in Western lands.

In 1967, the University of Urbino began a series of continuing Summer seminars which, through various excursions and alarums, and dramatic shifts in leadership, appear to have congealed into a functioning Centro Internazionale di Semiotica e di Linguistica (cf. Marcus, 1974). In part a Summer Session for students, in part a forum for established scholars convened to informally discuss diverse semiotic topics with one another in a modern university set in early Renaissance surroundings, Urbino has provided a rare site where representatives of workshops in Eastern Europe can freely mingle with those in Western Europe and the Americas, in a relaxed ambiance, Italian-style. Urbino has also launched, in 1971, a series of Working Papers and Prepublications, bewilderingly sectioned into six subseries (which can be safely disregarded); I have received 31 pamphlets so far, but the highest number reads C 46-47.

Several cities, like Paris and Toronto, have created disparate semiotic Circles (Jakobson, 1971a), or the like, meeting at irregular intervals, sometimes reported (e.g., *Semiotica* 4, 286-94; 7, 369-75), more often tacit. It is difficult enough to keep track of local happenings in places such as Bucharest (*Semiotica* 5, 301f.), Budapest (Hoppál, 1971, 1973),

---

was tentatively agreed that both sides would work, in the months ahead, towards an eventual bipartite North American Semiotics Federation, and that annual meetings may be alternately scheduled in Canada and the U.S.A. (The 1976 Annual Meeting will take place in Atlanta, Georgia, September 24-25.)

Buenos Aires (*Semiotica* 5, 297-300), or all of Czechoslovakia (Osolsobě, 1973b) and Poland (Pelc, 1974) in the absence of regularly published reports, but it is clear that semiotic associations of varying degrees of cohesion and continuity are multiplying even in such unexpected corners of the world as Sicily (the Circolo Semiologico Siciliano can boast of five monographs so far; cf. the fifth, Sparti, 1975), or Ribeirão Preto, a community in the State of São Paulo, which has set up a Centro de Estudos Semióticos A. J. Greimas (and which has published *Significação: Revista Brasileira de Semiótica* since August, 1974).

An exceptionally high number of conferences have been convened during the first half of our decade to debate particular semiotic topics of the most varied sort: on interaction ethology (Amsterdam, 1970 – see Sherzer, 1971), on pragmatics (Jerusalem, 1970 – see Staal, 1971), on the relation of semiotics to medicine and health problems (New York, 1970 – see Lewis, 1970), on the semiotics of the cinema (Oberlin, 1972 – see Koch, forthcoming), the First International Congress of Musical Semiotics (Belgrade, October 17-21, 1973 – see *Versus* 7, 101-04; the proceedings were published by the Centro di Iniziativa Culturale, in Pesaro), and a symposium on Peirce's concept of sign (Washington, 1975 – see *Peirce Newsletter*, April, 1975), to mention only a few, with many more scheduled to take place yet this year or, later on, during the second half of this decade. The most important among these will include several more Peirce-oriented events (Baltimore, 1975, and the First International Peirce Congress in Amsterdam, 1976, which will focus on Pragmatism and Semiotic – see 1. above, and *Peirce Newsletter*, April, 1975); a formative Semiotisches Colloquium convened by German practitioners (Berlin, 1975); an International Symposium on Semiotics and Theories of Symbolic Behavior in Eastern Europe and the West, to be held at Brown University (Providence, April, 1976); and three loosely intertwined successive symposia, still in the early planning stages, on, respectively, iconicity, indexical expressions, and the symbol.

By all accounts, the First Congress of the International Association for Semiotic Studies (Milan, June 2-6, 1974) "was a great success" (in the words of Nelson, 1975: 296, an inspired *aperçu* that should be read by two groups of semioticians – those who attended the Congress, and those who did not). Moreover, I think that, in historical perspective, the Congress will loom as the watershed of semiotics in its contemporary phase, the crucial event when the subject edged into the academic establishment. This is certainly not because of the answers provided by the motley assemblage of speakers and discussants (cf. Thomas, 1974: 185), but rather because of the cheerful atmosphere of self-criticism that prevailed and because so many of the right kinds of questions were insistently brought up, especially by the young people present. In short, semiotics is very much alive as it begins to emerge from its protracted infancy to find its rightful place among the law-seeking sciences of man; thus Saussure's oft-quoted prophetic utterance of some seventy years ago is about to be fulfilled: "Puisqu'elle n'existe pas encore, on ne peut dire ce qu'elle sera; mais elle a droit à l'existence, sa place est déterminée d'avance" (Saussure, 1972: 33).

6. TEACHING SEMIOTICS

Given, as Peirce once remarked, that "all this universe is perfused with signs, if it is not composed exclusively of signs" (5.448n), it should amaze no one that semiotics, or the doctrine of signs, is everywhere. Rather, what is surprising is that semiotics is nowhere — well, hardly anywhere at all — within the academy. For many, like Eco (1974: 16), "semiotics is a *scientific attitude*, a critical way of looking at the objects of other sciences", more a method than a discipline. Yet it was precisely Peirce who held the view that "The true and worthy idea of the science [of logic] was that it was the art of devising methods of research — the method of methods" (Fisch and Cope, 1952: 289), and who said, in a memorable public lecture at Johns Hopkins, in September, 1882: "This is the age of methods; and the university which is to be the exponent of the living condition of the human mind, must be the university of methods" (*ibid.*). The following year, Peirce's "contract was summarily terminated under obscure circumstances" (Macksey, 1970: 6), and he never held any other teaching post. Although he lectured extensively on implicitly semiotic topics after the Hopkins episode, I am reasonably certain that Morris' sporadic semiotic seminars of the early 1940s, to which I referred earlier (1., above), were, at least in this country's educational system, without any precedent.

During the thirty years or so after Morris, semiotics as such continued to flow beneath the surface of some of our most dis-tinguished campuses, erupting, geyser-like, only on the rarest of occasions, usually in response to irresistible student demand. To give a parochial example (only because I know it best): each of the last four visiting professorships I held – at the University of Colorado in 1969, at Stanford in 1971, and at the University of South Florida in 1972 and 1975 – required me to offer an introductory course on semiotics, as I have done, for the past few years, in the Honors Division on my home grounds. At several of our major universities, faculty groups joining forces in all sorts of combinations have tried to mount programs of varying ambition, design, level of funding, and, of course, different degrees of success. Thus Columbia announced the formation of "a theoretical group exploring alternatives in semiotics" (*Semiotext(e)* 1974: 1, 2), while an informal faculty committee from Berkeley asked to consult with me in San Francisco, in the Spring of 1972, about ways and means of developing semiotics in their branch of the University of California. In the meantime, chairs with a semiotics label attached were set up in such far-flung centers of learning as Bologna, Canberra, and Montreal. So far as I have been able to determine, however, Brown University can lay claim to pride of place, at least in the United States,[9] for having established a "semiotics concentration", or program for undergraduates, confidently expected in Providence to "become as central to modern humanistic education" as rhetoric was when it was added to curricula half a millennium ago; (cf. "Brown University Concentration in Semiotics", distributed by its English Department in April, 1975). It is heartening to note that although, because of financial exigencies, Brown is at present contemplating the elimination of as many as 75 of its 460 non-medical faculty positions over the next three years, the allure to students has been so intense that "What expansion takes place will occur in semiotics" (Scully, 1975: 11).

Motivated by my conviction that the most exciting developments in linguistics are bound to happen, in the years immediately ahead, at the periphery of its more traditional concerns – in neurolinguistics at the one extreme, and in 'pragmatics', or, to be a shade more precise, in respect to the "deictic anchorage of utterances" (Rommetveit, 1968: 185; Fillmore, 1973) at the other – I goaded the director of the 1975 Linguistic Institute to concentrate heavily on selected topics in just such zones (among others), and, for the first time in the history of this venerable enterprise, an array of explicitly labelled semiotic courses

---

[9] Tomás Maldonado had a carefully worked out semiotics program as part of the teaching curriculum at the Hochschule für Gestaltung, in Ulm, back in 1958, as evidenced by its teaching prospectus; (see also Maldonado, 1959).

was actually being offered not only of an introductory character, but also in such specialized fields as 'kinesics', the semiotics of the cinema, the semiotics of the performing arts and of the verbal arts, and examining the relationship prevailing between linguistics and semiotics in the last century and this. These studies were greatly enhanced by the visitors who graced the Colloquium mentioned under 5., above.

A singularly propitious development, laden with promise for a bright future of semiotics in American university life, may be assumed to eventuate from an imaginative grant the National Endowment for the Humanities recently made to Indiana University for a "Pilot Program in Semiotics in the Humanities", beginning in the Fall of 1975. This project was designed to inaugurate the teaching and facilitate the integration of semiotics into our curriculum. By mid-1976, in the light of extensive consultations with more than a dozen visiting scholars of eminence, our faculty and student community should be ready to present a solid, coherent program meeting the standards of both the federal Endowment and our University administration, tending to assure a steady course of reasonable systemic growth well into the 1980s. The fit of this Program with the Peirce project on our sister-campus in Indianapolis (1.) is exceptionally felicitous too.[10]

The image of the modern semiotic universe has, until lately, suffered from excessive fragmentation, much as the world of astronomy must have appeared to John Donne when he wrote, in 1611, " 'Tis all in pieces, all coherence gone;/All just supply, and all Relation." Many semiotic instruments have lately been heard, but most were being played separately rather than in harmony. The aim of our Program, and other efforts like it, is to make the experience whole again for the generations to follow, and to restore for them, as it were, its orchestral unity through the arts of teaching.

So much, for the time being, about the teaching *of* semiotics. But what about semiotics *in* teaching?[11] Let me momentarily dwell on an expression Morris introduced under the name of 'applied semiotic', that

---

[10] The unfolding of semiotics at Indiana University was, through 1975, recorded in a monthly *Newsletter*, copies of which are obtainable by writing to the Research Center for Language and Semiotic Studies, P.O. Box 1214, Bloomington, Indiana 47401. This has now been superseded by *The Semiotic Scene*, a bimonthly informatory publication of the Semiotic Society of America, edited by Margot D. Lenhart.

[11] For a glimpse of a Soviet view, advocating a semiotic approach to optimize the teaching process, "especially essential in programmed learning", see Kull (1965).

subdivision of the totality he defined as the one which "utilizes knowledge about signs for the accomplishment of various purposes" (Morris, 1971: 303, 366). One striking area of application, that may be cited from the field of bionics, consists of attempts to transfer the principles governing echolocation in, say, bats (radar) or marine mammals (sonar) — a solipsistic use of sign behavior — to the design of guidance devices for the benefit of blind humans (Rice, 1967; for further zoosemiotic illustrations, cf. Sebeok, 1972: 132f.). I have always favored Morris' understanding of this term, for I found it convenient; but I recognize that, for some other scholars, it carries quite different (and mutually inconsistent) connotations, as I have pointed out above (cf. pp. 32ff.). However, a fairly common usage confines applied semiotics strictly within the area of pedagogy, appearing to mean something like the teaching of, for instance, gSigns (see 2., above) to hearing persons who teach or otherwise serve the deaf (Oléron, 1974), to chimpanzees (Gardner and Gardner, 1971: 127-44), or to 'normal' humans, enabling such members of our species to acquire a range of social skills for role-playing (e.g., by the method proposed by Stanislavsky for budding actors), sensitivity training, behavior therapy, or the like (Argyle, 1969: x), and to supplement second-language acquisition in the classroom.

The foregoing suggests a few further observations. First, there is a rapidly accumulating literature (ultimately instigated by Darwin) dealing with the ontogeny of nonverbally coded motor signs in humans (Latif, 1934; Brannigan and Humphries, 1972; Blurton Jones in Hinde, 1972: 271-96), notably of facial expressions in infants and children (Charlesworth and Kreutzer, 1973), including tongue showing (Smith, et al., 1974: 222-27), all best studied as a part of the closely allied science of human ethology (McGrew, 1972: 14-16; Eibl-Eibesfeldt, 1970: Ch. 18). Second, and in sharp contrast, the literature dealing with the acquisition of further, that is, culturally alien, codes is very thin indeed. The question then boils down to this: if, as is the case, we lavish incalculable amounts of energy, time, and money to instill in children and adults a range of foreign language competencies, why are the indissolubly parallel foreign gesticulatory skills all but universally neglected, especially considering that even linguists are fully aware that what has been called the total communication package, "best likened to a coaxial cable carrying many messages at the same time" (Smith, 1969: 101), is hardly an exaggerated simile? Oddly, some of the teachers of the Western Romance languages, particularly of French

or Spanish, appear to have best appreciated the necessity for introducing "the gestures of the speakers of the target language along with
the linguistic patterns being taught" (Saitz, 1966: 33), and a modest
but not uninteresting flurry of suggestive books and articles has sprung
up here and there. (For French, cf. e.g., Brault, 1962, and, in a more
popular vein, Alsop, 1960; for Iberian Spanish, Green, 1968; for
Colombian, Saitz and Cervenka, 1972, where further references are
given. As a matter of fact, informal training in foreign gesticulations
sometimes reinforces language drills in some U.S. government programs,
for instance, of the Peace Corps; cf. Schnapper, 1969.)

Now one of the more fashionable methodologies currently pursued
by language teachers here (Alatis, 1968) and abroad (Nickel, 1971) goes
by the name of contrastive analysis, meaning the study of correspond-
ences, or the lack of them, between paired source and target languages,
mainly with a view to the effective teaching of the latter. What I should
like to urge here is that comparative studies throughout the rest of the
semiotic domain be immediately intensified, following Efron's (1972)
elegant contrastive analysis of tendencies in the gestural behavior of
several groups of Eastern Jews and Southern Italians, and expanded on
the model of Ekman's (1971) definitive work on universals and cultural
differences in facial expressions of emotion. The results of such
scholarly researches, effectively constituting a dialect-atlas of nonverbal
semiotic behavior, or another latticed pattern, should, then, as rapidly
as possible, be assimilated by foreign-language teachers and those
concerned with instruction in cross-cultural and cross-ethnic matters
(e.g., Taylor and Ferguson, 1975). I timidly venture to suggest that the
beginnings of a scarcely digested data-base may already exist for the
Southern and Western Romance populations, where the scrutiny of
motor signs seems for some time past to have been accepted as an
avocation (e.g., for Italian, see Cocchiara, 1932; for Portuguese, Basto,
1938; for Spanish, Poyatos, 1970, *inter alia*).

Six years back, I answered the question posed by myself, "Is a
comparative semiotics possible?" (see Ch. 3, above), in the affirmative,
and now I would like to go on to advocate that its pedagogical
consequences be also faced up to and opened to inquiry. I do so in full
awareness that applied semiotics lacks glamor, and even respectability
in certain quarters more partial to theory and/or description, a view
which I can but ruefully counter with a remark attributed to the famed
mathematician Richard Courant: "Pure mathematics is a small and not
very significant part of applied mathematics."

7. THE SEMIOTIC TRIPOD

In our semiotic Pantheon, the name of Saussure stands engraved as the emblem for the linguistic affinities and extensions of the hierarchically superordinate field, while that of Peirce, "the heir of the whole historical philosophical analysis of signs" (Morris, 1971: 337), and now manifestly the benchmark for all contemporary deliberations, epitomizes its manifold filiation with the profoundest strata of human wisdom. The third, admittedly uneven leg upon which semiotics rests, very likely the most deeply rooted, is medicine, the revered ancestral figure surely being Hippocrates (c. 460 - c. 377 B.C.,), "der Vater und Meister aller Semiotik" (Kleinpaul, 1972: 103). These three fundamental semiotic traditions – the medical, the philosophical, and the linguistic – have, of course, thoroughly intermingled at various points in Western intellectual history, although at other times they have striven for autonomy. For instance, Sextus Empiricus, the most prominent of the Skeptics, was, like Locke, a physician by profession (Stough, 1969: 11-15), with a decided interest in the theory of signs (Ogden and Richards, 1938: 266-68). But while the philosophical and linguistic strands are appreciated, more or less widely, I have found that the distinctive contributions of medical semiotics – or, to reinforce Shands' and Meltzer's apt coinage, 'clinical semiotics' (1975) – are seldom understood. Medical inquiry revolves around one particular subclass of signs called 'symptoms' (and their stable, rule-governed configurations, 'syndromes'), which are, in turn, often considered a species of a more basic grouping, 'indexes' (as shrewdly observed by Bühler, 1965: 28). It is a peculiarity of symptoms that their denotata are generally different for the addresser, viz.,· the patient ('subjective symptoms', confusingly called by many American medical practitioners 'signs') and the addressee, viz., the examining physician ('objective symptoms', or simply 'symptoms') (see further Section 2, pp. 124ff. above).[12] Symptomatology, also known as 'semeiology', or the like, in many Western languages (cf. Ch. 2, above), eventually developed into a branch of medicine foreseen and durably delineated by Galen (130-c. 200), who taught that semiotics – being one of the six principal branches of medicine – is to be divided into three parts, "in praeteri-

---

[12] This distinction between 'signs' and 'symptoms' in American medical practice was called to my attention by William O. Umiker, M.D. A Conference on "Sign and Symptom from the Clinical and Semiotic Viewpoints" is currently being planned.

tum cognitionem, in praesentium inspectionem et futurorum providentiam" (Galenus, 1965: 690), meaning that its threefold preoccupation
must be with diagnostics, focusing on the here and now, and its twin
temporal projections into the anamnestic past (i.e., case history) and
the prognostic future. Fifty years after Crookshank's neglected essay
(1923), a reasoned rapprochement between the general theory of signs
on the one hand, and medical theory and clinical praxis on the other, is
again in progress, stimulated in no small part by the pioneer works of
Michel Foucault (Barthes, 1972: 38), by such attempts as those of
Barthes himself (*ibid*.), and, in an entirely different vein, of Celan and
Marcus (1973). Conferences like the one reported by Lewis (1970), and
more specialized ones being actively planned (e.g., on specifically
psychiatric-psychotherapeutic aspects of clinical semiotics), will doubtless speed up the process of reconvergence given a decisive turn at the
Bloomington semiotic conference of 1962 (pp. 21f., above), where we
all profited immensely from the insights of the ten participating physicians, and where a not inconsiderable portion of the discussions was
devoted to the vital problem, "How the patient communicates about
disease with the doctor" (Sebeok, Bateson, and Hayes, 1972: 11-49;
Blum, 1972; Ostwald, 1973: 236-59). Physicians are also publishing
more and more through semiotic outlets: in the *Approaches to
Semiotics* series alone, four books have appeared by three M.D.'s
(Ostwald, 1973; Ruesch, 1972; Shands, 1970b, 1971; see also Bär,
1975, a volume which inaugurates the *Studies in Semiotics* series,
partially replacing the former).

The metaphor of the tripod is, I think, historically justified, and has
the right sorts of connotations for me personally — with a surveyor's
level, or transit, as well as with a kind of examination, Cambridge-
style — but it does become a bit awkward if pushed too far. For one
thing, I did observe that these three semiotic traditions have interwoven
in various ways and at various times, which does conjure up the
ungainly figure of a three-legged stand with rubbery legs of unequal
length. To take only one recent example of such blending, "Montague's
semiotic program" (as the editor of his posthumous papers has dubbed
it, 1974: 1ff.) illustrates how one man's framework for the study of a
natural language has brought metamathematical tools to bear on the
analysis, consisting of logical elements which "are natural developments
of standard logical theories", compounded with linguistic elements
(independent though they may be of current grammatical theories).
When one reflects further on the explosion of the 1960s, and the ways

in which semiotic theory, practice, and methods have pervaded a broad spectrum of late 20th century thought, ranging from architecture to zoology, the image does take on science-fiction attributes, with (for some of my conservative colleagues) menacing pseudopodial protrusions. It would be a salutary and informative exercise to assess, field by established field, the successes and failures of these intrusions. One wants to know, among other things, why semiotics has achieved great successes in application, for instance, to the cinematic crafts (cf. Bettetini, 1973; Lotman, 1973; Metz, 1974; Worth, 1969), whereas its impact on the art of dancing has, as far as I can judge, made only modest headway (Ikegami, 1971); or why its insidious encroachments on the study of culture have been far more robust (as mentioned before) than on descriptions of the conduct of international relations (Jervis, 1970); and so forth. An inquiry of this scope would clearly be out of place here, but I would like to inspect cursorily just two lines of lateral development, the first because it hints at what may be feasible, the second for the opposite reason, because it is an already flourishing enterprise.

In 1970, a Polish legal scholar (Studnicki, 1970; cf. Droste, 1972) published a remarkable paper, far-reaching in its implications, consisting of a sophisticated analysis, from a strictly semiotic point of view, of 'traffic signs', namely, that subclass of visual signs which are used in the regulation and control of traffic on public roads (danger signs, mandatory signs, prohibitory signs, information signs). What the author did not treat, nor, I believe, returned to elsewhere, was a detailed analysis of the prescriptions which form the legal basis of the system under consideration, the totality of which he succinctly referred to "under the name of 'Law'" (*ibid.*, 151). The Law standardizes the sign-types utilized in the system and its text includes a list of the corresponding patterns. The semantic rules contained in the text of the Law assign to each of the signs in the system "a definite utterance of the ethnic language", to wit, "the natural translations" of the appropriate signs (*ibid.*, 161). Studnicki's approach is relevant for a theory of normative languages in general, and thus opens up exciting new avenues for investigation. A 'legal semiotics' can be envisaged in outline: if the Law is regarded as a system of signs, the mechanisms of which are concretely institutionalized, difficult problems appear in a new light, for example, the age-old question of drawing an analytical boundary between the legal system and the environment in which it lies embedded, or how social norms, unspecific as these tend to be, nonetheless provide authoritative guides to conduct. Since the peculiar province of law seems to be juridical interpretation, the possibilities for a semiotic research strategy are boundless, but hitherto barely tested.

If legal semiotics is as yet hardly more than a gleam in someone's eye, musical semiotics has progressed, in the 1970s, far beyond the programmatic declarations and early attempts collected by Nattiez (*Musique en jeu* 1971; cf. the interesting review article by Osmond-Smith, 1974), and advanced by him in a notable lecture he delivered in the Indiana University School of Music the following year (Nattiez, 1972). Harking back directly to the work of Ruwet (1972), a scholar equally adept in linguistics and musicology, who has set forth an explicitly reproducible procedure allowing for the delimitation and definition of musical units, and to his conception of such units according to a hierarchic principle, Nattiez has pushed forward on several fronts: he continues as a vigorous anthologist of musical semiotics (*Musique en jeu* 1973; the first special thematic issue of *Semiotica*, in Vol. 15, No. 1 [forthcoming], entirely devoted to music, was likewise assembled by him), a foremost contributor to his chosen field (Nattiez, 1975), and a dedicated teacher who has promoted the University of Montreal into a mecca for students wishing to specialize in intricate questions of musical semiosis. This difficult domain of semiotics, marked by the absence, or very much diminished presence, of the referential function, has spread and matured sufficiently to have merited an international congress in 1973 (5.), and book-length publications are multiplying (e.g., Pagnini, 1974) whereas a handful of articles contained the sum total of knowledge only a few years ago.

As Morris has insisted, esthetics "becomes in its entirety a subdivision of semiotic", and the approach to it in terms of the theory of signs "is thus not merely significant for art, esthetics, and semiotic, but for the whole program of unified science" (Morris, 1971: 416, 433). Understanding the esthetic function of sign systems as displayed in the several arts, verbal and pictorial, two- and three-dimensional, pantomimic and choreographic, introversive and extroversive, and ranging in appeal from mass culture, like the comic strip, to more elitist strata, like the opera, thus becomes an essential concern and preoccupation of modern semiotics and in the human context beyond, with a vast, accreting, specialized literature. The dramatic forward thrust of musical semiotics is paralleled across the board, to be sure with variations in speed, intensity, and individual initiative, but the arachnoid semiotic movement envelops the totality of esthetic discourse, as Morris foresaw when he married axiology, or the study of preferential behavior, to the inherently interdisciplinary semiotic enterprise.

8. APPENDIX: NOTES TOWARD A CHECKLIST OF SERIAL
    PUBLICATIONS

Semiotica – the official organ of the IASS – will have published, from 1969 to the end of 1975, approximately 6,000 pages, distributed over 15 volumes of four fascicles each. *Semiotica* strives to maintain a reasonable balance among the various semiotic domains, and, at the same time, contributions of quality received from scholars who labor in different countries. The journal, now a monthly, routinely accepts articles in either French or English, sporadically also in German. The cardinal conception underlying the editorial policy of *Semiotica* is to provide a link between all the creative workshops of the world, as well as to be a forum for the most diverse scientific approaches to the doctrine of signs. Its founding editor likes to think of *Semiotica* as a sort of clearing-house for novel and stimulating ideas, and as the focal point in an international multidisciplinary network, or, in a word, web. A uniform, comprehensive set of indexes, especially of subjects, for all the volumes published so far, plus perhaps a glossary of technical terms used throughout, are a priority desideratum.[13]

There exists, of course, a multitude of outlets which have printed articles, or may do so in the future, concerned either directly or tangentially with semiotic topics. The mere listing of linguistic periodicals takes up 27 pages in the latest UNESCO bibliography (for the year 1972, published in 1975), to say nothing of those servicing philosophy, the verbal arts, and other specialized domains, including even theology (thus *Linguistica Biblica*, edited in Bonn, carries an ever increasing number of explicitly labeled semiotic pieces). I will, of necessity, mainly confine myself, in the list that follows, to the mere handful of periodicals which explicitly identify themselves with semiotics or are otherwise obviously relevant:

[13] Members of the Editorial Committee of *Semiotica* are Claude Bremond (France), Umberto Eco (Italy), Henry Hiż (U.S.A.), Julia Kristeva (France), Juri M. Lotman (U.S.S.R.), Jerzy Pelc (Poland), Nicolas Ruwet (France), Meyer Schapiro (U.S.A.), and Hansjakob Seiler (Germany, DBR); Roland Barthes (France) was a member from 1969 to 1974.

Cahiers internationaux de symbolisme, produced in Belgium; 26 issues have appeared through 1974.

Degrés: Revue de synthèse à orientation sémiologique, also produced in Belgium; six issues have appeared through 1974.

Le Journal Canadien de Recherche Sémiotique/The Canadian Journal of Research in Semiotics, produced in Edmonton; two volumes have appeared so far.

Semiosis: Zeitschrift für Semiotik und ihre Anwendungen, produced in the German Federal Republic; one issue appeared so far, in 1976, but announced as a quarterly.

Studia Semiotyczne, a publication of the Polish Semiotic Society, each issue of which is accompanied by a separate pamphlet, *Semiotic Studies*, containing English summaries of the Polish articles. I have seen four numbers, the latest dated 1973.

Versus: Quaderni di studi semiotici, produced in Italy; nine numbers have appeared through 1974.

It is very difficult to keep track of fugitive 'special issues' on semiotic topics which this or that journal features, because these are often improvisations directed at a particular segment of the total semiotic readership. An early case in point is *Sprache im Technischen Zeitalter*, a well-known German periodical, which unexpectedly blossomed forth with an issue (No. 27, 1968) entirely devoted to film semiotics: "Zeichensystem Film/Versuche zu einer Semiotik". Five years later, *Screen* came out with a 'special double issue' (Vol. 14, Nos. 1-2, 1973) on "Cinema Semiotics and the Work of Christian Metz". One could enumerate a host of similar epiphanies in architecture (e.g., *Sémiotique des plans en architecture* and *Sémiotique de l'espace*, both published in Paris, 1973, by the so-called Groupe 107), literature (*Helikon*, Vol. 19, Nos. 2-3, 1973), music (see 7., above, re *Musique en jeu* 1971, 1973), the visual arts (esp. *Communications* No. 15, 1970; cf. *idem*, No. 4, n.d.), ideology, as in the issue devoted to "Sémiologie et sociétés" of *Sociologie et société* (Vol. 5, No. 2, 1973), etc. Furthermore, a journal may simply present its readers with a bouquet of semiotic miscellanea in a random number (as in *Vozes*, Vol. 68, No. 8, 1974, on "Semiotica & semiologia").

An event of quite exceptional importance for the welfare of the field occurred in 1973, when the editor of *The Times Literary Supplement* commissioned nine articles on assigned semiotic topics, which then appeared in two successive special issues, together entitled "The Tell-Tale Sign: A Survey of Semiotics" (Nos. 3,735-3,736), of the *TLS*.

The timing (Oct. 5 and 12, 1973) was deliberately set on the occasion of the 25th Frankfurt Book Fair, where this conspectus of semiotics received maximum exposure and was, by all accounts, accorded an uncommonly warm reception by a wide circle beyond the specialized public. Most of the essays, revised and with materials added, were later included, and are now conveniently available, in a book (Sebeok, 1975a).

At the Milano Congress (5., above), some of the journal editors met to discuss ways and means of facilitating communication. One decision taken that Summer was to start a *Bulletin of Literary Semiotics*, an international newsletter designed to keep track of recent and forthcoming publications, to announce forthcoming conferences and the like, and to keep its readers informed of work in progress. The first issue, edited by Daniel Laferrière, appeared in May of 1975. Several other newsletters, rather informal in appearance and coverage, more or less regularly service those interested in aspects of nonverbal communication (the 12th number in four years of "Nonverbal Components of Communication, Paralanguage, Kinesics, Proxemics" came out in May, 1975), including zoosemiotics (viz., 'human ethology' – see the *Human Ethology Newsletter*, the 9th number of which appeared in May, 1975). Others are regional in orientation, as the *Szemiotikai Tájékoztató* of the Hungarian Academy of Sciences (No. 1, 1975), announced to appear six times a year, to be exclusively devoted to semiotic activities in Hungary.

As for serials designed to accommodate booklength contributions to the theory of signs – monographs, including reprints of classics in the field, translations of important foreign-language books into some other tongue, collections of articles by a single author or on some unified theme, and pertinent conference proceedings – the following can be singled out.

Approaches to Semiotics: Since 1969, about fifty volumes have been published in this series (in The Netherlands), many of them listed among the references in this book. In addition, two new series have now appeared, both under the auspices of Indiana University – *Advances in Semiotics* (Eco, 1976; Bouissac, 1976), and *Studies in Semiotics* (Bär, 1975; Jakobson, 1975; Wallis, 1975; Fiordo, 1976).

The French house Mame has published six books, since 1972, in a collection with the over-all title, *Univers Sémiotiques*. In Italy, Bompiani has a series, *Il campo semiotico*, with four books out so far; Feltrinelli has another series, *Semiotica e Pratica Sociale*, with one book published in 1975. In *Studies in African Semiotics* (edited by S.O. Anozie), a series "presenting contemporary interpretations and evaluations of language and communication in Africa", there are two anthologies and one monograph available as of 1975, and a Semiotic Association of Africa, "to be formally inaugurated in the near future", has just been proclaimed. Rumors of still other series, soon to be activated in at least three West European countries, are currently being bruited about, but concrete information about these is lacking.

11

Drum and Whistle Systems*

> *Of very great interest and importance is the possibility of transferring the whole system of speech symbolism into other terms than those that are involved in the typical process . . . a transfer, direct or indirect, from the typical symbolism of language as spoken and heard. . . . The ease with which speech symbolism can be transferred from one sense to another, from technique to technique, itself indicates that the mere sounds of speech are not the essential fact of language, which lies rather in the classification, in the formal patterning, and in the relating of concepts (Sapir, 1921: 19-21).*

1. THE SEMIOTIC NATURE OF DRUM AND WHISTLE SURROGATES

In his terse and penetrating remarks on the varieties of surrogate systems, which he defines as "un sème dont la signification est constituée par le signifiant d'une autre sémie", Buyssens (1967: 45) correctly warns against confusing semiotic systems which are independent of but translatable into natural language with truly substitutive systems, such as the drum and whistle surrogates dealt with in Sebeok and Umiker-Sebeok (1976), which are dependent on spoken language to such an extent that persons wishing to use them must share a common base language if they are to make themselves understood.

* This article, written in collaboration with Donna Jean Umiker-Sebeok, is reprinted, with minor alterations, from Sebeok and Umiker-Sebeok, 1976, pp. xiii-xxiv.

Il faut se garder d'inclure parmi les sémies substitutives toute sémie qui n'est pas discours, sous prétexte qu'on peut traduire en discours tout sème non linguistique. Les symboles graphiques des mathématiciens, des logiciens, des chimistes ne représentent pas des unités linguistiques: si l'on trouvait dans la rue un papier sur lequel une main inconnue aurait tracé de tels signes, il serait impossible de découvrir quelle est la langue maternelle de leur auteur, et pourtant la signification serait claire . . . Certes, nous nous servons du discours pour enseigner les autres sémies: un texte légal fait connaître la signification de chaque panneau de signalisation routière; mais il ne serait pas difficile d'apprendre ces sémies par la méthode qui nous a servi à apprendre notre langue maternelle (Buyssens, 1967: 48).

True substitutive systems instigate a particular process of what Jakobson (1971b: 261) calls *transmutation*, or intersemiotic (as opposed to intra- or interlingual) translation, which is the "interpretation of verbal signs by means of signs of nonverbal sign systems". There may be nonverbal sign systems (such as the sign languages of the deaf or those of the native peoples of North America and Australia) which are dependent on the same basic type of semiotic patterning ability which underlies human speech, but this semiotic competence is put to use directly in the signs produced by such systems; the decoding of messages is direct rather than through linguistic symbolism.

The isolation of actual cases of substitution from instances of translation between independent semiotic systems is made difficult by the proclivity of the human mind to constantly establish equivalences between the signs which it encounters, whether these signs are verbal or nonverbal, from the same or different systems. This psychological interdependency is so pervasive, in fact, that it becomes almost impossible, except in the very broadest terms, to clearly distinguish 'dependent' from 'independent' codes. The goal eventually becomes one of establishing degrees and types of dependency between semiotic systems (e.g., see Buyssen's discussion of Chinese writing, 1967: 46-47). One may even go so far as to say, as does Steiner in his recent, masterful study of translation (1975), that any act of interpretation is an act of 'translation'. In this view, translation takes on a significant biological value, becoming central to the survival of the individual and the species.

The life of the individual and of the species depends on the rapid and/or accurate reading and interpretation of a web of vital information. There is a vocabulary, a grammar, possibly a semantic of colours, sounds, odours, textures, and gestures as multiple as that of language, and there may be dilemmas of decipherment and translation as resistant as any we have met. Though it is polysemic, speech cannot identify, let alone paraphrase, even a fraction of the sensory data which man . . . can . . . register (Steiner, 1975: 415).

The number and type of truly substitutive transmutations devised by the human mind is itself staggering, and is complicated by the fact that substitutive systems have been created for nonverbal as well as verbal semiotic systems, with language itself occasionally serving as a surrogate.

Le discours n'est pas le seule sémie directe à avoir donné naissance à des sémies substitutives. On représente graphiquement les sonneries de clairon ou celles des cloches; ces graphies ont pour signifiés les signifiants des sonneries. Si, en voyant écrit 3/5, on dit *trois cinquièmes* ou *trois divisé par cinq*, on nomme successivement chacun des signes, et ce que l'on dit n'a de sens que si l'on se réfère à la formule mathématique car en français, *trois sur cinq* signifie *trois individus parmi un groupe de cinq* (Buyssens, 1967: 48).

The transfer systems dealt with in Sebeok and Umiker-Sebeok, 1976, may be characterized by the fact that they are *first-order* (Jakobson, 1974: 29) as opposed to second-order systems. In this respect, drum and whistle surrogates are similar to many (but not all) forms of writing, for in both the surrogate sign serves as the *signans*, the sign of natural language the *signatum*. In contrast to these 'direct' systems, the *signans* of a second-order, or 'indirect' surrogate, has for its *signatum* the *signans* of a first-order system. The dots and dashes of the Morse Code, for instance, have for their *signata* the letters of the alphabet. In drum and whistle systems, signs stand for signs; second-order surrogate signs stand for signs of signs. There are cases reported in Sebeok and Umiker-Sebeok (1976) of drum systems themselves being represented by a second-order system in which the tones of the drums are imitated (by humming or whistling) rather than the sounds of the spoken language; (see the discussion of such 'secret codes' in the articles by Meinhof and Nekes).

In addition to being first-order systems, the speech surrogates represented in the articles gathered together in Sebeok and Umiker-Sebeok (1976) are characterized by the fact that they all make use of the acoustic channel and therefore do not involve a transfer of speech symbolism from one sense to another, as in visual surrogates, such as some forms of writing, where the auditory *signans* of a spoken language is transferred into the *signatum* of a visual *signans*. Drum and whistle systems involve a different sort of transmutation – namely, from what Sapir refers to as one 'technique' to another. Linguistic signs become the *significata* of sign vehicles made up of the sounds produced not by the usual speech articulations but (1) with various instruments (we use the term 'drum' surrogates only as an abbreviated way of referring to instrumental systems in general), (2) the mouth (usually with the aid of one or more fingers) in a simple whistle, or (3) the mouth forming a whistle in combination with speech articulations.

Like any semiotic system, drum and whistle surrogates have access to the three basic types of signifying relationships first systematically explored by Charles S. Peirce.[1] Burks (1949: 674) has succinctly restated Peirce's early tripartite classification of signs as follows:

A sign represents its object to its interpretant symbolically, indexically, or iconically according to whether it does so (1) by being associated with its object by a conventional rule . . . (as in the case of [the English word] 'red'); (2) by being in existential relation with its object (as in the case of the act of pointing); or (3) by exhibiting its object (as in the case of the diagram).

Using another set of terms commonly found in the literature on the classification of signs, the semiotic principle which informs the icon is similarity, the index contiguity, and the symbol (Peirce's own term) 'imputed character'.

Because they employ the same channel of communication as the semiotic system which they represent, there is a tendency for drum and whistle systems to be highly iconic. Drum and whistle signs often physically resemble their spoken *signata*, and rely heavily on this iconic

---

[1] For our purposes in this introductory article, we prefer to make reference to only the most fundamental of Peirce's classification of signs. Those interested in the complex refinements of his original tripartite division of signs should consult Peirce, 1965-66, especially Vol. 2, Bk. 2, Ch. 2, pp. 134-55 ("Division of Signs"). Sebeok has combined the Peircian semiotic framework with a communication model in a detailed description of the six most common species of signs in Ch. 8 of this book.

relationship for their meaning. The drum and whistle systems which signify primarily in consequence of their physical resemblance to spoken language have been called 'abridgment' systems by Stern (in Sebeok and Umiker-Sebeok, 1976: 124-148). As will be clear from a reading of the papers included in that book, each drum and whistle system differs somewhat in the precise number and combination of verbal elements (tone, loudness, rhythm, etc.) which they reproduce. Each abridges the flow of speech in a slightly different manner, but the semiotic principle of iconicity pertains to each such abridgment.

The process of abridgment frequently results in the creation of homophonous surrogate signs from non-homophonous lexical items of the base language (e.g., two words with identical tone patterns will become homophonous when transferred into a drum system which relies on the reproduction of tone levels but not other features by which the units are distinguished in speech). In order to avoid homophonic clashes, a technique of enphrasing is employed, where the individual lexical unit is replaced by or embedded in a phrase, much as synonyms are used to replace homonymic or near-homonymic pairs or pair parts in spoken language (see Ullmann, 1951: 144-46, and, following him, Coates, 1968: 473-74). Carrington (in Sebeok and Umiker-Sebeok, 1976: Part II) gives the example of the Kele *songe* 'moon' and *kɔkɔ* 'fowl', which would be homophonous when drummed, being replaced, respectively, by 'the moon looks down at the earth' and 'the fowl, the little one which says *kiokio*'. Alexandre (in Sebeok and Umiker-Sebeok, 1976: 816-824) reports the substitution of the phrase 'tribe without penises' for the Bulu word for 'women'.

The drum and whistle substitute phrases are, of course, iconic in relation to the spoken units they directly represent (the words of the phrase). They are probably not iconic with respect to the word which they stand for as a whole, at least on the phonetic level, but frequently are iconic on the semantic level. In recognition of this, Alexandre suggests that substitutive systems such as drum and whistle surrogates can be classified according to their 'distance' from ordinary speech, that is, according to the amount of iconicity they reflect and at what structural levels. Some surrogates, for example, reproduce a large proportion of verbal elements (such as the whistle talk of La Gomero, which is actually a whistle superimposed on articulated speech, or even, as Stern has suggested in a personal communication, any whispered speech), so that their distance from the spoken language which they represent would not be great. Farther from their base language would be those surrogates which represent a smaller number of verbal characteristics on the phonetic level, but with iconicity on the semantic level in an attempt to assure intelligibility (e.g., in many of the drum systems based on tone languages). Even farther from the base language are those substitutive systems where only a very restricted number of speech units are produced (as in Alexandre's examples of certain *jeux de langage*).

In his discussion of the metaphoric (iconic) and metonymic (indexical) aspects of language, Jakobson (1971b: 255) points out that "... either of these two relations (similarity and contiguity) can appear – and each in either of two aspects [positional and semantic]". Using the examples given by Jakobson (pp. 254-55) of word association tests, a response to the stimulus word *hut* such as *burnt out* provides a case of 'positional contiguity', *is a poor house* one of positional (syntactic) contiguity plus 'semantic similarity', *cabin* or *hovel* one of 'positional similarity' as well as semantic similarity, and *thatch* one of positional similarity with 'semantic contiguity'. So far we have discussed the iconic relation with respect to one of the aspects mentioned by Jakobson – the semantic – and to one aspect which he does not mention – the phonetic. Drum and whistle systems also take advantage of the metaphoric relation on the positional level, as when archaic synonyms are used as substitutes for a potentially homophonous pair of modern terms. This practice is widespread among drum and whistle surrogates and in fact may account for many of the early claims that the drum and whistle messages were not directly related to spoken language. Drum and whistle messages are also iconic on the positional level in that they normally follow the word order, or syntactic patterning, of the speech they represent.

Abridgment systems, while largely iconic, nevertheless do not rely solely on either physical or semantic similarity with spoken language, but make use as well of indexical and symbolic relationships on all three of the levels discussed above: phonetic, semantic, and positional. On the phonetic level, indexicality is found in the very act of abridging speech, for the representation of a whole unit of spoken language by one or more of its parts brings into play the principle of metonymy (or *pars pro toto*). The principle of association by conventional rule which underlies symbolic signs is also found on the phonetic level, in the manner in which drum and whistle signs are often punctuated (with opening calls to attention, message boundary markers within a text, as well as closing signals).

On the semantic level, indexicality is represented in the phrases used as substitutes for potentially ambiguous words. In the examples from the Carrington and Alexandre materials mentioned above, for instance, the existential relationship between the moon and the earth, and between the sexual organs and the entire female anatomy are as important to the signification of 'moon' and 'women' as is the exhibiting of 'fowl', in the third example, by the sound it makes. The principle of conventional rule applies to these examples as well to the extent that the substitute phrases in a sense arbitrarily pick out one or more features of the object of the base word to be represented, whether these features are to serve indexically, iconically, or both.

Drum and whistle messages often follow the word order of spoken language, but they may, for one reason or another, delete certain entire words or parts of words (such as verb endings), much in the way that telegraphic messages abridge the spoken messages they represent. When this happens, a part of a sentence must stand for a whole sentential unit in the base language, and so once again the principle of indexicality reveals itself in drum and whistle surrogates, this time on the positional level. Conventional rule or imputed character applies on this level by virtue of the fact that most drum and whistle systems, while displaying some degree of flexibility with regard to the creation of relatively novel messages (especially in situations where contextual cues are available to aid interpretation), do employ texts which are made up of fairly stereotyped message units.

While drum and whistle signs are frequently iconic in several respects, then, they may simultaneously be indexical and symbolic as well. They are further evidence of the principle that "There is no question of three categorically separate types of signs but only of a different hierarchy assigned to the interacting types of relation between signans and signatum of the given signs . . ." (Jakobson, 1970: 7). In drum and whistle systems the principle of similarity usually dominates those of contiguity and conventional rule; it is this hierarchical arrangement of semiotic principles, and the constant shifting of the elements within it, that is of interest here, not the iconicity itself.

In some drum and whistle systems, particularly those observed in Oceania and South America,[2] the symbolic principle appears to be dominant over the iconic (see especially the cases reported by Eilers

[2] Note that some investigators report the existence of abridgment systems in these parts of the world; in Sebeok and Umiker-Sebeok, 1976, see the articles by Nekes, Thiesen, and Caughley.

and Zemp and Kaufmann, for Melanesia, and Stern's discussion of the
South American literature, all reprinted in Sebeok and Umiker-Sebeok,
1976). In this type of surrogate, signs stand for whole semantic units
much as the Chinese form of writing does in the visual mode. Signs of
this type have been variously called *lexical ideographs* (Stern),
ideogrammes (Zemp and Kaufmann), and *logograms* (Umiker, 1974).
As the terms themselves indicate, the status of the *significata* of these
systems is not yet clear, for it is difficult to determine precisely
whether they are images, or concepts, as such ('ideo- . . .'), or true
lexical units, or words ('logo- . . .'). More work is necessary on this sort
of drum and whistle surrogate before it will be possible to discuss in
detail its exact semiotic nature.

2. DRUM AND WHISTLE SURROGATES IN CONTEXT

Drum and whistle surrogates are of interest, then, as specimens of one
species of transmutation, one which is (a) a true substitutive system, (b)
a first-order rather than a second-order system, and (c) in the acoustic
modality, with the attendant potential for the utilization of iconicity
as the dominant semiotic principle. These surrogates are noteworthy
objects of study not only for this ability to represent spoken language,
however, but also as semiotic systems in their own right. Like some
other surrogates, such as writing, drum and whistle systems frequently
become partially independent of spoken language due, on the one hand,
to the different contextual pressures exerted on them and, on the
other, to the systemic requirements of the surrogate itself.
   Drum and whistle surrogates may be needed for communication in
situations where normal speech is either inadequate (as across great
distances[3] or inappropriate (e.g., during courtship). In transforming
language into a form which can be heard at a distance, drum and

---

[3] References to the facility with which drum and whistle messages may be
successfully transmitted across considerable distance are found in many of the
articles in Sebeok and Umiker-Sebeok (1976). With regard to the physical
explanation of this capacity, consider the following remarks of Classe
(1957: 117):

   What makes speech unintelligible at a distance is the loss of the weak
   harmonics and transients [of the complex speech waves] . . . A whistled signal,
   whose meaning does not depend on timbre but is determined solely by pitch,
   will be understood perfectly so long as it is heard at all.

whistle surrogates may produce potentially ambiguous signs such as the homophonous pairs of lexical items discussed above. To avoid these ambiguities, surrogate texts must be organized in ways which would not be required in normal speech situations. There are two basic sources from which drum and whistle systems draw in order to increase the intelligibility of their messages. The first is the recourse to the base language itself, already mentioned above: archaic terms, synonymic words or phrases, poetic devices, and the like. The second source – music – is independent of spoken language. Redundancy is added to drum and whistle messages by the orchestration of the transferred verbal structures with musical rhythmic patterns. We are all familiar with the device of putting words to musical motifs (such as to bugle calls like reveille; cf. the examples given in Buyssens, 1967: 28), where the verbal element, among other things, makes the music more accessible to recall. In drum and whistle surrogates the reverse process takes place, with melodies being added to verbal elements (cf., on another level, the setting of a second-order surrogate, the alphabet, to music, as in the 'alphabet song' familiar to all American school-children).

The superimposition of musical structures upon verbal ones – most notably in instrumental surrogates – not only increases the intelligibility of messages but may serve certain aesthetic goals as well. This explains the wide range of contexts in which these surrogates have been found and the large number of functions which they can serve. The titles of the papers which make up Sebeok and Umiker-Sebeok (1976) give some indication of this flexibility: drum and whistle surrogates are variously described as a form of 'talk', 'communication', 'language', 'poetry', 'music', 'mass media', 'telephone', 'telegraph', and so on. In everyday life, drum and whistle messages have been reported to serve the exchange of information in situations ranging from private (personal business transactions or courtship) to public (announcements of significant community events such as births, deaths, arrival and departure of important individuals or groups), from informal (such as calling the family pet dog or joking with a rival) to formal (calls to war, recitation of a monarch's lineage). Before the advent of modern broadcasting techniques, drum and whistle surrogates were frequently made to fill the functions which in Western society are performed by a wide variety of devices (including church bells, town criers, telegraph, radio, military signal systems, telephone, newspapers, and so forth).

The combination of poetic devices in the base texts and musical structures in the surrogate messages promotes drum and whistle surrogates into something like an art form as well as a tool for the straightforward communication of information. Over and over again, for example, we find descriptions of the use of drum texts as an integral part of formal ritual performances as well as in everyday life, and frequently in combination with song, dance, or purely musical accompaniments. In such situations, drum texts may serve several functions, setting the tone of the occasion through lyrical poetry and appropriate rhythms, explaining or embellishing the action through epic poetry, advancing the action by responding to the dynamic behavior of the ritual participants or giving instructions to them. Drum texts thus function in ways similar to those of a chorus in Western culture, in addition to their role as providers of the musical background of dramatic or ritual actions.

3. CONTENT AND ORGANIZATION OF *SPEECH SURROGATES: DRUM AND WHISTLE SYSTEMS*

Drum and whistle surrogates have fascinated a wide range of investigators during the last hundred or so years, with ethnographers, ethnomusicologists, linguists, phoneticians, and students of literary forms alike being attracted to their study. The articles presented in the cited volume have been selected in such a way that together they will provide the reader with an insight into the historical development of and the variety of approaches to the investigation of drum and whistle surrogates. Care has also been exercised that the papers represent the full geographical distribution of various drum and whistle systems, their peculiar semiotic structure, and the scope of their expression in the life of the society in which they are found.

The papers in that volume range in date from the early nineteenth century German investigations to 1975, with two previously unpublished articles (nos. 46 and 55). Judging from the average number of publications per year which are devoted to them, interest in drum and whistle systems has remained stable over the years. In the first twenty-year period covered by this collection (1887-1907), the publication rate was an average of .4 items per year; over the next two twenty-year periods (1908-1928 and 1929-1949), the rate climbed to 1.1 and 1.2, respectively, and, since 1950, to 2.3 (1950-1970) and 2.5 (1971-1975).

Interest in each of the geographical areas represented in the volume has been steady as well, over the years, with Africa continuing to account, in each twenty-year period, for the largest number of publications (71% of all publications in 1887-1907, 40% in 1971-1975, overall representing 50% of all publications). Apart from the studies of African systems, publications tend to be more or less equally distributed among the other areas, with Eurasia and the Americas receiving a slightly higher overall amount of attention (15% and 17%, respectively) than Oceania (10%).

The quantity of articles concentrating on Eurasian systems jumped significantly in the 1950-1970 period, due principally to a renewal of interest, during the late fifties and early sixties, in the phonetic aspects of the 'articulated' whistle system of La Gomero and, in the late sixties, the discovery of a previously unrecorded whistle system in Küskoy, Turkey. Another significant areal development is the considerable increase in number of publications, beginning in the fifties and accelerating after 1970, devoted to whistle surrogates found in Mexico.

What does the future hold for studies of drum and whistle surrogates? First, the investigation of Asian, Oceanic, and South American systems has, in our estimation, only just begun, and we can expect additional materials from these parts of the world in the years to come. New drum and (especially) whistle surrogates continue to crop up from time to time, and we have reason to believe that this will be the case in the future. To take only two examples, M. Frantz, of The Summer Institute of Linguistics, has, by personal communication, announced the discovery of a new whistle system based on the Gadsup language of East New Guinea Highlands Phylum. See also the recent survey of nonverbal communication in Northeast New Guinea by Eilers (forthcoming).

Secondly, major monographic treatment of whistle surrogates remains to be done. A. Classe, in a personal communication, reports that he and R.-G. Busnel are currently at work on a book about whistle systems, especially those which are 'articulated'.

We can also expect to see additional book-length contributions to the study of individual drum and whistle systems. J. H. K. Nketia, for example, has in press a volume on the drum system of Akan (*The Poetry of Akan Drums* [The Hague: Mouton]).

4. BIBLIOGRAPHICAL NOTE

References to articles and books on drum and whistle surrogates not included in Sebeok and Umiker-Sebeok (1976) can be found in the Annotated Bibliography in Umiker (1974: 520-36), with the exception of Cowan (1971), *Drums and Shadows* (1972), and Knappert (1961).

References

Aaron, R. I.
1955 [1937[1]] *John Locke* (London: Oxford University Press).
Adey, W. Ross
1967 "Historical Review", in: *Information and Control Processes in Living Systems*, ed. by Diane M. Ramsey (New York: New York Academy of Sciences), pp. 20-22.
Alatis, James E.
1968 (ed.) *Report on the Nineteenth Annual Round Table Meeting on Linguistics and Language Studies* (Washington D.C.: Georgetown University Press).
Albrecht, Erhard
1967 *Sprache und Erkenntnis: Logisch-Linguistische Analysen* (Berlin: VEB).
Alsop, Stewart
1960 "How to Speak French Without Saying a Word", *The Saturday Evening Post* 233, 26-29.
Altmann, Stuart A.
1967 (ed.) *Social Communication among Primates* (Chicago: University of Chicago Press).
1967 "The Structure of Primate Social Communication", in: Altmann (ed.), 1967, pp. 325-62.
Andrew, R. J.
1963 "Evolution of Facial Expression", *Science* 142, 1034-41.
Apel, Karl-Otto
1973 "Charles W. Morris und das Programm einer pragmatisch integrierten Semiotik", in: *Zeichen, Sprache und Verhalten*, by Charles W. Morris (Düsseldorf: Schwann), pp. 9-66.

Arbib, Michael A.
1971 "How We Know Universals: Retrospect and Prospect", *Mathematical Biosciences* 11, 95-107.

Ardener, E.
1971 (ed.) *Social Anthropology and Language* (London: Tavistock).

Ardrey, Robert
1970 *The Social Contract: A Personal Inquiry into the Evolutionary Sources of Order and Disorder* (New York: Dell).

Argyle, Michael
1969 *Social Interaction* (New York: Atherton).
1975 *Bodily Communication* (London: Methuen).

Armstrong, Edward A.
1963 *A Study of Bird Song* (London: Oxford University Press).

Arnauld, Antoine, and Pierre Nicole
1816 [1662] *La logique, ou l'art de penser* (Paris: Delalain).

Arrivé, Michel
1974 "Sémiologie ou semiotique?", *Le Monde*, June 7.

Auzias, J.-M.
1967 *Clefs pour le structuralisme* (Paris: Seghers).

Ayala, F.J.
1968 "Biology as an Autonomous Science", *American Scientist* 56, 207-21.

Bach-Y-Rita, P., *et al.*
1969 "Vision Substitution by Tactile Image Projection", *Nature* 221, 963-64.

Back, Kurt W.
1972 *Beyond Words: The Story of Sensitivity Training and The Encounter Movement* (New York: Russell Sage Foundation).

Backus, R. H., and W. E. Schevill
1966 "*Physeter* Clicks", in: *Whales, Dolphins, and Porpoises*, ed. by Kenneth S. Norris (Berkeley: University of California Press), pp. 510-27.

Baldassare, Mark, and Susan Feller
1975 "Cultural Variations in Personal Space: Theory, Methods, and Evidence", *Ethos* 3/4, 481-503.

Bally, Charles
1939 "Qu-est-ce qu'un signe?", *Journal de Psychologie* 1939, 161-74.

Bang, Preben, and Preben Dahlstrom
1974 *Animal Tracks and Signs* (London: Collins).

Bär, Eugen
1971 "The Language of the Unconscious According to Jacques Lacan", *Semiotica* 3, 241-68.
1975 *Semiotic Approaches to Psychotherapy* (= *Studies in Semiotics* 1) (Bloomington: Research Center for Language and Semiotic

Studies).
1976 Review – see Verdiglione, 1975.
Bar-Hillel, Yehoshua
1954 "Indexical Expressions", *Mind* 63, 359-79.
1968 "The Future of Man-Machine Languages", in: *Purposive Systems: Proceedings of the First Annual Symposium of the American Society for Cybernetics*, ed. by Heinz von Foerster, *et al.* (New York: Spartan), pp. 141-52.
1970a "Argumentation in Pragmatic Languages", *Proceedings of the Israel Academy of Sciences and Humanities* 4:8, 15.
1970b *Aspects of Language: Essays and Lectures on Philosophy of Language, Linguistic Philosophy and Methodology of Linguistics* (Jerusalem: Magnes Press).
Barthes, Roland
1964 *Éléments de sémiologie* (Paris: Seuil). [English version – 1967a: *Elements of Semiology* (London: Jonathan Cape); the first American edition appeared, in 1968, under the imprint of Hill and Wang, New York.]
1967b *Système de la mode* (Paris: Seuil).
1972 "Sémiologie et médecine", in: *Les sciences de la folie*, ed. by Roger Bastide (Paris: Mouton), pp. 37-46.
1974 "L'aventure sémiologique", *Le Monde*, June 7.
Bastide, Roger
1962 (ed.) *Sens et usages du terme structure dans les sciences humaines et sociales* (The Hague: Mouton).
Basto, Claudio
1938 "A linguagem dos gestos em Portugal", *Revista Lusitana* 36, 5-72.
Bateson, Gregory
1970 *Form, Substance and Difference* (Hawaii: Oceanic Institute, Contribution No. 65).
Bateson, Mary Catherine
1968 "Linguistics in the Semiotic Frame", *Linguistics* 39, 5-17.
Baumann, H.-H.
1969 "Über französischen Strukturalismus: Zur Rezeption moderner Linguistik in Frankreich und in Deutschland", *Sprache im technischen Zeitalter* 30, 157-83.
Beer, C. G.
1963-64 "Ethology – The Zoologist's Approach to Behaviour", *Tuatara* 2, 170-77 and 3, 16-39.
Bellour, Raymond, and Christian Metz
1971 "Entretien sur la sémiologie du cinéma", *Semiotica* 4, 1-30.
Bendix, E. H.
1966 *Componential Analysis of General Vocabulary: The Semantic Structure of a Set of Verbs in English, Hindi, and Japanese*

(Bloomington: Indiana University).

Bense, Max
1965 "Semiotik und Linguistik", *Grundlagenstudien aus Kybernetik und Geisteswissenschaft* 6, 97-108.
1967 *Semiotik: Allgemeine Theorie der Zeichen* (Baden-Baden: Agis).

Bense, Max, and Elisabeth Walther
1973 (eds.) *Wörterbuch der Semiotik* (Cologne: Kiebnheuer & Witsch). [Cf. Kenneth Laine Ketner and Christian J. W. Kloesel's 1975 review article, "The Semiotic of Charles Sanders Peirce and the First Dictionary of Semiotics", *Semiotica* 13, 395-414.]

Benveniste, Émile
1969 "Sémiologie de la langue", *Semiotica* 1, 1-12; 127-35.

Bertin, Jacques
1967 *Sémiologie graphique* (Paris: Mouton).

Bettetini, Gianfranco
1968 *Cinema: Lingua e scrittura* (Milan: Bompiani).
1973 *The Language and Technique of Film* (= *Approaches to Semiotics* 28) (The Hague: Mouton).

Bierwisch, Manfred
1966 "Strukturalismus. Geschichte, Probleme und Methoden", *Kursbuch* 5, 77-152.
1969 "On Certain Problems of Semantic Representation", *Foundations of Language* 5, 153-84.
1972 "Generative Grammar and European Linguistics", in: *Current Trends in Linguistics*, Vol. 9, *Linguistics in Western Europe*, ed. by Thomas A. Sebeok (The Hague: Mouton), pp. 313-42.

Bilz, Rudolf
1940 *Pars pro toto: Ein Beitrag zur Pathologie menschlicher Affekte und Organfunktionen* (Leipzig: Georg Thieme).

Birdwhistell, Ray L.
1963 "The Kinesic Level of the Investigation of the Emotions", in: *Expression of the Emotions in Man*, ed. by P. H. Knapp (New York: International Universities Press).
1968a "Communication", *International Encyclopedia of the Social Sciences* 3, 24-28.
1968b "Kinesics: Inter- and Intra-Channel Communication Research", *Social Science Information* 7:6, 9-26.
1970 *Kinesics and Context: Essays on Body Motion Communication* (Philadelphia: University of Pennsylvania Press). [Cf. Paul A. R. Bouissac's 1972 review article, "What Does the Little Finger Do? An Appraisal of Kinesics", *Semiotica* 6, 279-88.]

Black, M.
1968 *The Labyrinth of Language* (New York: Praeger).

Bleibtreu, John N.
1968   *The Parable of the Beast* (London: Gollancz).
Blest, A. D.
1961   "The Concept of 'Ritualization' ", in: *Current Problems in Animal Behaviour*, ed. by W. H. Thorpe and O. L. Zangwill (Cambridge: University Press), pp. 102-24.
Bloomfield, Leonard
1933   *Language* (New York: Holt).
1939   "Linguistic Aspects of Science", *International Encyclopedia of Unified Science* 1:4, 55.
Blum, Lucille Hollander
1972   *Reading Between the Lines: Doctor-Patient Communication* (New York: International Universities Press).
Bocheński, J. M.
1956   *Formale Logik* (Freiburg: K. Alber).
1968² [1965¹]   *The Methods of Contemporary Thought* (New York: Harper & Row).
Bock, Kenneth E.
1966   "The Comparative Method in Anthropology", *Comparative Studies in Society and History* 8, 269-80.
Bogatyrev, Petr
1971² [1937¹]   *The Functions of Folk Costume in Moravian Slovakia* (= *Approaches to Semiotics* 5) (The Hague: Mouton). [Cf. Henry Glassie's 1973 review article, "Structure and Function, Folklore and the Artifact", *Semiotica* 7, 312-51.]
Bolinger, Dwight
1949   "The Sign Is Not Arbitrary", *Thesaurus: Boletín del Instituto Caro y Cuerva* 5, 52-62.
1968   *Aspects of Language* (New York: Harcourt, Brace and World).
Bonfante, Giuliano, and Thomas A. Sebeok
1944   "Linguistics and the Age and Area Hypothesis", *American Anthropologist* 46, 382-86.
Bonner, John T.
1963   "How Slime Molds Communicate", *Scientific American* 209, 84-94.
Bosmajian, Haig A.
1971   *The Rhetoric of Nonverbal Communication: Readings* (Glenview: Scott, Foresman).
Bouissac, Paul
1968   "Volumes sonores et volumes gestuels dans un numéro d'acrobatie", *Langages* 10, 128-31.
1969   "Le numéro d'acrobatie en tant que structure narrative". Oral communication delivered at the Troisième Symposium International sur l'étude des structures narratives, August, 1969.
1970   "Pour une sémiotique du cirque", *Semiotica* 3, 93-120.

1972   Review – see Birdwhistell, 1970.
1973   *La mesure des gestes: Prolégomènes à la sémiotique gestuelle* (= *Approaches to Semiotics*, paperback series 3) (The Hague: Mouton).
1976   *Circus and Culture: A Semiotic Approach* (= *Advances in Semiotics* 2) (Bloomington: Indiana University Press).
Brain, Lord
1961   "The Neurology of Language", *Brain* 84, 145-46.
Brannigan, Christopher R., and David A. Humphries
1972   "Human Non-verbal Behaviour, A Means of Communication", in: *Ethological Studies of Child Behaviour*, ed. by N. Blurton Jones (Cambridge: University Press), pp. 37-64.
Brault, Gérard J.
1962   "Kinesics and the Classroom: Some Typical French Gestures", *French Review* 36, 374-82.
Bréal, Michel
[1900]   *Semantics. Studies in the Science of Meaning* (New York: Holt).
Brekle, Herbert E.
1964   "Semiotik und linguistische Semantik in Port-Royal", *Indogermanische Forschungen* 69, 103-21.
1966   (ed.) *Grammaire générale et raisonnée, ou La grammaire de Port-Royal, par Claude Lancelot et Antoine Arnauld.* Critical edition, facsimile printing of the 3rd ed. of 1676. (Stuttgart-Bad Cannstatt: Friedrich Frommann).
Brilliant, Richard
1963   *Gesture and Rank in Roman Art: The Use of Gestures to Denote Status in Roman Sculpture and Coinage* (= *Memoirs of the Connecticut Academy of Arts & Sciences* 14) (New Haven: Academy).
Bronowski, Jacob
1967   "Human and Animal Language", in: *To Honor Roman Jakobson* (The Hague: Mouton), pp. 374-94.
Bronowski, Jacob, and Ursula Bellugi
1970   "Language, Name, and Concept", *Science* 168, 669-73.
Brower, Lincoln P., Jane van Zandt Brower, and Joseph Corvino
1967   "Plant Poisons in a Terrestrial Foodchain", *Proceedings of the National Academy of Sciences* 57, 893-98.
Brown, Jerram L.
1975   *The Evolution of Behavior* (New York: W.W. Norton).
Brown, Roger
1958   *Words and Things* (Glencoe, Ill.: Free Press).
1970   "The First Sentences of Child and Chimpanzee", in: *id., Psycholinguistics: Selected Papers* (New York: Free Press), pp.

208-31.

Brun, Theodore
1969   *The International Dictionary of Sign Language: A Study of Human Behaviour* (London: Wolfe).

Bucher, Gérard
1975   Review – see Martinet, 1973.

Bühler, Karl
1965²   [1934¹]   *Sprachtheorie: Die   Darstellungsfunktion   der Sprache* (Stuttgart: Gustav Fischer).
1968²   [1933¹]   *Ausdruckstheorie: Das   System   an   der   Geschichte aufgezeigt* (Stuttgart: Gustav Fischer).

Burghardt, Gordon M.
1970   "Defining 'Communication' ", in: *Communication by Chemical Signals*, ed. by James W. Johnson, Jr., David G. Moulton, and Amos Turk (New York: Appleton-Century-Crofts), pp. 5-18.

Burke, Kenneth
1966   *Language as Symbolic Action: Essays on Life, Literature, and Method* (Berkeley and Los Angeles: University of California Press).

Burkhardt, D., W. Schleidt, H. Altner, *et al.*
1967   *Signals in the Animal World* (New York: McGraw-Hill).

Burks, Arthur W.
1949   "Icon, Index, and Symbol", *Philosophy and Phenomenological Research* 9, 673-89.

Bursill-Hall, Geoffrey L.
1963   "Some Remarks on Deixis", *Canadian Journal of Linguistics/ Revue Canadienne de linguistique* 8, 82-96.
1971   *Speculative Grammars of the Middle Ages: The Doctrine of Partes Orationis of the Modistae* (= *Approaches to Semiotics* 11) (The Hague: Mouton). [Cf. Jean Stefanini's 1973 review article, "Les modistes et leur apport à la theorie de la grammaire et du signe linguistique", *Semiotica* 8, 263-75.]

Buyssens, Eric
1943   *Les langages et le discours: Essai de linguistique fonctionnelle dans le cadre de la sémiologie* (Brussels: J. Lebègue). [A revised version is incorporated in Buyssens, 1967, pp. 9-74.]
1956   "Le langage par gestes chez les moines", *Revue de l'Institut de Sociologie de Bruxelles* 29, 537-45.
1967   *La communication et l'articulation linguistique* (Brussels: Presses Universitaires).
1973   "Les noms singuliers", *Cahiers Ferdinand de Saussure* 28, 25-34.

Calvet, Louis-Jean
1973   *Roland Barthes: un regard politique sur le signe* (Paris: Payot).

1974 "Une sémiologie politique", *L'Arc: Roland Barthes* 56, 25-29.

1975 *Pour et contre Saussure: vers une linguistique sociale* (Paris: Payot).

Carnap, Rudolf

1942 *Introduction to Semantics* (Cambridge, Mass.: Harvard University Press).

1956[2] [1947[1]] *Meaning and Necessity: A Study in Semantics and Modal Logic* (Chicago: University of Chicago Press).

Carpenter, Clarence R.

1969 "Approaches to Studies of the Naturalistic Communicative Behavior in Nonhuman Primates", in: Sebeok and Ramsay (eds.), 1969, pp. 40-70.

Carpenter, Edmund S.

1960 *Eskimo* (Toronto: University of Toronto Press).

Carroll, John B.

1956 (ed.) *Language, Thought and Reality: Selected Writings of Benjamin Lee Whorf* (Cambridge, Mass.: MIT Press).

1964 *Language and Thought* (Englewood Cliffs: Prentice-Hall).

Cassirer, Ernst

1923 *Die Philosophie der Symbolischen Formen* (Berlin: Bruno Cassirer, 1923, 1924, 1929).

1944 *An Essay on Man: An Introduction to a Philosophy of Human Culture* (New Haven: Yale University Press).

Caws, Peter

1969 "The Structure of Discovery", *Science* 166, 1375-80.

Celan, Eugen, and Solomon Marcus

1973 "Le diagnostic comme langage, I", *Cahiers de Linguistique* 10, 163-73.

Chafe, Wallace

1968 Review of Lamb, 1966. *Language* 44, 593-603.

Chao, Yuen Ren

1968 *Language and Symbolic Systems* (Cambridge: University Press).

Charbonnier, G.

1961 *Entretiens avec Claude Lévi-Strauss* (Paris: Plon and Julliard).

Charlesworth, William R., and Mary Anne Kreutzer

1973 "Facial Expressions of Infants and Children", in: *Darwin and Facial Expression: A Century of Research in Review*, ed. by Paul Ekman (New York: Academic Press), pp. 91-168.

Cherry, Colin

1966 *On Human Communication: A Review, a Survey, and a Criticism* (Cambridge: Mass.: MIT Press).

Chevalier, Jean, and Alain Gheerbrant

1973-74 [1969[1]] (eds.) *Dictionnaire des symboles: mythes, rêves, coutumes, gestes, formes, figures, couleurs, nombres* (Paris: Seghers).

Chomsky, Noam
1965 *Aspects of the Theory of Syntax* (Cambridge, Mass.: MIT Press).
1967 "The General Properties of Language", in: Darley (ed.), 1967, pp. 73-88.
1971 "Deep Structure, Surface Structure, and Semantic Interpretation", in: *Studies in General and Oriental Linguistics Presented to Shirô Hattori on the Occasion of His Sixtieth Birthday*, ed. by Roman Jakobson and Shigeo Kawamoto (Tokyo: TEC Company), pp. 59-91.
1972 *Language and Mind* (New York: Harcourt, Brace, Jovanovich).
Ciolek, T. M.
1975 "Human Communicational Behavior: A Provisional Checklist of References to the Use of Gesture, Postures, Bodily Contact, Spacing, Orientation, Facial Expressions, Looking Behavior, and Appearance in the Course of Face-to-Face Interactions", *Sign Language Studies* 6, 1-64.
Clark, B. F. C., and K. A. Marcker
1968 "How Proteins Start", *Scientific American* 218, 36-42.
Clark, Herbert H.
1972 "Semantics and Comprehension", in: Sebeok (ed.), 1974b, pp. 1291-1428.
Classe, André
1957 "The Whistle Language of La Gomero", *Scientific American* 196, 111-20.
Clastres, P.
1962 "Échange et pouvoir: Philosophie de la chefferie Indienne", *L'Homme* 2, 51-65.
Clerk, Christian
1975 "The Cannibal Sign", *Royal Anthropological Institute News* 8, 1-3.
Coates, W. A.
1968 "Near-homonymy as a Factor in Language Change", *Language* 44, 467-79.
Cocchiara, Giuseppe
1932 *Il linguaggio del gesto* (Turin: Fratelli Bocca).
Coquet, Jean-Claude, and Julia Kristeva
1972 "Sémanalyse: Conditions d'une sémiotique scientifique", *Semiotica* 5, 324-49.
Corti, Maria
1973 "Le jeu comme génération du texte: des tarots au recit", *Semiotica* 7, 33-48.
Coseriu, Eugenio
1967 "L'arbitraire du signe: zur Spätgeschichte eines aristotelischen Begriffes", *Archiv für das Studium der Neueren Sprachen und*

Literaturen 204, 81-112.

1969, 1972 *Die Geschichte der Sprachphilosophie von der Antike bis zur Gegenwart. Eine Übersicht.* (*Teil I: Von der Antike bis Leibniz. Teil II: Von Leibniz bis Rousseau.*)(Stuttgart: Vogt KG).

Coseriu, Eugenio, and Horst Geckeler

1974 "Linguistics and Semantics", in: Sebeok (ed.), 1974b, pp. 103-71.

Count, Earl W.

1969 "Animal Communication in Man-Science", in: Sebeok and Ramsay (eds.), 1969, pp. 71-130.

Cowan, George M.

1971 "Segmental Features of Tepehua Whistle Speech", in: *Proceedings of the VIIth International Congress of Phonetic Sciences. Drums and Shadows*

1972 Survival studies among the Georgian Coastal Negroes (Garden City, New York: Doubleday).

Cowan, M.

1963 (Tr.) *Humanist without Portfolio: An Anthology of the Writings of Wilhelm von Humboldt* (Detroit: Wayne State University Press).

Crick, F. H. C.

1966 "The Genetic Code – Yesterday, Today and Tomorrow", in: *The Genetic Code* (= *Cold Spring Harbor Symposia on Quantitative Biology* 31) (Cold Spring Harbor, L. I., N.Y.).

Critchley, Macdonald

1939 *The Language of Gesture* (London: Arnold).

1975 *Silent Language* (London: Butterworth).

Croneberg, Carl G.

1965 "Sign Language Dialects", in: *A Dictionary of American Sign Language*, ed. by William C. Stokoe, Jr., *et al.* (Washington: Gallaudet College Press), Appendix D.

Crookshank, F. G.

1923 "The Importance of a Theory of Signs and a Critique of Language in the Study of Medicine", in: Ogden and Richards, 1938, pp. 337-55.

Crystal, David

1969 *Prosodic Systems and Intonation in English* (Cambridge: University Press).

1974 "Paralinguistics", in: Sebeok (ed.), 1974b, pp. 265-95.

Culler, Jonathan

Forthcoming *Saussure.* Fontana Modern Masters (London: Collins).

Daanje, A.

1950 "On Locomotory Movements in Birds and Their Intention

Movements", *Behaviour* 3, 48-99.

Dante Alighieri
1957 *De vulgarī eloquentiā*, ed. by Aristide Marigo (Firenze: Le Monnier).

Darley, F. L.
1967 (ed.) *Brain Mechanisms Underlying Speech and Language* (New York: Grune and Stratton).

Darwin, Charles
1872 *The Expression of the Emotions in Man and Animals* (London: John Murray).

Dascal, Marcelo
1972 *Aspects de la sémiologie de Leibniz* (Jerusalem: Hebrew University).
1975 "Quelques fonctions des signes et du langage d'après Leibniz et ses contemporains", in: *Akten des II. Internationalen Leibniz-Kongresses, Hannover, 17-22. Juli 1972*, Bd. 4 (Wiesbaden: Franz Steiner), pp. 239-55.

Davidson, Donald
1970 "Semantics for Natural Languages", *Linguaggi nella società e nella tecnica*, 177-88.

Davis, Flora
1970 "The Way We Speak 'Body Language' ", *The New York Times Magazine*, May 31, pp. 8-9, 29-34, 41-42.
1971 *Inside Intuition: What We Know About Nonverbal Communication* (New York: McGraw-Hill).

Davis, Martha
1972 *Understanding Body Movement: An Annotated Bibliography* (New York: Arno).

Deely, John N.
1974 "The Two Approaches to Language: Philosophical and Historical Reflections on the Point of Departure of Jean Poinsot's Semiotic", *The Thomist* 38, 856-907.
1975 " 'Semeiotica': dottrina dei segni", *Renovatio: Rivista di Teologia e Cultura* 10, 472-90.

De Lacy, Phillip and Estelle DeLacy
1941 (eds.) *Philodemus: On Methods of Inference; A Study in Ancient Empiricism* (=*Philological Monograph* 10) (Philadelphia: American Philological Association).

Deledalle, Gérard
1974 Review — see Greenlee, 1973.

De Marinis, Marco, and Patrizia Magli
1975 "Materiali bibliografici per una semiotica del teatro", *VS: Quaderni di studi semiotici* 11, 53-128.

de Vries, Ad.
1974 *Dictionary of Symbols and Imagery* (Amsterdam: North-Holland).
Dewan, Edmond M.
1969 "Rhythms", *Science and Technology*, January, 20-28.
Dewey, John
1946 "Peirce's Theory of Linguistic Signs, Thought, and Meaning", *The Journal of Philosophy* 43, 85-95.
Dittmann, Allen T.
1973 Review – see Efron, 1972.
Dreyfuss, Henry
1972 *Symbol Source Book: An Authoritative Guide to International Graphic Symbols* (New York: McGraw-Hill).
Droste, Frederik G.
1972 "The Grammar of Traffic Regulations", *Semiotica* 5, 257-62.
Dubois, Jean, *et al.*
1973 (eds.) *Dictionnaire de linguistique* (Paris: Larousse).
Ducrot, Oswald, *et al.*
1968 *Qu'est ce que le structuralisme?* (Paris: Seuil).
Ducrot, Oswald, and Tzvetan Todorov
1972 *Dictionnaire encyclopédique des sciences du langage* (Paris: Seuil).
Dummett, Michael
1973 *Frege: Philosophy of Language* (London: Duckworth).
Duncan, Hugh D.
1968 *Symbols in Society* (New York: Oxford University Press).
Eakins, Barbara Westbrook
1972 "Charles Morris and the Study of Signification". Dissertation. The University of Iowa.
Eco, Umberto
1968 *La struttura assente: Introduzione alla ricerca semiologica* (Milan: Bompiani). [German version – 1972a. *Einführung in die Semiotik* (Munich: Fink).] [Cf. Paolo Valesio's 1971 review article, "Toward a Study of the Nature of Signs", *Semiotica* 3, 155-85.]
1972b "Introduction to a Semiotics of Iconic Signs", *VS: Quaderni di studi semiotici* 2, 1-15.
1973 *Il segno* (Milan: ISEDI).
1974 "Closing Statement at the First Congress of the International Association for Semiotic Studies", *Le Journal Canadien de Recherche Sémiotique* 2:2, 7-16.
1975 *Trattato di semiotica generale* (Milan: Bompiani).
1976 *A Theory of Semiotics* (= *Advances in Semiotics* 1) (Bloomington: Indiana University Press).

Forthcoming "The Influence of Roman Jakobson on the Development of Semiotics", in: van Schooneveld and Armstrong, 1976.

Efron, David
1972[2] [1941[1]] *Gesture, Race and Culture* (= *Approaches to Semiotics* 9) (The Hague: Mouton). [Cf. Allen T. Dittmann's 1973 review article, "Style in Conversation", *Semiotica* 9, 241-51.]

Egger, V.
1904 *La parole intérieure* (Paris: Alcan).

Ehrmann, Jacques
1966 *Structuralism* (= *Yale French Studies* 36-37) (New Haven: Yale University Press).

Eibl-Eibesfeldt, Irenäus
1970 *Ethology: The Biology of Behavior* (New York: Holt, Rinehart and Winston).

Eibl-Eibesfeldt, Irenäus, and H. Hass
1967 "Film Studies in Human Ethology", *Current Anthropology* 8, 477-79.

Eilers, Franz-Josef
1967 *Zur Publizistik schriftloser Kulturen in Nordost-Guinea* (St. Augustin: Steiger).
Forthcoming "Non-verbal Communication in Northeast New Guinea", in: *New Guinea Area Languages and Language Study*, ed. by S. A. Wurm (= *Pacific Linguistics* series C) (Canberra: Department of Linguistics, Research School of Pacific Studies, The Australian National University).

Eimermacher, Karl
1971 "Entwicklung, Charakter und Probleme des sowjetischen Strukturalismus in der Literaturwissenschaft", in: *Teksty sovetskogo literaturovedčeskogo strukturalizma*, ed. by Karl Eimermacher (Munich: Fink), pp. 9-40.
1974 *Arbeiten sowjetischer Semiotiker der Moskauer und Tartuer Schule (Auswahlbibliographie)*. (Kroneberg Ts.: Scriptor).

Eisenberg, Abne N., and Ralph R. Smith, Jr.
1971 *Nonverbal Communication* (Indianapolis: Bobbs-Merrill).

Ekman, Paul
1971 "Universals and Cultural Differences in Facial Expressions of Emotion", *Current Theory and Research in Motivation* 19, 207-83.

Ekman, Paul, and Wallace V. Friesen
1969a "Nonverbal Leakage and Clues to Deception", *Psychiatry* 32, 88-106.
1969b "The Repertoire of Nonverbal Behavior: Categories, Origins, Usage, and Coding", *Semiotica* 1, 49-98.

1974 "Detecting Deception from the Body or Face", *Journal of Personality and Social Psychology* 29, 288-98.

1975 *Unmasking the Face: A Guide to Recognizing Emotions from Facial Clues* (Englewood Cliffs: Prentice-Hall).

Engler, Rudolf

1962 "Théorie et critique d'un principe saussurien: l'arbitraire du signe", *Cahiers Ferdinand de Saussure* 19, 5-66.

1968 *Lexique de la terminologie saussurienne* (Utrecht and Anvers: Spectrum).

Ennion, Eric A. R., and Niko Tinbergen

1967 *Tracks* (London: Oxford University Press).

Ervin, Susan M.

1965[2] "Information Transmission with Code Translation", in: *Psycholinguistics: A Survey of Theory and Research Problems*, ed. by Charles E. Osgood and Thomas A. Sebeok (Bloomington: Indiana University Press), pp. 185-92.

Eschbach, Achim

1974 *Zeichen – Text – Bedeutung: Bibliographie zu Theorie und Praxis der Semiotik* (Munich: Fink).

Evans, William E., and Jarvis Bastian

1969 "Marine Mammal Communication: Social and Ecological Factors", in: *The Biology of Marine Mammals*, ed. by Harald T. Andersen (New York: Academic Press), pp. 425-75.

Faccani, Remo, and Umberto Eco

1969 (eds.) *I sistemi di segni e lo strutturalismo Sovietico* (Milan: Bompiani).

Fages, J.-B.

1968 *Comprendre le structuralisme* (Paris: Privat).

Fast, Julius

1970 *Body Language* (New York: M. Evans).

Fedorenko, N. P.

1970 (ed.) *Ekonomičeskaja Semiotika* (Moscow: Nauka). [German version – 1972. *Ökonomische Semiotik* (Berlin: Akademie Vlg.).]

Feigl, Herbert

1969 "The Wiener Kreis in America", in: *Intellectual Migration: Europe and America, 1930-1960*, ed. by Donald Fleming and Bernard Bailyn (Cambridge, Mass.: Harvard University Press, The Belknap Press), pp. 630-73.

Fillmore, Charles J.

1972 "A Grammarian Looks to Sociolinguistics", *Georgetown University Monograph Series on Languages and Linguistics* 25, 273-87.

1973 "May We Come In?", *Semiotica* 9, 97-116.

Fiordo, Richard Anthony
1976   *Charles Morris and the Criticism of Discourse* (= *Studies in Semiotics* 4) (Bloomington: Research Center for Language and Semiotic Studies).
Firth, Raymond
1973   *Symbols: Public and Private* (Ithaca: Cornell University Press).
Fisch, Max H.
1972   "Peirce and Leibniz", *Journal of the History of Ideas* 33, 485-96.
Fisch, Max H., and Jackson I. Cope
1952   "Peirce at the Johns Hopkins University", in: *Studies in the Philosophy of Charles Sanders Peirce*, ed. by Philip P. Wiener and Frederic H. Young (Cambridge, Mass.: Harvard University Press), pp. 277-311, 355-60.
Fischer-Jørgensen, Eli
1957   Introduction to Uldall, 1957 (= *Travaux du Cercle Linguistique de Copenhague* 10).
Fitzgerald, John J.
1966   *Peirce's Theory of Signs as Foundation for Pragmatism* (The Hague: Mouton).
Fleming, Ilah
1969   "Stratificational Theory: An Annotated Bibliography", *Journal of Linguistics* 3, 37-65.
Fokkema, Douwe W.
1974   "Semiotiek en Structuralisme in de Sovjetunie", *Forum der Letteren* 15, 138-56.
Fónagy, Iván
1975   Review – see Ostwald, 1973.
Frank, L. K.
1957   "Tactile Communication", *Genetic Psychology Monographs* 56, 209-55.
Frazer, James G.
1951   *The Golden Bough: A Study in Magic and Religion* (New York: Macmillan).
Frege, Gottlob
1892   "Über Sinn und Bedeutung", *Zeitschrift für Philosophie und philosophische Kritik* 100, 25-50.
Frei, Henri
1944   "Systèmes de déictiques", *Acta Linguistica Hafniensia* 4, 111-29.
1950   "Zéro, vide et intermittent", *Zeitschrift für Phonetik, Sprachwissenschaft und Kommunikationsforschung* 4, 161-91.
1963   "Le signe de Saussure et le signe de Buyssens", *Lingua* 12, 423-28.

Fresnault-Deruelle, Pierre
1975 "L'espace interpersonnel dans les comics", in: Helbo, *et al.* (eds.), 1975, pp. 129-50.
Freud, Sigmund
1959 [1905] "Fragment of an Analysis of a Case of Hysteria", in: *Collected Papers*, Vol. 3 (New York: Basic Books).
Friedmann, Herbert
1955 "The Honey-Guides" (= *U.S. National Museum Bulletin* 208) (Washington, D.C.: Smithsonian).
Frisch, Joseph C.
1969 *Extension and Comprehension in Logic* (New York: Philosophical Library).
Frisch, Karl von
1962 "Dialects in the Language of Bees", *Scientific American* 207, 79-87.
1967 *The Dance Language and Orientation of Bees* (Cambridge, Mass.: Harvard University Press).
Gale, R. M.
1967 "Indexical Signs, Egocentric Particulars, and Token-Reflexive Words", *The Encyclopedia of Philosophy* 4, 151-55.
Galenus, Claudius
1965 *Opera Omnia* 14 (Hildesheim: Georg Olms).
Gandelsonas, Mario, *et al.*
1970 "Semiología arquitectonica", *Summa* 32, 69-82.
Gardner, Beatrice T., and R. Allen Gardner
1969 "Teaching Sign Language to a Chimpanzee", *Science* 165, 664-72.
1971 "Two-Way Communication with an Infant Chimpanzee", in: *Behavior of Nonhuman Primates: Modern Research Trends*, ed. by Allan M. Schrier and Fred Stollnitz (New York: Academic Press), Vol. 4, pp. 117-84.
Gardner, Martin
1968 "Combinatorial Problems Involving 'Tree' Graphs and Forests of Trees", *Scientific American* 218, 118-20.
Garrison, Fielding H.
1929[4] *An Introduction to the History of Medicine: With Medical Chronology, Suggestions for Study and Bibliographic Data* (Philadelphia: Saunders).
Garroni, Emilio
1968 *Semiotica ed estetica* (Bari: Laterza).
Geertz, Clifford
1973 *The Interpretation of Cultures* (New York: Basic Books).
Geldard, Frank
1960 "Some Neglected Possibilities of Communication", *Science*

131, 1583-88.

Genette, Gérard
1969   "The Reverse Side of the Sign", *Social Science Information*
       8:4, 169-82.

Gerard, Ralph
1957   "Units and Concepts of Biology", *Science* 125, 429-33.
1960   "Becoming: The Residue of Change", in: *Evolution after
       Darwin* II, ed. by Sol Tax (Chicago: University of Chicago
       Press), pp. 255-67.

Giedion, Sigfried
1960   "Space Conception in Prehistoric Art", in: *Explorations in
       Communication: An Anthology*, ed. by E. Carpenter and M.
       McLuhan (Boston: Beacon, 1966), pp. 71-89.

Gilliard, E. Thomas
1963   "The Evolution of Bowerbirds", *Scientific American* 209,
       38-46.

Glasersfeld, Ernst von
1974   "Signs, Communication, and Language", *Journal of Human
       Evolution* 3, 465-74.

Glass, D. C.
1967   "Genetics and Social Behavior", Social Science Research
       Council *Items* 21, 1-5.

Glassie, Henry
1973   Review – see Bogatyrev, 1971.

Godel, Robert
1953   "La question des signes zéro", *Cahiers Ferdinand de Saussure*
       11, 31-41.
1957   *Les sources manuscrites du* Cours de linguistique générale *de
       F. de Saussure* (Geneva: Droz).
1969   (ed.) *A Geneva School Reader in Linguistics* (Bloomington:
       Indiana University Press).

Goffman, Erving
1963   *Stigma: Notes on the Management of Spoiled Identity*
       (Englewood Cliffs: Prentice-Hall).

Golopenția-Eretescu, Sanda
1971   "Explorări semiotice", *Studii și cercetări linguistice* 22,
       283-91.

Gorn, Saul
1968   "The Identification of the Computer and Information
       Sciences: Their Fundamental Semiotic Concepts and Relation-
       ships", *Foundations of Language* 4, 339-72.

Grace, George W.
1970   "Languages of Oceania". Paper prepared for presentation at the
       Center for Applied Linguistics World's Languages Conference,

April 23-25, Washington.

Graham, Jean Ann, and Michael Argyle

1975 "A Cross-Cultural Study of the Communciation of Extra-Verbal Meaning by Gestures", *International Journal of Psychology* 10, 57-67.

Green, Jerald R.

1968 *A Gesture Inventory for the Teaching of Spanish* (New York: Chilton).

Greenberg, Joseph H.

1963 (ed.) *Universals of Language* (Cambridge, Mass.: MIT Press).

1964 "Linguistics and Ethology", in: *Language in Culture and Society*, ed. by Dell Hymes (New York: Harper & Row), pp. 27-31.

1966 "Language Universals", in: *Current Trends in Linguistics*, Vol. 3, *Theoretical Foundations*, ed. by Thomas A. Sebeok (The Hague: Mouton), pp. 61-112.

Greenlee, Douglas

1973 *Peirce's Concept of Sign* (= *Approaches to Semiotics*, paperback series 5) (The Hague: Mouton). [Cf. Gérard Deledalle's 1974 review article, "Qu'est-ce qu'un signe? Apropos de *Peirce's Concept of Sign* de Douglas Greenlee", *Semiotica* 10, 383-97.]

Greimas, Algirdas J.

1966 *Sémantique structurale* (Paris: Larousse).

[1968] *Modelli semiologici* (Urbino: Argalia).

1970 *Du sens: Essais sémiotiques* (Paris: Seuil).

Greimas, Algirdas J., *et al.*

1970 (eds.) *Sign, Language, Culture* (The Hague: Mouton).

Griffin, Donald R.

1968 "Echolocation and Its Relevance to Communication Behavior", in: Sebeok (ed.), 1968b, pp. 154-64.

Grossman, Reinhardt

1969 *Reflections on Frege's Philosophy* (Evanston: Northwestern University Press).

Guiraud, Pierre

1971 *La sémiologie* (Paris: Presses Universitaires de France). [English version – 1975: *Semiology* (London and Boston: Routledge & Kegan Paul).]

Gutiérrez Lopez, Gilberto A.

1975 *Estructura de lenguaje y conocimiento: Sobre la epistemologia de la semiotica* (Madrid: Fragua).

Haas, Willy

1957 "Zero in Linguistic Description", *Studies in Linguistic Analysis*, Special volume of The Philological Society of London

(Oxford: Blackwell), pp. 33-53.

Hadas, Moses
1954 *Ancilla to Classical Reading* (New York: Columbia University Press).

Haldane, J. B. S.
1955 "Animal Communication and the Origin of Human Language", *Science Progress* 43, 385-401.

Hall, Edward T.
1959 *The Silent Language* (Garden City: Doubleday).
1966 *The Hidden Dimension* (Garden City: Doubleday).
1968 "Proxemics", *Current Anthropology* 9, 83-108.

Hall, K. R. L.
1963, 1966 "Tool-using Performances as Indicators of Behavioral Adaptability, *Current Anthropology* 4, 479-94, and 7, 215-16.

Hall, K. R. L., and George B. Schaller
1964 "Tool-using Behavior of the California Sea Otter", *Journal of Mammalology* 45, 287-98.

Hamilton, A. Mc.
1878 *Nervous Diseases: Their Description and Treatment* (Philadelphia: Henry C. Lee).

Harrison, Randall P., *et al.*
1972 "The Nonverbal Communication Literature", *The Journal of Communication* 22, 460-76.

Haugen, Einar
1951 "Directions in Modern Linguistics", *Language* 27, 211-22.

Hayes, Alfred S.
1964 "Paralinguistics and Kinesics: Pedagogical Perspectives", in: Sebeok, Hayes, and Bateson (eds.), 1964, pp. 145-75, with discussion, pp. 175-90.

Hayes, Francis C.
1957 "Gestures: A Working Bibliography", *Southern Folklore Quarterly* 21, 218-317.

Hediger, Heini
1955 *Studies in the Psychology and Behaviour of Captive Animals in Zoos and Circuses* (London: Butterworth's Scientific Publications).
1965 "Man as a Social Partner of Animals and Vice Versa", *Symposia of the Zoological Society of London* 14, 291-300.
1967 "Verstehens- und Verständingungsmöglichkeiten zwischen Mensch und Tier", *Schweizerische Zeitschrift für Psychologie und ihre Anwendungen* 26, 234-55.
1968 *The Psychology and Behaviour of Animals in Zoos and Circuses* (New York: Dover).
1970 "Zur Sprache der Tiere", *Der Zoologische Garten* 38, 171-79.

1974   "Communication between Man and Animal", *Image Roche* 62, 27-40.

Helbo, André
1974   "Prolégomènes à la sémiologie théâtrale: Une lecture de *Port Royal*", *Semiotica* 11, 359-74.

Helbo, André, *et al.*
1975   (eds.) *Sémiologie de la représentation: Théatre, television, bande dessinée* (Brussels: Complexe).

Hendricks, Gordon
1975   *Eadweard Muybridge: The Father of the Motion Picture* (London: Secker and Warburg).

Herculano de Carvalho, José G
1969   "Segno e significazione in João de São Tomás", *Estudos Linguísticos* (Coimbra: Atlântida) 2, 129-68.

Hermes, Hans
1938   *Semiotik: eine Theorie der Zeichengestalten als Grundlage für Untersuchungen von formalisierten Sprache. Forschungen zur Logik und zur Grundlegung der Exakten Wissenschaften* 5 (Leipzig: Hirzel).

Hess, Eckhard H.
1962   "Ethology: An Approach Toward the Complete Analysis of Behavior", in: *New Directions in Psychology*, ed. by Roger Brown, *et al.* (New York: Holt, Rinehart and Winston), pp. 157-266.
1975   *The Tell-Tale Eye: How Your Eyes Reveal Hidden Thoughts and Emotions* (New York: Van Nostrand Reinhold).

Hewes, Gordon W.
1975   *Language Origins: A Bibliography* (= *Approaches to Semiotics* 44) (The Hague: Mouton).

Hill, Archibald A.
1948   "The Use of Dictionaries in Language Teaching", *Language Learning* 1, 9-13.
1958   *Introduction to Linguistic Structures: From Sound to Sentence in English* (New York: Harcourt Brace).
1969   (ed.) *Linguistics Today* (New York: Basic Books).

Hill, Jane H.
Forthcoming   "Language Contact Systems and Human Adaptation", *Science*.

Hinde, Robert A.
1966   *Animal Behaviour: A Synthesis of Ethology and Comparative Psychology* (New York: McGraw-Hill).
1972   (ed.) *Non-verbal Communication* (Cambridge: University Press).
1974   *Biological Bases of Human Social Behaviour* (New York:

Mc Graw-Hill).

Hinton, H. E.
1973 "Natural Deception", in: *Illusion in Nature and Art*, ed. by R. L. Gregory and E. H. Gombrich (London: Duckworth), pp. 97-159.

Hjelmslev, Louis
1953 [Danish original 1943] *Prolegomena to a Theory of Language* (Baltimore: Waverly).

Hockett, Charles F.
1955 "How To Learn Martian", *Astounding Science Fiction*, May.
1963 "The Problem of Universals in Language", in: Greenberg (ed.), 1963, 1-29.

Hofstadter, Albert
1941-42 "Objective Teleology", *The Journal of Philosophy* 38, 29-39.
1942 "Subjective Teleology", *Philosophy and Phenomenological Research* 2, 88-97.

Holenstein, Elmar
1976 *Linguistik Semiotik Hermeneutik: Plädoyers für eine strukturale Phänomenologie* (Frankfurt a/M: Suhrkamp).

Hollander, John
1959 "The Metrical Emblem", *Kenyon Review* 21, 279-96.

Hooff, J. A. R. A. M. van
1972 "A Comparative Approach to the Phylogeny of Laughter and Smiling", in: Hinde (ed.), 1972, pp. 209-38.

Hoppál, Mihály
1971 "Szemiotikai kutatások Magyarországon", *Fotómüvészet* 14:2, 9-18, 34.
1973 "Semiotic Research in Hungary", *Acta Ethnographica* 22, 204-16.

Horányi, Özséb, and Csaba Pléh
1975 "Jelek a rajzfilmben", in: *Tanulmányok a magyar animácios filmről* (Budapest: Magyar Filmtudományi Intézet és Filmarchivum), pp. 226-48.

Horányi, Özséb, and György Szépe
1975 (eds.) *A jel tudománya* (Budapest: Gondolat).

Hotopf, W. H. N.
1965 *Language, Thought and Comprehension: A Case Study of the Writings of I. A. Richards* (Bloomington: Indiana University Press).

Hrushovski, Benjamin, and Itamar Even-Zohar
1972 "A Short Hebrew-English-French-German-Russian Dictionary of Terms in Semiotics, Semantics, and Allied Fields", *Hasifrut: Quarterly for the Study of Literature* 3, 412-26.

Huggins, W. H., and Doris R. Entwisle
1974 *Iconic Communication: An Annotated Bibliography* (Baltimore: The Johns Hopkins University Press).
Husserl, Edmund
1970 [1890[1]] "Zur Logik der Zeichen (Semiotik)", in: *Philosophie der Arithmetik*, ed. by Lothar Elegy (The Hague: Martinus Nijhoff), pp. 340-72.
Hutt, Clelia
1968 "Etude d'un corpus: Dictionnaire du langage gestuel chez les Trappistes", *Langages* 10, 107-18.
Huxley, Aldous
1963 *Literature and Science* (New York: Harper & Row).
Huxley, Julian
1966 "A Discussion of Ritualization of Behaviour in Animals and Men", *Philosophical Transactions of the Royal Society of London* 251, 247-526.
Hymes, Dell
1968a Foreword to Peacock, 1968.
1968b Review of Burke, 1966. *Language* 44, 664-69.
1969 Review of Duncan, 1968. *Science* 164, 695-96.
Ičas, M.
1969 *The Biological Code* (Amsterdam: North-Holland).
Ikegami, Yoshihiko
1971 "A Stratificational Analysis of the Hand Gestures in Indian Classical Dancing", *Semiotica* 4, 365-91.
Ivanov, V. V.
1969 "L'évolution des signes — symboles", *Semiotica* 1, 218-21.
Ivanov, V. V., and V. Toporov
1965 *Slavjanskie jazykovyie modelurujuščie semiotičeskie sistemy* (Moscow: Nauk).
Jackson, J. H.
1932 "On Affections of Speech from Disease of the Brain", in: *Selected Writings of John Hughlings Jackson* (London: Hodder and Staughton), Vol. 2, pp. 155-70.
Jacob, François
1974 *The Logic of Living Systems: A History of Heredity* (London: Allen Lane).
Jakobson, Roman
1940 "Das Nullzeichen", *Bulletin du Cercle Linguistique de Copenhague* 5, 12-14.
1963 [1957] *Essais de linguistique générale* (Paris: Minuit).
1964 "On Visual and Auditory Signs", *Phonetica* 11, 216-20.
1965 "Quest for the Essence of Language", *Diogenes* 51, 21-37.
1966 [1939] "Signe zéro". Reprinted in *Readings in Linguistics* II, ed. by E. Hamp, F. Householder, and R. Austerlitz (Chicago:

University of Chicago Press, 1966), pp. 109-15.

1967 "About the Relation Between Visual and Auditory Signs", in: *Models for the Perception of Speech and Visual Form*, ed. by W. Wathen-Dunn (Cambridge, Mass.: MIT Press).

1968 "Language in Relation to Other Communication Systems". Address before Conference on Language in Society and in the Technical World, Milan, Olivetti. Reported in de Mauro and Grassi, 1969.

1969 "Linguistics in Relation to Other Sciences", in: *Actes du X^è Congrès International des Linguistes, Bucarest, 28 août-2 septembre 1967*, ed. by A. Graur (Bucharest: Académie de la République Socialiste de Roumanie), Vol. 1, p. 78.

1970 "Language in Relation to Other Communication Systems", *Linguaggi nella società e nella tecnica: Convegno promosso dalla Ing. C. Olivetti & C., S. p. A. per il centenario della nascita di Camillo Olivetti* (Milan: Communità), pp. 3-16.

1971a "An Example of Migratory Terms and Institutional Models", *Selected Writings* 2 (The Hague: Mouton), pp. 257-38.

1971b "On Linguistic Aspects of Translation", in: Jakobson, 1971d, pp. 260-66.

1971c "Two Aspects of Language and Two Types of Aphasic Disturbances", in: Jakobson, 1971d, pp. 239-59.

1971d "Word and Language", *Selected Writings* 2 (The Hague: Mouton).

1972 "Motor Signs for 'Yes' and 'No' ", *Language in Society* 1, 91-96.

1974 [1970] *Main Trends in the Science of Language* (New York: Harper & Row, Harper Torchbooks).

1975 *Coup d'oeil sur le développement de la sémiotique* (= *Studies in Semiotics* 3) (Bloomington: Research Center for Language and Semiotic Studies).

Jaulin, Robert
1970 "Formal Analysis of Geomancy", *Semiotica* 2, 195-246.

Jencks, C., and G. Baird
1969 *Meaning in Architecture* (London: Barrie & Jenkins).

Jervis, Robert
1970 *The Logic of Images in International Relations* (Princeton: University Press). [Cf. Anatol Rapoport's 1973 review article, "Games Nations Play", *Semiotica* 9, 272-88.]

Jespersen, Otto
1964 [1922] *Language, Its Nature, Development, and Origin* (New York: Norton).

Joos, Martin
1958 "Semology: A Linguistic Theory of Meaning", *Studies in Linguistics* 13, 53-70.

Jorio, Andrea de
1832 *La mimica degli antichi investigata nel gestire Napoletano* (Naples: Stamperia e Cartiera del Fibreno).
Jung, Carl G., *et al.*
1968 (eds.) *Man and His Symbols* (New York: Dell).
Kahn, David
1967 *The Codebreakers* (New York: Macmillan).
Kahn, Theodore C.
1969 "Symbols and Man's Nature", *The International Journal of Symbolology* 1, 5-6.
Kainz, Friedrich
1961 *Die "Sprache" der Tiere. Tatsachen – Problemschau – Theorie* (Stuttgart: Enke).
Kang, Wook
Forthcoming *G. H. Mead's Concept of Rationality: A Study of the Use of Symbols and Other Implements* (= *Approaches to Semiotics* 54) (The Hague: Mouton).
Kantor, Jacob R.
1936 *An Objective Psychology of Grammar* (= *Indiana University Publications*, Science Series 1) (Bloomington).
Katz, Jerrold J.
1966 *The Philosophy of Language* (New York: Harper & Row).
1967 "Recent Issues in Semantic Theory", *Foundations of Language* 3, 124-94.
Katz, Jerrold J., and Paul Postal
1964 *An Integrated Theory of Linguistic Descriptions* (Cambridge, Mass.: MIT Press).
Kauffman, Lynne
1971 "Tacesics, the Study of Touch: A Model for Proxemic Analysis", *Semiotica* 4, 149-61.
Kecskemeti, Paul
1952 *Meaning, Communication, and Value* (Chicago: University of Chicago Press).
Kelemen, János
1974 Review – see *VS: Quaderni di studi semiotici, 1971-74.*
1976 "Locke's Theory of Language and Semiotics", *Language Sciences* 40, 16-24.
Kendon, Adam
1972a "Some Relationships between Body Motion and Speech: An Analysis of an Example", in: *Studies in Dyadic Communication*, ed. by Aron Wolfe Siegman and Benjamin Pope (New York: Pergamon).
1972b Review of Birdwhistell, 1970. *American Journal of Psychology* 85, 441-55.

1977 *Studies in the Behavior of Social Interaction* (= *Studies in Semiotics* 6) (Bloomington: Research Center for Language and Semiotic Studies).

Ketner, Kenneth Laine, and Christian J. W. Kloesel
1975 Review – see Bense and Walther, 1973.

Key, Mary Ritchie
1974 "U.S.A. – Nonverbal Communication", *VS: Quaderni di studi semiotici* 8/9, 248-80.

Klaus, Georg
1963 *Semiotik und Erkenntnistheorie* (Munich: Frank).

Kleinpaul, Rudolph
1888 *Sprache ohne Worte: Idee einer allegemeinen Wissenschaft der Sprache* (Leipzig: Friedrich). [Reprinted as *Approaches to Semiotics* 19 (The Hague: Mouton, 1972).]

Kloft, W.
1959 "Versuch einer Analyse der trophobiotischen Beziehungen von Ameisen zu Aphiden", *Biologisches Zentralblatt* 78, 863-70.

Kluckhohn, Clyde
1953 "Universal Categories of Culture", in: *Anthropology Today: An Encyclopedic Inventory*, ed. by A. L. Kroeber (Chicago: University of Chicago Press).

Knapp, Mark L.
1972 *Nonverbal Communication in Human Interaction* (New York: Holt, Rinehart and Winston).

Knappert, J.
1961 "Seintrom en taalmelodie in Afrika", *Mededelingen van het Afrika Instituut* 15:5, 155-61.

Koch, Christian
Forthcoming (ed.) *Semiotics and Cinema* (= *Approaches to Semiotics* 52) (The Hague: Mouton).

Koch, Walter A.
1974 "Semiotik und Sprachgenese", in: *Perspektiven der Linguistik* 2, ed. by Walter A. Koch (Stuttgart: Kröner), pp. 312-46.

Koestler, A.
1967 *The Ghost in the Machine* (New York: Macmillan).

Kortland, Adriaan, and M. Kooij
1963 "Protohominid Behaviour in Primates", *Symposia of the Zoological Society of London* 10, 61-88.

Kowzan, Tadeusz
1975 *Littérature et spectacle* (= *Approaches to Semiotics* 58) (The Hague: Mouton).

Krampen, Martin
1965 "Signs and Symbols in Graphic Communication", *Design*

Quarterly 62, 3-31.

Krenn, Herwig, and Klaus Müller
1970 "Generative Semantik", *Linguistische Berichte* 5, 85-106.

Kretzmann, Norman
1967 "Semantics, History of", in: *The Encyclopedia of Philosophy* 7, 358-406.

Kristeva, Julia
1967 "L'expansion de la sémiotique", *Social Science Information* 6, 169-81.
1969a "La sémiologie comme science des idéologies", *Semiotica* 1, 196-204.
1969b *Semeiotikè: Recherches pour une sémanalyse* (Paris: Seuil).
1970 "La mutation sèmiotique", *Annales économies, sociétés, civilisations* 25, 1497-522.

Kristeva, Julia, Josette Rey-Debove, and Donna Jean Umiker
1971 (eds.) *Essays in Semiotics/Essais de sémiotique* (= *Approaches to Semiotics* 4) (The Hague: Mouton).

Kroeber, A. L., and Clyde Kluckhohn
1952 *Culture: A Critical Review of Concepts and Definitions* (Cambridge, Mass.: Peabody Museum).

Krueger, John R.
1968 "Language and Techniques of Communication as Theme or Tool in Science-Fiction", *Linguistics* 39, 68-86.

Kuckuk, Erwin
1936 "Tierpsychologische Beobachtungen an zwei jungen Braunbären", *Zeitschrift für vergleichende Physiologie* 24, 14-41.

Kull, I. G.
1965 "Semiotika i obučenie", *Semeiotikè* 2, 11-21.

La Barre, Weston
1964 "Paralinguistics, Kinesics, and Cultural Anthropology", in: Sebeok, Hayes, and Bateson (eds.), 1964, pp. 191-220, with discussion, pp. 221-37.

Labov, William
1973 "The Social Setting of Linguistic Change", in: *Current Trends in Linguistics*, Vol. 11, *Diachronic, Areal, and Typological Linguistics*, ed. by Thomas A. Sebeok (The Hague: Mouton), pp. 195-251.

Lacan, Jacques
1966 *Écrits* (Paris: Seuil).
1968 *The Language of Self: The Function of Language in Psychoanalysis*, trans. with notes and commentary by A. Wilden (Baltimore: The Johns Hopkins University Press).

Lamb, Sydney M.
n.d. [1966] *Outline of Stratificational Grammar* (Washington D. C.:

Georgetown University Press).
Lambert, J. H.
1764 *Neues Organon oder Gedanken über die Erforschung und Bezeichnung des Wahren und desen Unterscheidung vom Irrthum und Schein*, 2. Band (Leipzig: Wendler).
Land, Stephen K.
1974 *From Signs to Propositions: The Concept of Form in Eighteenth-Century Semantic Thought* (London: Longman).
Landar, Herbert
1966 *Language and Culture* (New York: Oxford University Press).
Lane, Michael
1970 (ed.) *Introduction to Structuralism* (New York: Basic Books).
Langer, Susanne K.
1948 [1942] *Philosophy in a New Key: A Study in the Symbolism of Reason, Rite, and Art* (New York: Penguin).
Lange-Seidl, Annemarie
1975 "Ansatzpunkte für Theorien nichtverbaler Zeichen", in: *Sprachtheorie*, ed. by Brigitte Schlieben-Lange (Hamburg: Hoffman und Campe), pp. 241-75.
Latif, Israil A.
1934 "The Physiological Basis of Linguistic Development and of the Ontogeny of Meaning", *Psychological Review* 41, 55-85, 153-76, 246-64.
Lawick-Goodall, Jane van
1968 *The Behaviour of Free-living Chimpanzees in the Gombe Stream Reserve* (= *Animal Behaviour Monographs* 1, Part 3).
Laziczius, Gyula
1932 *Bevezetés a fonológiába* (Budapest: Magyar Nyelvtudományi Társaság).
1942 *Általános nyelvészet: alapelvek és módszertani kérdések* (Budapest: Magyar Tudományos Akadémia).
1966 *Selected Writings of Gyula Laziczius*, ed. by Thomas A. Sebeok (The Hague: Mouton).
Le Boeuf, Burney J., and Richard S. Peterson
1969 "Dialects in Elephant Seals", *Science* 166, 1654-56.
Lenneberg, Eric H.
1967 *Biological Foundations of Language* (New York: John Wiley).
1969 "Problems in the Systematization of Communicative Behavior", in: Sebeok and Ramsay (eds.), 1969, Ch. 5.
1971 "Of Language Knowledge, Apes, and Brains", *Journal of Psycholinguistic Research* 1, 1-29.
Lévi-Strauss, Claude
1945 "L'analyse structurale en linguistique et en anthropologie", *Word* 1, 33-53.

1956 "Structure et dialectique", in: *For Roman Jakobson* (The Hague: Mouton).

1958 *Anthropologie structurale* (Paris: Plon).

1962a *La pensée sauvage* (Paris: Plon).

1962b "Les limites de la notion de structure en ethnologie", in: Bastide (ed.), 1962.

1966 "The Culinary Triangle", *Partisan Review* 33, 586-95.

1973 *Anthropologie structurale deux* (Paris: Plon).

Lewis, C. I.

1946 *An Analysis of Knowledge and Valuation* (La Salle, Ill.: Open Court).

Lewis, Kathleen

19/0 "Conference on Language and Medicine", *Language Sciences* 12, 14-16.

Liapunov, A. A.

1963 (ed.) *Problemy Kibernetiki* (Moscow: State Publishing House).

Lieb, Irwin C.

1953 (ed.) *Charles S. Peirce's Letters to Lady Welby* (New Haven: Whitlock's).

Lindekens, René

1971 *Éléments pour une sémiotique de la photographie* (Brussels: AIMAV).

Lloyd, James E.

1965 "Aggressive Mimicry in *Photuris*: Firefly Femmes Fatales", *Science* 149, 653-54.

1966 *Studies on the Flash Communication System in Photinus Fireflies* (= *Ann Arbor, Museum of Zoology, University of Michigan* series 130).

1975 "Aggressive Mimicry in *Photuris* Fireflies: Signal Repertoires by Femmes Fatales", *Science* 187, 452-53.

Locke, John

1690 *Essay Concerning Humane Understanding* (London: Basset).

Loewenstein, W. R.

1970 "Intercellular Communication", *Scientific American* 222, 79-86.

Lorenz, Konrad

1965 *Evolution and Modification of Behavior* (Chicago: University of Chicago Press).

Lorenz, Konrad, and Paul Leyhausen

1968 *Antriebe tierischen und menschlichen Verhaltens* (Munich: Piper).

Lotman, Jurij M.

1965, 1967, 1969, 1971, 1975 (ed.) *Semeiotikè. Trudy po znakovym systemam* II, III, IV, V, VI. (= *Transactions of the Tartu State University* 189, 198, 236, 284).

1973   *Semiotika kino i problemi kinoestetiki* (Tallin: Eesti Raa-
       mat).
Lotman, Jurij M., *et al.*
1975   "Theses on the Semiotic Study of Cultures (As Applied to
       Slavic Texts)", in: Sebeok, 1975a, pp. 57-83.
Lotman, Juri M., and A. M. Pjatigorskij
1969   "Le texte et la fonction", *Semiotica* 1, 205-17.
Lotman, Jurij M., and Boris A. Uspenskij
1973   (eds.) *Ricerche semiotiche: Nuove tendenze delle scienze
       umane nell'URSS* (Turin: Einaudi).
Lotz, John
1950   "Speech and Language", *Journal of the Acoustical Society of
       America* 22, 712-17.
1966 [1954]   "Plan and Publication of Noreen's Vårt Språk", in:
       Portraits of Linguists 2, ed. by Thomas A. Sebeok (Bloom-
       ington: Indiana University Press), pp. 56-65.
1972   "A Select Bibliography on Script and Language", *Visible
       Language: The Journal for Research on the Visual Media of
       Language Expression* 6, 79-80.
Lowie, R. H.
1937   *The History of Ethnological Theory* (New York: Farrar &
       Rinehart).
Luria, A. R.
1967   "Problems and Facts in Neural Linguistics", *International
       Social Science Journal* 19, 36-51.
1974   "Basic Problems of Neurolinguistics", in: Sebeok (ed.), 1974b,
       pp. 2561-94.
Lurker, Manfred
1968   (ed.) *Bibliographie zur Symbolik, Ikonographie und Mythol-
       ogie* (Baden-Baden: Heitz).
Lyons, John
1963   *Structural Semantics: An Analysis of Part of the Vocabulary
       of Plato* (Oxford: Blackwell).
1968   *Introduction to Theoretical Linguistics* (Cambridge: University
       Press).
McCawley, James D.
1968   "The Role of Semantics in Grammar", in: *Universals in
       Linguistic Theory*, ed. by E. Bach and R. T. Harms (New
       York: Holt, Rinehart and Winston), pp. 124-69.
McGrew, W. C.
1972   *An Ethological Study of Children's Behavior* (New York:
       Academic Press).
MacKay, D. M.
1961   "The Informational Analysis of Questions and Commands",
       in: *Information Theory*, ed. by Colin Cherry (Washington,

D.C.: Butterworth).

1972 "Formal Analysis of Communicative Processes", in: Hinde (ed.), 1972, pp. 3-25.

Macksey, Richard

1970 "Lions and Squares: Opening Remarks", in: Macksey and Donato (eds.), 1970, pp. 1-14.

Macksey, Richard, and Eugenio Donato

1970 (eds.) *The Languages of Criticism and the Sciences of Man: The Structuralist Controversy* (Baltimore: The Johns Hopkins Press).

Mahl, George F., and Gene Schulze

1964 "Psychological Research in the Extralinguistic Area", in: Sebeok, Hayes, and Bateson (eds.), 1964, pp. 51-124, with discussion, pp. 125-43.

Mahmoudian, Mortéza

1969 "Signe", in: *La linguistique: Guide alphabétique*, ed. by A. Martinet (Paris: Denoël), pp. 345-53, 428-29.

Maldonado, Tomás

1959 "Communication and Semiotics", *Quarterly Bulletin of the Hochschule für Gestaltung* (Ulm), July, 69-78.

1961 *Beitrag zur Terminologie der Semiotik* (Ulm: J. Ebner).

Malinowski, B.

1923 *The Problem of Meaning in Primitive Languages.* Supplement to Ogden and Richards, 1938.

Mallery, Garrick

1972[2] [1881[1]] *Sign Language Among North American Indians Compared with that Among Other Peoples and Deaf-Mutes* (= *Approaches to Semiotics* 14) (The Hague: Mouton). [Cf. Georges Mounin's 1973 review article, "Une analyse du langage par gestes des Indiens (1881)", *Semiotica* 7, 154-62.]

Malmberg, Bertil

1973 *Teckenlära: En introduktion till tecknens och symbolernas problematik* (Stockholm: Aldus/Bonniers).

Malson, Lucien

1973 "Un entretien avec Claude Lévi-Strauss", *Le Monde*, Dec. 8, 20.

Mannoury, G.

1969 "A Concise History of Significs", *Methodology and Science* 2, 171-80.

Mar, Timothy T.

1974 *Face Reading: The Chinese Art of Physiognomy* (New York: Signet).

Marcus, Solomon

1974 "Din activitatea Centrului international de semiotică şi linguistică al Universității din Urbino—Italia", *Studii şi cercetări lingvistice* 25, 645-46.

Maritain, Jacques
1943 "Sign and Symbol", in: *Redeeming the Time* (London: Bles), Ch. 9.

Marler, Peter
1956 "The Voice of the Chaffinch and Its Function as a Language", *Ibis* 98, 231-61.
1961 "The Logical Analysis of Animal Communication", *Journal of Theoretical Biology* 1, 295-317.
1963 "Inheritance and Learning in the Development of Animal Vocalizations", in: *Acoustic Behavior*, ed. by R.-G. Busnel (Amsterdam).
1965 "Communication in Monkeys and Apes", in: *Primate Behavior: Field Studies of Monkeys and Apes*, ed. by Irven De-Vore (New York: Holt, Rinehart and Winston), pp. 566-67.
1967 "Animal Communication Signals", *Science* 157, 769-74.

Marler, Peter and Andrew Gordon.
1968 "The Social Environment of Infant Macques", in: *Environmental Influences: Proceedings of a Conference Under the Auspices of Russell Sage Foundation and The Rockefeller University*, ed. by David C. Glass (= *Biology and Behavior Series* 3) (New York: The Rockefeller University Press and Russell Sage Foundation), pp. 113-29.

Marler, Peter, and Miwako Tamura
1962 "Song 'Dialects' in Three Populations of White-crowned Sparrows", *The Condor* 64, 368-77.

Marshall, Alexander J.
1954 *Bower-birds: Their Displays and Breeding Cycles* (Oxford: Clarendon).

Martinet, André
1968 (ed.) *Le Langage*. Encyclopédie de la Pléiade (Paris: Gallimard).

Martinet, Jeanne
1973 *Clefs pour la sémiologie* (Paris: Seghers). [Cf. Gérard Bucher's 1975 review article, "L'Objet de la sémiologie", *Semiotica* 14, 181-96.

Massin
1970 *Letter and Image* (New York: Van Nostrand Reinhold).

Masters, Roger D.
1970 "Genes, Language, and Evolution", *Semiotica* 2, 295-320.

Matson, Floyd W., and Ashley Montagu
1967 (eds.) *The Human Dialogue: Perspectives on Communication* (New York: Free Press).

Mauro, Tullio de, and Letizia Grassi
1969 "I linguaggi nella società e nella tecnica", *Lingua e Stile* 4, 249-63.
Mayenowa, Maria R.
1967 "Semiotics Today: Reflections on the Second International Conference on Semiotics", *Social Science Information* 6, 59-64.
Mead, Margaret
1964 "Vicissitudes of the Study of the Total Communication Process", in: Sebeok, Hayes, and Bateson (eds.), 1964, pp. 277-87.
1969 "From Intuition to Analysis in Communication Research", *Semiotica* 1, 13-25.
Meader, Clarence L., and John H. Muyskens
1962 *Handbook of Biolinguistics* 1 (Toledo: Herbert C. Weller).
Meetham, A. R., and R. A. Hudson
1969 (eds.) *Encyclopaedia of Linguistics, Information and Control* (Oxford: Pergamon).
Mehrabian, Albert
1972 *Nonverbal Communication* (Chicago: Aldine, Atherton). [Cf. Murray Melvin's 1974 review article, "Some Issues in Nonverbal Communication", *Semiotica* 10, 293-304.]
Meiland, Jack W.
1970 *The Nature of Intention* (London: Methuen).
Meletinskij, Eleazar M.
1969a Afterword to V. Ja. Propp, *Morfologia skazki* (Moscow: Nauk).
1969b "Zur strukturell-typologischen Erforschung des Volksmärchens", *Deutsches Jahrbuch für Volkskunde* 15, 1-30.
Meletinsky, Eleazar, and Dmitri Segal
1971 "Structuralism and Semiotics in the USSR", *Diogenes* 73, 88-115.
Melvin, Murray
1974 Review – see Mehrabian, 1972.
Metz, Christian
1968a "Propositions méthodologiques pour l'analyse du film", *Social Science Information* 7, 107-19.
1968b *Essais sur la signification au cinéma* (Paris: Klincksieck).
1974 *Language and Cinema* (= *Approaches to Semiotics* 26) (The Hague: Mouton).
Miller, David L.
1973 *George Herbert Mead: Self, Language, and the World* (Austin: University of Texas Press).
Miller, George A., Karl Pribram, and Eugene Galanter
1960 *Plans and the Structure of Behavior* (New York: Holt,

Rinehart and Winston).

Miller, Robert L.
1968 *The Linguistic Relativity Principle and Humboldtian Ethno-linguistics: A History and Appraisal* (The Hague: Mouton).

Moles, Abraham A.
1964 "Les voies cutanées: compléments informationnels de la sensibilité de l'organisme", *Studium Generale* 17, 589-95.
1971 (ed.) *La communication* (Paris: Centre d'Etude et de Promotion de la Lecture).

Montagu, Ashley
1971 *Touching: The Human Significance of the Skin* (New York: Columbia University Press).

Montague, Richard
1974 *Formal Philosophy: Selected Papers ...*, ed. by Richmond H. Thomason (New Haven: Yale University Press).

Morawski, Stefan
1970 "Mimesis", *Semiotica* 2, 35-58.

Morin, Edgar, and Massimo Piattelli-Palmarini
1974 (eds.) *L'Unité de l'homme: Invariants biologiques et universaux culturels* (Paris: Seuil).

Morris, Charles W.
1938 *Foundations of the Theory of Signs* (= *International Encyclopedia of Unified Science* 1:2) (Chicago: University of Chicago Press).
1946 *Signs, Language and Behavior* (New York: Prentice-Hall).
1964 *Signification and Significance: A Study of the Relation of Signs and Values* (Cambridge, Mass.: MIT Press).
1971 *Writings on the General Theory of Signs* (= *Approaches to Semiotics* 16) (The Hague: Mouton). [Cf. Ferruccio Rossi-Landi's 1975 review article, "Signs About a Master of Signs", *Semiotica* 13, 155-97.]

Mounin, Georges
1959 "Les systèmes de communication non-linguistique et leur place dans la vie du XXè siècle", *Bulletin de la Société de Linguistique de Paris* 54, 176-200.
1968 *Saussure ou le structuraliste sans le savoir* (Paris: Seghers). [Cf. Jean-Jacques Nattiez's 1973 review article, "Quelques problèmes de la sémiologie fonctionnelle", *Semiotica* 9, 157-90.]
1970 *Introduction à la sémiologie* (Paris: Minuit).
1973 Review — see Mallery, 1972.

Mulder, J. W. F., and S. G. J. Hervey
1972 *Theory of the Linguistic Sign* (The Hague: Mouton).

Munn, Nancy D.
1973 *Walbiri Iconography: Graphic Representation and Cultural Symbolism in a Central Australian Society* (Ithaca: Cornell University Press).

Murdock, G. P.
1945 "The Common Denominator of Cultures", in: *The Science of Man in the World Crisis*, ed. by R. Linton (New York: Columbia University Press).

Musique en jeu
1971, 1973 "Dossier: la sémiologie de la musique" 5, 3-98; "Analyse méthodologie sémiologie" 10, 3-90.

Nagel, Ernest
1959 "Charles Sanders Peirce, A Prodigious but Little Known American Philosopher" (review article), *Scientific American* 200, 185-92.

Nattiez, Jean-Jacques
1972 "Is a Descriptive Semiotics of Music Possible?", *Language Sciences* 23, 1-7.
1973 Review – see Mounin, 1968.
1974 Review – see Ruwet, 1972.
1975 *Fondements d'une sémiologie de la musique* (Paris: Union générale d'éditions).

Naville, Adrien
1901[2] *Nouvelle classification des sciences* (Paris: Alcan).

Nelson, Lowry, Jr.
1975 "Signs of the Times: Semiotics 1974", *The Yale Review* 64, 296-320.

Nickel, Gerhard
1971 (ed.) *Papers in Contrastive Linguistics* (Cambridge: University Press).

Nida, Eugene A.
1964 *Toward a Science of Translating* (Leiden: Brill).
1969 "Science of Translation", *Language* 45, 483-98.
1975 *Exploring Semantic Structures* (Munich: Fink).

Nida, Eugene A., and Charles R. Taber
1969 *The Theory and Practice of Translation* (Leiden: Brill).

Northrop, F. S. C.
1953 "Cultural Values", in: *Anthropology Today: An Encyclopedic Inventory*, ed. by A. L. Kroeber (Chicago: University of Chicago Press), pp. 668-81.

Nöth, Winfried
1975 *Semiotik: Eine Einführung mit Beispielen für Reklameanalysen* (Tübingen: Niemeyer).

Nottebohm, Fernando
1970 "Ontogeny of Bird Song", *Science* 167, 950-56.

1975   "A Zoologist's View of Some Language Phenomena with Particular Emphasis on Vocal Learning", *Foundations of Language Development: A Multidisciplinary Approach*, ed. by Eric H. and Elizabeth Lenneberg (New York: Academic Press), Vol. 1, pp. 61-103.

O'Brien, James F.
1969   *Design by Accident* (New York: Dover).

Ogden, C. K., and I. A. Richards
1938[5] [1923[1]]   *The Meaning of Meaning: A Study of the Influence of Language upon Thought and of the Science of Symbolism* (New York: Harcourt, Brace).

Ohm, Thomas
1948   *Die Gebetsgebärden der Völker und das Christentum* (Leiden: Brill).

Oléron, Pierre
1974· *Éléments de repertoire du langage gestuel des sourds-muets* (Paris: CNRS).

Osgood, Charles E., G. J. Suci, and P. H. Tannenbaum
1957   *The Measurement of Meaning* (Urbana: University of Illinois Press).

Osgood, Charles E., and Thomas A. Sebeok
1965[2]   (eds.) *Psycholinguistics: A Survey of Theory and Research Problems* (Bloomington: Indiana University Press).

Osmond-Smith, David
1974   "Problems of Terminology and Method in the Semiotics of Music", *Semiotica* 11, 269-94.

Osolsobě, Ivo
1967   "Ostenze jako mezni případ lidského sdělování a její význam pro umění", *Estetika* 1, 2-23, 101.
1973a   "Fifty Keys to Semiotics", *Semiotica* 7, 226-81.
1973b   "Czechoslovak Semiotics Past and Present", *Semiotica* 9, 140-45.
1974   *Divadlo, které mluví, zpívá a tančí* [The Theatre Which Speaks, Sings, and Dances (Semiotics of the Musical Theatre)] (Prague: Supraphon).

Ostwald, Peter F.
1964   "How the Patient Communicates about Disease with the Doctor", in: Sebeok, Hayes, and Bateson (eds.), 1964, pp. 11-34, with discussion, pp. 35-49.
1968   "Symptoms, Diagnosis and Concepts of Disease: Some Comments on the Semiotics of Patient-Physician Communication", *Social Science Information* 7:4, 95-106.
1973   *The Semiotics of Human Sounds* (= *Approaches to Semiotics*

36) (The Hague: Mouton). [Cf. Iván Fónagy's 1975 review article, "Analyses sémiotiques de la voix", *Semiotica*, 13, 97-108.]

Pagnini, Marcello
1974 *Lingua e musica: Proposta per un'indagine strutturalistico-semiotica* (Bologna: Il Mulino).

Papp, Ferenc
1969 "Jelentés, közlés, szemiótika a Szovjet nyelvtudományban", in: *Nyelv és kommunikáció*, ed. by Tamás Szecskő and György Szépe (Budapest: A MRT Tömegkommunikációs Kutatóközpontjának kiadása), Vol. 2, pp. 95-125. ·

Parkinson, Frank
1975 Review of Mulder and Hervey, 1972. *Lingua*, 35, 173-93.

Parret, Herman
1975 "Idéologie et sémiologie chez Locke et Condillac: La question de l'autonomie du langage devant la pensée", in: *Ut Videam: Contributions to an Understanding of Linguistics*, ed. by Werner Abraham (Lisse: The Peter de Ridder Press), pp. 225-48.

Pawlowski, T.
1974 "Linguistics and the Semiotic Theory of Culture", *Scientia* 5-8, 1-5.

Pazukhin, Rościsław
1972 "The Concept of Signal", *Lingua Posnaniensis* 16, 25-43.

Peacock, James L.
1968 *Rites of Modernization: Symbolic and Social Aspects of Indonesian Proletarian Drama* (Chicago: University of Chicago Press).

Pedersen, Holger
1962 *The Discovery of Language: Linguistic Science in the Nineteenth Century*, trans. J. W. Spargo (Bloomington: Indiana University Press).

Peirce, Charles S.
1906 "Prolegomena to an Apology for Pragmaticism", *The Monist* 16, 492-546.
1934 (c. 1906) "Pragmatism in Retrospect: A Reformulation", in: *Collected Papers* (1965-66), Vol. 5.
1965-66 *Collected Papers of Charles Sanders Peirce*, ed. by Charles Hartshorne, Paul Weiss, and Arthur W. Burks, 6 vols. (Cambridge, Mass.: Harvard University Press). [References are to volumes and paragraphs, not pages.]

Peirce Newsletter, The Charles S.
1974- [Institute for Studies in Pragmaticism (Lubbock: Texas Tech University).]

Pelc, Jerzy
1969 "Meaning as an Instrument", *Semiotica*, 1, 26-48.

1971   *Studies in Functional Logical Semiotics of Natural Languages* (The Hague: Mouton).
1974   "The Development of Polish Semiotics in the Post-War Years", *Semiotica* 10, 369-81.
Pfeiffer, John E.
1969   *The Emergence of Man* (New York: Harper & Row).
Phillips, Herbert P.
1959-60   "Problems of Translation and Meaning in Fieldwork", *Human Organization* 18, 184-92.
Piaget, Jean
1968   *Le structuralisme* (Paris: PUF).
Pignatari, Decio
1971[5]   *Informação. Linguagem. Communicação* (São Paulo: Perspectiva).
Pinborg, Jan
1962   "Das Sprachdenken der Stoa und Augustins Dialektik", *Classica et Mediaevalia* 23, 148-77.
1972   *Logik und Semantik im Mittelalter: ein Überblick* (Stuttgart: Fromann-Holzboog).
Pitts, Walter, and Warren S. McCulloch
1947   "How We Know Universals: The Perception of Auditory and Visual Forms", *Bulletin of Mathematical Biophysics* 9, 127-49.
Poetics, Poetyka, Poetika I, II
1961, 1965   [Warsaw: PWN.]
Pohl, Jacques
1968   *Symboles et langages* 1: *Le symbole, clef de l'humain* (Paris: Sodi).
Poinsot, Jean
Forthcoming   *Treatise on Signs* (*Tractatus de Signis*), ed. by John N. Deely (= *Advances in Semiotics* 3) (Bloomington: Indiana University Press).
Poiret, Maude
1970   *Body Talk: The Signs of Kinesics* (New York: Award Books).
Pop, Mihai
1972   "Le laboratoire de sémiotique de l'Université de Bucarest, Roumanie", *Semiotica* 5, 301-02.
Postgate, J. P.
1900   "The Science of Meaning, Inaugural Address", in: Bréal (ed.), 1900, pp. 311-36.
Pottier, Bernard
1973   (ed.) *Le langage: Les dictionnaires du savoir moderne* (Paris: Centre d'Etude et de Promotion de la Lecture).
Poyatos, Fernando
1970   "Kinesica del Español actual", *Hispania* 53, 444-52.
1975   Review — see Saitz and Cervenka, 1972.

Praz, Mario
1964[2] *Studies in Seventeenth-Century Imagery* (Rome: Edizioni di Storia e Letteratura).
Prieto, Luis J.
1966 *Messages et signaux* (Paris: Presses Universitaires de France).
1968 "La sémiologie", in: Martinet, 1968, pp. 93-144.
1975 *Études de linguistique et de sémiologie générales* (Geneva: Droz).
Proceedings of the Eighth International Congress of Linguists
1958 [Oslo: Oslo University Press.]
Proceedings of the International Union of Physiological Sciences, Vol. 3
n.d. [1964] [Amsterdam, Excerpta Medica Foundation, International Congress Series 49.]
Propp, V. Ja.
1928 *Morfologia skazki* (Moscow: Nauk). [English version – 1958, 1968[2]: *Morphology of the Fairytale* (Bloomington: Indiana University Research Center in Anthropology, Folklore, and Linguistics).]
Pumphrey, R. J.
1951 *The Origin of Language* (Liverpool: University Press).
Quine, Willard Van Orman
1963 *From a Logical Point of View* (New York: Harper & Row).
Rapoport, Anatol
1973 Review – see Jervis, 1970.
Rastier, François
1972 *Idéologie et théorie des signes* (= *Approaches to Semiotics* 17) (The Hague: Mouton).
Read, A. W.
1948 "An Account of the Word Semantics", *Word* 4, 78-97.
Rector, Monica
1974 "Glossario de Semiotica", *Vozes* 68, 5-17.
1975 "Código e mensagem do carnaval as escolas de samba", *Cultura* 5/19.
Reichenbach, Hans
1948 *Elements of Symbolic Logic* (New York: Macmillan).
Resnikow, Lasar Ossipowitsch
1968 *Erkenntnistheoretische Fragen der Semiotik* (Berlin: VEB Deutscher Verlag der Wissenschaften). [Enlarged edition from the original Russian, 1964; in 1967, an Italian translation was published under the title, *Semiotica e Marxismo: I problemi gnoseologici della semiotica* (Milan: Bompiani).]
Revzina, Olga G.
1972 "The Fourth Summer School on Secondary Modeling Systems", (Tartu, 17-24 August 1970)", *Semiotica* 6, 222-43.

Rey, Alain
1969   "Remarques sémantiques", *Langue Française* 4, 5-29.
1971   "La théorie positiviste des langages: Auguste Comte et la sémiotique", *Semiotica* 4, 52-74.
1973   *Théories du signe et du sens. Lectures* 1. (Paris: Klincksieck).
Rey-Debove, Josette
1973   (ed.) *Recherches sur les systèmes signifiants: Symposium de Varsovie 1968* (= *Approaches to Semiotics* 18) (The Hague: Mouton).
Rice, Charles E.
1967   "The Human Sonar System", in: *Animal Sonar Systems: Biology and Bionics*, ed. by René-Guy Busnel (Paris: Masson), pp. 719-55.
Richards, I. A.
1933   "Preface to a Dictionary", *Psyche* 13, 10-24.
1936   *The Philosophy of Rhetoric* (London: Oxford).
1969   "Tipi e campioni", *Strumenti Critici* 3, 187-93.
Rijnberk, Gérard van
1953   *Le langage par signes chez moines* (Amsterdam: North-Holland).
Robert, Paul
1967   *Dictionnaire alphabétique & analogique de la langue française* (Paris: Société du Nouveau Littré, Le Robert).
Roberts, Don D.
1973   *The Existential Graphs of Charles S. Peirce* (= *Approaches to Semiotics* 27) (The Hague: Mouton).
Rommetveit, Ragnar
1968   *Words, Meanings, and Messages: Theory and Experiments in Psycholinguistics* (New York: Academic Press).
Rosetti, Alexandru
1965 [1942[1]]   *Linguistica* (The Hague: Mouton).
Rossi-Landi, Ferruccio
1953   *Charles Morris* (Rome: Fratelli Bocca).
1968   "Ideologie della relatività linguistica", *Ideologie* 4, 3-69.
1974   "Linguistics and Economics", in: Sebeok (ed.), 1974b, pp. 1787-2026.
1975a   *Charles Morris e la semiotica nove centesca* (Milan: Feltrinelli).
1975b   Review – see Morris, 1971.
Rowell, Thelma
1972   *The Social Behaviour of Monkeys* (Harmondsworth: Penguin).
Ruesch, Jurgen
1957   *Disturbed Communication: The Clinical Assessment of Normal and Pathological Communicative Behavior* (New York: Norton).

1961   *Therapeutic Communication* (New York: Norton).

1972   *Semiotic Approaches to Human Relations* (= *Approaches to Semiotics* 25) (The Hague: Mouton).

Ruesch, Jurgen, and Gregory Bateson

1951   *Communication: The Social Matrix of Psychiatry* (New York: Norton).

Ruesch, Jurgen, and Weldon Kees

1956   *Nonverbal Communication: Notes on the Visual Perception of Human Relations* (Berkeley and Los Angeles: University of California Press).

Rüppel, G.

1969   "Eine 'Lüge' als gerichtete Mitteilung beim Eisfuchs (Alopex lagopus L.)", *Zeitschrift für Tierpsychologie* 26, 371-74.

Russell, Bertrand

1940   *An Inquiry into Meaning and Truth* (London: Allen and Unwin).

Russell, L. J.

1939   "Note on the Term *Semeiotike* in Locke", *Mind* 64, 405-06.

Russell, Patrick J., Jr.

1973   *The Philip Mills Arnold Semeiology Collection* (St. Louis: Rare Books and Special Collections Department, Washington University Libraries).

Ruwet, Nicolas

1967   "Musicology and Linguistics", *International Social Science Journal* 19, 79-87.

1972   *Langage, musique, poésie* (Paris: Seuil). [Cf. Jean-Jacques Nattiez's 1974 review article, "Problèmes de sémiologie musicale et de poétique structurale", *Semiotica* 11, 247-68.]

Ryle, Gilbert

1957   "The Theory of Meaning", in: *British Philosophy in Mid-century*, ed. by C. A. Mace (London: Allen and Unwin), pp. 239-64.

Saitz, Robert L.

1966   "Gestures in the Language Classroom", *English Language Teaching* 21, 33-37.

Saitz, Robert L., and Edward J. Cervenka

1972   *Handbook of Gestures: Colombia and the United States* (= *Approaches to Semiotics* 31) (The Hague: Mouton). [Cf. Fernando Poyatos' 1975 review article, "Gesture Inventories: Fieldwork Methodology and Problems", *Semiotica* 13, 199-227.]

Sanders, Gary

1970   "Peirce's Sixty-six Signs?", *Transactions of the Charles S. Peirce Society* 6, 3-16.

Sapir, Edward
1921 *Language* (New York: Harcourt, Brace & Co.).
1929 "The Status of Linguistics as a Science", *Language* 5, 207-14.
Saussure, Ferdinand de
1967 [1916[1]] *Cours de linguistique générale*, ed. by R. Engler (Wiesbaden: Otto Harrassowitz). [Cf. also 1960[5] (Paris: Payot); and for the most recent version, see the critical edition by Tullio de Mauro (Paris: Payot, 1972).]
Savan, David
Forthcoming *An Introduction to C. S. Peirce's Completed System of Semiotics* (= *Studies in Semiotics*) (Bloomington: Research Center for Language and Semiotic Studies).
Schaeder, Burkhard
1969 "Die Sprachinhaltforschung im deutschen sprachraum: Wortschatz- und Grammatiktheorie", *Studium Generale* 22, 294-309.
Schaff, Adam
1962 *Introduction to Semantics* (Oxford: Pergamon).
Schapiro, Meyer
1969 "On Some Problems in the Semiotics of Visual Art: Field and Vehicle in Image-Signs", *Semiotica* 1, 223-42.
Scheflen, Albert E.
1972 *Body Language and the Social Order: Communication as Behavioral Control* (Englewood Cliffs: Prentice-Hall).
1974 *How Behavior Means* (Garden City: Anchor).
Schenk, Günter
1973 *Zur Geschichte der logischen Form*, Vol. 1, *Einige Entwicklungstendenzen von der Antike bis zum Ausgang des Mittelalters* (Berlin: VEB Deutscher Verlag der Wissenschaft).
Scherer, Klaus R.
1970 *Non-verbale kommunikation: Ansätze zur Beobachtung und Analyse der aussersprachlichen Aspekte von Interaktionsverhalten* (Hamburg: Buske).
Schmidt, Siegfried J.
1969 *Bedeutung und Begriff: Zur Fundierung einer sprachphilosophischen Semantik* (Braunschweig: Vieweg).
Schnapper, Melvin
1969 "Your Actions Speak Louder ...", *Peace Corps Volunteer*, June, 7-10.
Schooneveld, C. H. van, and Daniel Armstrong
1976 (eds.) *Roman Jakobson: Echoes of His Scholarship* (Lisse: The Peter de Ridder Press).
Schuchardt, H.
1912 "Geschichtlich verwandt oder elementar verwandt?", *Magyar*

Nyelvőr 44, 3-13.

Scully, Malcolm G.

1975 "A Special Kind of Literacy", *Chronicle of Higher Education* 10, 11.

Sebeok, Thomas A.

1953 Review. *International Journal of American Linguistics* 19, 159-60.

1958 Review. *International Journal of American Linguistics* 24, 79-82.

1960 (ed.) *Style in Language* (Cambridge, Mass.: MIT Press).

1962a "Coding in the Evolution of Signalling Behavior", *Behavioral Science* 7, 430-42.

1962b "The Texture of a Cheremis Incantation", *Mémoires de la Société Finno-ougrienne* 125, 523-27.

1963 "Communication among Social Bees; Porpoises and Sonar; Man and Dolphin" (review article), *Language* 39, 448-66.

1965 "Animal Communication", *Science* 147, 1006-14.

1966 "Introduction" to *Portraits of Linguists: A Biographical Source Book for the History of Western Linguistics 1746-1963*, ed. by Thomas A. Sebeok (Bloomington: Indiana University Press).

1967a "Animal Communication", *International Social Science Journal* 19, 88-95.

1967b "Colloque international de sémiologie", *Linguistic Reporter* 9, 1-3.

1967c "Discussion of Communication Processes", in: Altmann (ed.), 1967, pp. 363-69.

1967d "On Chemical Signs", in: *To Honor Roman Jakobson* (The Hague: Mouton), pp. 1775-82.

1968a "A Selected and Annotated Guide to the Literature of Zoosemiotics and Its Background", *Social Science Information* 7, 103-17.

1968b (ed.) *Animal Communication: Techniques of Study and Results of Research* (Bloomington: Indiana University Press).

1968c "Communication Models and Signaling Behavior", *International Encyclopedia of the Social Sciences* 3, 33-40.

1968d "Goals and Limitations in the Study of Animal Communication", in: Sebeok (ed.), 1968b, pp. 3-14.

1968e "Zoosemiotics", *American Speech* 43, 142-44.

1969a (ed.) *Approaches to Semiotics* 1-   (The Hague: Mouton).

1969b "Semiotics and Ethology", in: Sebeok and Ramsay (eds.), 1969, pp. 200-31.

1969c "The Comparison of Human Communication with Animal Communication", *Actes du Xè Congrès International des*

Linguistes, Bucarest, 28 août-2 Septembre 1967, ed. by A. Graur (Bucharest: Académie de la Republique Socialiste de Roumanie), Vol. 1, pp. 433-36.

1970a   "The Word 'Zoosemiotics' ", *Language Sciences* 10, 36-37.

1970b   "Zoosemiotic Structures and Social Organization", *Linguaggi nella società e nella tecnica. Convegno promosso dalla Ing. C. Olivetti & C., S. p. A. per il centenario della nascita di Camillo Olivetti* (Milan: Communità), 113.

1972   *Perspectives in Zoosemiotics* (The Hague: Mouton).

1973   "Semiotica e affini", *VS: Quaderni di studi semiotici* 3, 1-11.

1974a   "Az állati kommunikáció", in: *A nyelv keletkezése*, ed. by Mária Papp (Budapest: Kossuth), pp. 191-212.

1974b   (ed.) *Current Trends in Linguistics*, Vol. 12, *Linguistics and Adjacent Arts and Sciences* (The Hague: Mouton).

1975a   (ed.) *The Tell-Tale Sign: A Survey of Semiotics* (Lisse: The Peter de Ridder Press).

1975b   "Zoosemiotics: A Bibliography", *VS: Quaderni di studi semiotici* 10.

1975c   "Iconicity". Opening address delivered at the Charles Sanders Peirce Symposium on Semiotics and the Arts, The Johns Hopkins University Centennial Celebration, Baltimore, September 25.

1975d   (ed.) *Current Trends in Linguistics*, Vol. 13, *Historiography of Linguistics* (The Hague: Mouton).

1977a   (ed.) *How Animals Communicate* (Bloomington: Indiana University Press).

1977b   "Semiosis in Nature and Culture" in: *A Perfusion of Signs: Transactions of the North American Semiotics Colloquium* (= *Advances in Semiotics* 4), ed. by Thomas A. Sebeok (Bloomington: Indiana University Press).

1977c   "The Pertinence of Peirce to Linguistics". Presidential address delivered to the Linguistic Society of America, San Francisco, December 30, 1975. *Language* 53.

1977d   *Semiotics* (Harmondsworth: Penguin).

Sebeok, Thomas A., Alfred S. Hayes, and Mary Catherine Bateson

1972[2] [1964[1]] (eds.) *Approaches to Semiotics: Cultural Anthropology, Education, Linguistics, Psychiatry, Psychology* (The Hague: Mouton).

Sebeok, Thomas A., and Alexandra Ramsay

1969   (eds.) *Approaches to Animal Communication* (The Hague: Mouton).

Sebeok, Thomas A., and Donna Jean Umiker-Sebeok

1976   (eds.) *Speech Surrogates: Drum and Whistle Systems* (= *Approaches to Semiotics* 23) (The Hague: Mouton).

Forthcoming *Aboriginal Sign Languages: Gestural Systems Among
            Native Peoples of the Americas and Australia* (New York:
            Plenum).
Sechehaye, Albert, Charles Bally, and Henri Frei
1940-41 "Pour l'arbitraire du signe", in: Godel (ed.), 1969, pp.
         191-95.
Segre, Cesare
1969 "Fra strutturalismo e semiologia", in: *I segni e la critica*, ed.
      by C. Segre (Turin: Einaudi), pp. 61-92.
1973 *Semiotics and Literary Criticism* (= *Approaches to Semiotics*
      35) (The Hague: Mouton).
Sellars, Wilfrid
1950 "Language, Rules, and Behavior", in: *John Dewey: Philosophy
      of Science and Freedom*, ed. by Sidney Hook (New York:
      Dial), pp. 289-315.
Semeiotikè: Trudy po znakovym systemam [Works on Semiotics]
1965-75 [Tartu: Acta et Commentationes Universitatis Tartuensis;
         Jurij M. Lotman's *Lekcii po struktural'noj poetike* was
         published as Trudy 1 (1964).]
Semiotext(e): Alternatives in Semiotics
1974-   1- . (New York: 560 West 113th Street).
Shands, Harley C.
1970a "Momentary Deity and Personal Myth: A Semiotic Inquiry
       Using Recorded Psychotherapeutic Material", *Semiotica* 2,
       1-34.
1970b *Semiotic Approaches to Psychiatry* (= *Approaches to Semi-
       otics* 2) (The Hague: Mouton).
1971 *The War with Words: Structure and Transcendence* (= *Ap-
      proaches to Semiotics* 12) (The Hague: Mouton).
Shands, Harley C., and James D. Meltzer
1975 "Clinical Semiotics", *Language Sciences* 38, 21-24.
Shepherd, Walter
1971 *Shepherd's Glossary of Graphic Signs and Symbols* (New
      York: Dover).
Sherzer, Joel
1971 "Conference on Interaction Ethology", *Language Sciences* 14,
      19-21.
1973 "Verbal and Nonverbal Deixis: The Pointed Lip Gesture
      among the San Blas Cuna", *Language in Society* 2, 117-31.
Sign Language Studies
1972-   Vols. 1- (Silver Spring, Md.: Linstok Press).
Simon, John
1975 "Antonioni: *The Passenger* will please refrain . . .", *Esquire*,
      July, pp. 16ff.
Simone, Raffaele
1972 "Sémiologie augustinienne", *Semiotica* 6, 1-31.

Simpozium po strukturnomu izučeniju znakovyx sistem
1962 [Moscow: Nauk].

Simpson, George G.
1966 "The Biological Nature of Man", *Science* 152, 472-78.

Smith, Henry Lee, Jr.
1969 "Language and the Total System of Communication", in: Hill (ed.), 1969, pp. 89-102.

Smith, W. John
1965 "Message, Meaning, and Context in Ethology", *American Naturalist* 99, 405-09.
1968 "Message-meaning Analysis", in: Sebeok (ed.), 1968b, Ch. 4.
1969a "Displays and Messages in Intraspecific Communication", *Semiotica* 1, 357-69.
1969b "Messages of Vertebrate Communication", *Science* 165, 145-50.

Smith, W. John, *et al.*
1974 "Tongue Showing: A Facial Display of Humans and Other Primate Species", *Semiotica* 11, 201-46.

Snider, James G., and C. E. Osgood
1969 (eds.) *Semantic Differential Technique: A Sourcebook* (Chicago: Aldine).

Söder, Karl
1964 "Beiträge J. H. Lamberts zur formalen Logik und Semiotik. Dissertation. Greifswald.

Sommer, Robert
1969 *Personal Space: The Behavioral Basis of Design* (Englewood Cliffs: Prentice-Hall).

Sørensen, Holger S.
1963 *The Meaning of Proper Names: With a Definiens Formula for Proper Names in Modern English* (Copenhagen: Gad).
1967 "Meaning", in: *To Honor Roman Jakobson* (The Hague: Mouton), Vol. 3, pp. 1876-99.

Spang-Hanssen, Henning
1954 [1948] "Recent Theories on the Nature of the Language Sign", *Travaux du Cercle Linguistique de Copenhague* 9.

Sparti, Antonino di
1975 *Linguaggio pubblicitario: analisi linguistica di un corpus pubblicitario di sigarette americane. Quaderni del Circolo Semiologico Siciliano* 5.

Sperber, Dan
1974 *Le symbolisme en général* (Paris: Hermann).

Staal, J. F.
1971 "What Was Left of Pragmatics in Jerusalem", *Language Sciences* 14, 29-32.

Stammerjohann, Harro, *et al.*
1975 *Handbuch der Linguistik: Allegemeine und angewandte Sprachwissenschaft* (Munich: Nymphenburger).
Stankiewicz, Edward
1964 "Problems of Emotive Language", in: Sebeok, Hayes, and Bateson (eds.), 1964, pp. 239-64, with discussion, pp. 265-76.
1974 "Structural Poetics and Linguistics", in: Sebeok (ed.), 1974b, pp. 629-59.
Forthcoming *Aspects of Emotive Language* (= *Studies in Semiotics*) (Bloomington: Research Center for Language and Semiotic Studies).
Stanosz, Barbara
1970 "Formal Theories of Extension and Intension of Expressions", *Semiotica* 2, 102-14.
Stefanini, Jean
1973 Review — see Bursill-Hall, 1971.
Steiner, George
1971 *Extraterritorial: Papers on Literature and the Language Revolution* (New York: Atheneum).
1975 *After Babel: Aspects of Language and Translation* (London: Oxford University Press).
Steinthal, Heyman
1881[2] [1871[1]] *Einleitung in die Psychologie und Sprachwissenschaft* (Berlin: Dümmlers).
Stender-Petersen, A.
1949 "Esquisse d'une théorie structurale de la littérature", *Travaux du Cercle Linguistique de Copenhague* 5, 277-87.
Stent, Gunther S.
1969 *The Coming of the Golden Age: A View of the End of Progress* (Garden City: Natural History Press).
Stepanov, Yu. S.
1971 *Semiotika* (Moscow: Nauka). [In Russian.] [A Hungarian edition, *Szemiotika*, appeared in 1976, published by Akadémiai Kiadó, Budapest.]
Stern, Theodore
1957 "Drum and Whistle Languages: An Analysis of Speech Surrogates", *American Anthropologist* 59, 487-506.
Stetson, R. H.
1951 *Motor Phonetics: A Study of Speech Movements in Action* (Amsterdam: North-Holland).
Stokoe, William C., Jr.
1972 *Semiotics and Human Sign Languages* (= *Approaches to Semiotics* 21) (The Hague: Mouton). [Cf. Bernard Th. Tervoort's 1973 review article, "Could There Be a Human Sign

Language?", *Semiotica* 9, 347-82.]
1974   "Motor Signs as a First Form of Language", *Semiotica* 10, 117-30.
Stough, Charlotte L.
1969   *Greek Skepticism: A Study in Epistemology* (Berkeley and Los Angeles: University of California Press).
Strehle, Hermann
1974[5] [1954[1]]   *Mienen Gesten und Gebärden: Analyse des Gebarens* (Munich/Basel: Reinhardt).
Studia z Historii Semiotyki 1, 2.
1971, 1973   Monografie z Dziejów Nauki i Techniki, Zakład Historii Nauki i Techniki Polskiej Akademii Nauk 68, 88 (Warsaw: PAN).
Studnicki, Franciszek
1970   "Traffic Signs", *Semiotica* 2, 151-72.
Sturtevant, Edgar H.
1947   *An Introduction to Linguistic Science* (New Haven: Yale University Press).
Tavolga, William N.
1974   "Application of the Concept of Levels of Organization to the Study of Animal Communication", in: *Nonverbal Communication*, ed. by Lester Krames, Patricia Pliner, and Thomas Alloway (New York: Plenum), pp. 51-76.
Taylor, Orlando, and Dianna Ferguson
1975   "A Study of Cross-cultural Communication between Blacks and Whites in the U.S. Army", *The Linguistic Reporter* 17:3, 8, 11.
Tervoort, Bernard Th.
1973   Review – see Stokoe, 1972.
Thibaud, Pierre
1975   *La logique de Charles Sanders Peirce: De l'algèbre aux graphes* (Aix-en-Provence: Université de Provence).
Thielcke, Gerhard
1969   "Geographic Variation in Bird Vocalizations", in: *Bird Vocalizations: Their Relations to Current Problems in Biology and Psychology*, ed. by R. A. Hinde (Cambridge: University Press), 311-39.
Thielcke, Gerhard, and Helga Thielcke
1964   "Beobachtungen an Amseln (*Turdus merula*) und Singdrosseln (*T. Philomelos*)", *Die Vogelwelt* 85, 46-53.
Thom, René
1973   "De l'icône au symbole: Esquisse d'une théorie du symbolisme", *Cahiers internationaux de symbolisme* 22/23, 85-106.

1974 *Modèles mathématiques de la morphogénèse: Recueil de textes sur la théorie des catastrophes et ses applications* (Paris: Inédit).

Thomas, Jean-Jacques
1974 "The Semiotic *Parole*", *Sub-stance: A Review of Theory and Literary Criticism* 10, 182-89.

Thomas, L. L.
1957 *The Linguistic Theories of N. Ja. Marr* (Berkeley and Los Angeles: University of California Press).

Thorpe, W. H.
1963 "Antiphonal Singing in Birds as Evidence for Avian Reaction Time", *Nature* 197, 774-76.
1965 "Ethology as a New Branch of Biology", in: *Readings in Animal Behavior*, ed. by Thomas E. McGill (New York: Holt, Reinhart and Winston), pp. 34-49.
1967 "Vocal Imitation and Antiphonal Song and Its Implications", *Proceedings of the XIV International Ornithological Congress*, ed. by D. W. Snow (Oxford and Edinburgh: Blackwell), pp. 245-63.
1968 "Perceptual Basis for Group Organization in Social Vertebrates, Especially Birds", *Nature* 220, 124-28.

Tiger, Lionel, and Robin Fox
1966 "The Zoological Perspective in Social Science", *Man* 1, 75-81.

Tinbergen, Niko
1951 *The Study of Instinct* (New York: Oxford).
1963 "On Aims and Methods of Ethology", *Zeitschrift für Tierpsychologie* 20, 410-33.

Todorov, Tzvetan
1966 "Recherches sémantiques", *Langages* 1, 5-43.
1971 (ed.) "Documents: Sémiologie du théâtre" [Consists of French translations of Petr Bogatyrev, *Les signes du théâtre*, 1938; and Roman Ingarden, *Les fonctions du langage au théâtre*, 1958], *Poétique* 8, 515-38.
1973 "Semiotics", *Screen* 14, 15-23.

Tomkins, Gordon M.
1975 "The Metabolic Code", *Science* 189, 760-63.

Trabant, Jürgen
1976 *Elemente der Semiotik* (Munich: C. H. Beck).

Transactions of the Charles S. Peirce Society. A Quarterly in American Philosophy
1965-75 Vols. 1-11.

Trier, J.
1931 *Der deutsche Wortschatz im Sinnbezirk des Verstandes: Die Geschichte eines sprachlichen Feldes*, Vol. 1, *Von den*

Visit us online at
Economist.com

Just as you expected: They want the world.

Give the gift of *The Economist* and save up to 80% off the cover price.

Gift subscriptions include full access to *The Economist* on iPhone®, iPad™ and Android™*

First gift subscription:

51 issues for $109 - **SAVE 69%** and receive *Pocket World in Figures 2012* as a FREE gift.

☐ For myself   ☐ For a friend
☐ Bill me later   ☐ Payment enclosed
(Make checks payable to *The Economist*)

BILL TO: _____

Address: _____

City: _____

State: _____ Zip: _____

Email: _____
(Email address is for subscription correspondence only)

▲ **Order online at: www.economist.com/gift11/us and enter code: PB021**

Additional gift subscription:

51 issues for just $69 - **SAVE 80%**, receive *Pocket World in Figures 2012* **AND** our new *Economist* journal as a bonus.

GIFT TO: _____

Address: _____

City: _____

State: _____ Zip: _____

▲ **First Gift**

▲ **Bonus Gift when you give 2 or more gifts**

Anfängen bis zum Beginn des 13. Jahrhunderts (Heidelberg: Winter).

Turner, Victor
1975 "Symbolic Studies", *Annual Review of Anthropology* 4, 145-61.

Tyler, Stephen A.
1969 (ed.) *Cognitive Anthropology* (New York: Holt, Rinehart and Winston).

Uexküll, Jakob von, and Georg Kriszat
1970 [1940] *Streifzüge durch die Umwelten von Tieren und Menschen: ein Bilderbuch unsichtbaren welten; und Bedeutungslehre* (Frankfurt a/M: Fischer).

Uldall, Hans J.
1957 *Outline of Glossematics*, Part I: *General Theory* (Copenhagen: Nordisk Sprog- og Kulturforlag).

Ullmann, Stephen
1951 *The Principles of Semantics* (Glasgow: Jackson, Son & Co.)
1962 *Semantics: An Introduction to the Science of Meaning* (Oxford: Blackwell).
1967 Review of A. J. Greimas, 1966. *Lingua* 18, 296-303.
1972 "Semantics", in: *Current Trends in Linguistics* Vol. 9, *Linguistics in Western Europe*, ed. by Thomas A. Sebeok (The Hague: Mouton), pp. 343-95.

Umiker, Donna Jean
1974 "Speech Surrogates: Drum and Whistle Systems", in: Sebeok (ed.), 1974b, pp. 497-536.

Valesio, Paolo
1969 "Icons and Patterns in the Structure of Language", *Actes du Xè Congrès International des Linguistes, Bucarest, 28 août-2 Septembre 1967*, ed. by A. Graur (Bucharest: Académie de la République Socialiste de Roumanie), Vol. 1, pp. 383-87.
1971 Review — see Eco, 1968.

Veltsos, Giorgos S.
1975 *Semeiologia tonpolitikon thesmon* (Athens: Ekdoseis Papazisis).

Venclova, Tomas
1967 "Le colloque sémiotique de Tartu", *Social Science Information* 6, 123-29.

Verdiglione, Armando
1975 (ed.) *Psicanalisi e semiotica* (Milan: Feltrinelli). [Cf. Eugen Bär's 1976 review article, "Psychoanalysis and Semiotics", *Semiotica* (forthcoming).]

Verón, Eliseo
1971 "Ideology and Social Sciences: A Communicational Ap-

proach", *Semiotica* 3, 59-76.

Verplanck, William S.
1962 "Unaware of Where's Awareness: Some Verbal Operants – Notates, Monents, and Notants", in: *Behavior and Awareness: A Symposium of Research and Interpretation*, ed. by Charles W. Ericksen (Durham: Duke University Press), pp. 130-58.

VS: Quaderni di studi semiotici
1971-74 Nos. 1-9. [Cf. János Kelemen's 1974 review article, "The Semiotic Conception of *VS*", *Semiotica* 11, 75-97.]

Viet, Jean
1965 *Les méthodes structuralistes dans les sciences sociales* (The Hague: Mouton).

Voigt, Vilmos
1969a "Modellálás a folklorisztikában", *Studia Ethnographica* 5, 347-430.
1969b Modellálási kisérletek a folklorisztikában", *Ethnographia* 80, 355-92.

Vygotsky, L. S.
1962 *Thought and Language*, ed. and trans. by E. Hanfmann and G. Vakar (Cambridge, Mass.: MIT Press).

Wallis, Mieczysław
1975 *Arts and Signs* (= *Studies in Semiotics* 2) (Bloomington: Research Center for Language and Semiotic Studies).

Walther, Elisabeth
1974 *Allgemeine Zeichenlehre: Einführung in die Grundlagen der Semiotik* (Stuttgart: Deutsche Verlags-Anstalt).

Watson, O. Michael
1970 *Proxemic Behavior: A Cross-cultural Study* (= *Approaches to Semiotics* 8) (The Hague: Mouton).

Watt, W. C.
1967 *Morphology of the Nevada Cattlebrands and Their Blazons* (Pittsburgh: Department of Computer Science, Carnegie-Mellon University).

Weinreich, Uriel
1958 Review of Osgood, Suci, and Tannenbaum, 1957. *Word* 14, 346-66.
1963 "Lexicology", in: *Current Trends in Linguistics*, Vol. 1, *Soviet and East European Linguistics*, ed. by Thomas A. Sebeok (The Hague: Mouton), pp. 60-93.
1966 "Explorations in Semantic Theory", in: *Current Trends in Linguistics*, Vol. 3, *Theoretical Foundations*, ed. by Thomas A. Sebeok (The Hague: Mouton), pp. 395-477.
1968 "Semantics and Semiotics", in: *International Encyclopedia of the Social Sciences* 14, 164-69.

Weinrich, Harald
1966 *Linguistik der Lüge* (Heidelberg: Schneider).
Weiss, Paul
1940 "The Essence of Peirce's System", *Journal of Philosophy* 37, 253-64.
Weiss, Paul, and Arthur Burks
1945 "Peirce's Sixty-six Signs", *Journal of Philosophy* 42, 383-88.
Weitz, Shirley
1974 (ed.) *Nonverbal Communication: Readings with Commentary* (New York: Oxford University Press).
Wells, Rulon
1954 "Meaning and Use", *Word* 10, 235-50.
1967 "Distinctly Human Semiotic", *Social Science Information* 6, 103-24.
Weltring, Georg
1910 *Das Semeion in der aristotelischen, stoischen, epikureischen und skeptischen Philosophie. Ein Beitrag zur Geschichte der Antiken Methodenlehre* (Bonn: Hauptmann'sche Buchdruckerei).
Wenner, Adrian M.
1969 "The Study of Animal Communication: An Overview", in: Sebeok and Ramsay (eds.), 1969, pp. 232-43.
Werner, Oswald, *et al.*
1974 "Some New Developments in Ethnosemantics and the Theory and Practice of Lexical/Semantic Fields", in: Sebeok (ed.), 1974b, pp. 1477-1543.
Wertheimer, Max
1923 "Untersuchungen zur Lehre von der Gestalt, II", *Psychologische Forschungen* 4, 301-50.
Wescott, Roger W.
1966 "Introducing Coenetics: A Biosocial Analysis of Communication", *American Scholar* 35, 342-56.
1971 "Linguistic Iconism", *Language* 47, 416-28.
White, Leslie A.
1940 "The Symbol: The Origin and Basis of Human Behavior", *Philosophy of Science* 7, 451-63.
Whiteside, Robert L.
1974 *Face Language* (New York: Frederick Fell).
Wickler, Wolfgang
1968 *Mimicry in Plants and Animals* (New York: McGraw-Hill).
1971 *Die Biologie der Zehn Gebote* (Munich: R. Piper).
1973 *The Sexual Code* (Garden City: Anchor/Doubleday).
Wiener, Norbert
1950 *The Human Use of Human Beings* (Boston: Houghton Mifflin).

Wilder, Harris Hawthorne, and Bert Wentworth
  1918 *Personal Identification: Methods for the Identification of Individuals, Living or Dead* (Boston: Badger).
Wilson, Edward O.
  1971 "The Prospects for a Unified Sociobiology", *American Scientist* 59, 400-03.
  1975 *Sociobiology: The New Synthesis* (Cambridge Mass.: Harvard University Press).
Windelband, W.
  1894 *Geschichte und Naturwissenschaft* (Strasbourg: Heitz).
Wollen, Peter
  1969 *Signs and Meaning in the Cinema* (Bloomington: Indiana University Press).
Worth, Sol
  1969 "The Development of a Semiotic of Film", *Semiotica* 1, 282-321.
Wundt, Wilhelm
  1973 *The Language of Gestures* (= *Approaches to Semiotics*, paperback series 6) (The Hague: Mouton).
Wynne-Edwards, V. C.
  1962 *Animal Dispersion in Relation to Social Behaviour* (New York: Hafner).
Yerkes, Robert M., and Henry W. Nissen
  1939 "Pre-linguistic Sign Behavior in Chimpanzee", *Science* 89, 585-87.
Zaliznjak, A. A., *et al.*
  1962 "O vozmožnosti strukturno-tipologičeskogo izučenija nekotorych modelirujuščich semiotičeskich sistem", in: *Strukturno-tipologičeskie issledovanija*, ed. by G. N. Mološnaja (Moscow: Sbornik Statej), pp. 134-43.
"Zeichensystem Film − Versuche zu einer Semiotik"
  1968 Special issue of *Sprache im technischen Zeitalter*, No. 27.
Zeman, J. Jay
  1964 "The Graphical Logic of C. S. Peirce". Dissertation. University of Chicago.
Zeuner, Frederick E.
  1963 *A History of Domesticated Animals* (New York: Harper & Row).
Zołkiewski, Stefan
  1969 *Semiotika a kultura* (Bratislava: Nakladatel'stvo Epocha).
Zvegintsev, V.
  1967 "Structural Linguistics and Linguistics of Universals", *Acta Linguistica Hafniensia* 10, 129-44.

Index of Proper Names